Predicting the Bite

By
Ronald W. Reinhold

First Edition

ISBN: 978-0-578-04734-8

Published by:
Pressure Publishing, LLC
4446 Westridge Drive
Williamsburg, Michigan 49690

www.PredictingTheBite.com

Printed in the United States of America

Contents

Sidebars

Acknowledgments

Throughout this book project I was repeatedly reminded that no man is an island. I was constantly seeking advice, reviews, records, scientific facts and interpretations, local knowledge from local experts, and much more. Although I did the writing, about three dozen very smart, very busy people gave me their time and knowledge in the most unselfish manner possible — they were just glad to help. Their help shaved many years off the time that would have been required to otherwise complete the work. I am deeply appreciative of every one of them because each contributed something special that made the book better. I mention all of them here as a humble attempt to immortalize their kindnesses to me.

First and foremost I thank my wife, Laura L. Reinhold, for her infinite patience and understanding, and her stoic suffering at work while my income flagged during the years I was researching and writing. The book would not have been possible without her. I must surely be destined for Perdition because I am, no doubt, already receiving my heavenly reward on Earth by having her as my partner.

I'm probably incapable of adequately thanking Dr. Gary Litman, PhD, Immunology and Genetics, Professor and Vice-Chairman of the Dept. of Pediatrics at University of South Florida Medical School, Director of the Children's Research Institute, and author-editor of hundreds of scientific publications; and Dr. Steve Brocco, PhD, Invertebrate Zoology and Marine Biology, Environmental consulting with emphasis on freshwater and marine ecosystems, and founding member of the Northwest Atlantic Salmon Fly Tying Guild; and Dr. Charles Vestal, PhD, P.E., Chemical Engineering, Lecturer of Thermodynamics at the Colorado School of Mines, and 32 years of research engineering for an international oil company; for the countless hours they spent ruminating on the details of the material. Their scholarly advice and encouragement was responsible for some of the most invigorating moments of this work. I shall be forever grateful for their wisdom and generosity.

I must also thank Dennis Dokken, BA, Entomology and Biology; Rob Roden, BS, Marine Biology; and David White, MS, Hydrogeology, for their meticulous science editing; and Paul Rossman, BFA, Photography, MFA, Painting, for his keen feedback and corroborative stream testing of the principles contained in the work.

Brief but important contributions were also made by Dr. Erwin "Duke" Elsner, PhD, Entomology, Agricultural Extension Agent for Michigan State University; Tom Kelly, MS, Fisheries Biology, Executive Director of Inland Seas Education Assn.; Todd Kalish, MS, Aquatic Science, Fisheries Management Biologist, Michigan Dept. of Natural Resources; and Mike Borkovich, BS, Resource Development, Law Enforcement of Natural Resources — Michigan Dept of Natural Resources, Conservation Officer 28 years.

I also thank my amazing son, Jabin Reinhold, BS, Electrical Engineering, for his computer wizardry help; and his wife, Laura E. Reinhold, BS, Mechanical Engineering and CPA, for her masterful mathematical help.

This work reflects a lifetime of my own fishing experiences, but also the circumstances contained in hundreds, perhaps thousands, of fishing reports that I received from many fishermen friends over the years. Voss Guntzviller, acclaimed local taxidermist and fisherman, has been an unfailing friend and informant regarding fish caught by him or his customers on certain dates, places, and times. His careful observations have helped me verify untold numbers of predictions that support this work. His sons, Jeremy Guntzviller and Curt Guntzviller also shared reports and careful records that were vital over the years. My friends Dan Morrison, Dan Hanna, Bob Powers, John McLain, and Alonzo Knowles related many valuable stories and reports as well.

Respected river guide, Russ Madden, and local business man, Rock Wilson, both provided fishing information that only astute observers are capable of providing. Rock also selflessly persevered as a fishing editor throughout the entire work. I am so indebted.

Dennis Gretel graciously lent me his extensive fishing logs for a long period of examination, as did Ed Bussa who lent me his deceased father's (Paul Bussa) 20 year log book; two great acts of generosity.

Eric Palo, local financial advisor, and a meticulous keeper of detailed logs, also shared his insights unselfishly throughout this effort. Our early conversations about barometric pressure were the impetus that led me down a path to closer examination of pressure. It was a long and convoluted path, but it eventually produced a series of epiphanies that led to the pressure rules. Upon sharing them with Eric, he deftly and quickly adapted the information to the hatches and bites on his beloved local rivers, and Canadian lakes, and periodically emailed his exciting results for this work.

My nephew, Christopher Reinhold, and I shared many long distance conversations discussing fishing conditions and fishing results near my boyhood latitude, a hundred and forty miles south of my current residence, where he still lives. His information has been critical in support of my observations of natural sequences and various fishing situations. His experiences as a tournament fisherman are intricately woven into the work.

Mitch Rompola, likely the greatest trophy whitetail deer hunter that ever lived, has unselfishly shared with me the incredible accuracy and value of natural sequences for predicting whitetail deer behavior. His mastery of sequences has proved to be a guiding compass in much of my work. During twenty-plus years of friendship, we've spent hundreds of hours in conversation about natural sequences and how to use them to make predictions for hunting and fishing alike. He literally has stacks of logs, field notes, and maps that he readily admits have been the foundation for his success.

No one has provided me with more freshwater reports and tested my thinking more than Bill Rosinski. Just when I thought I had a situation figured out, Bill's observations often caused me to think a lot deeper. He's a steelhead specialist, catching many hundreds of them since we first met on the Elk River in year 2003. He has a detailed report for every fish he's caught, and has shared every one with me. I have also shared my work with him every step of the way, which has been a revelation to him because so much of it deals with aquatic insects and crustaceans. Bill generally prefers spinning gear, and, like most spin fishermen, knowledge about aquatic insects has not been a major part of his strategic repertoire. As I began introducing him to the study of insects (entomology), Bill was noticeably intimidated, and could never quite remember the word "entomology." He compensated, however, by coining the word "bugtomologist." He now knows, and admits with a chuckle, that he has become a much more successful fisherman as he has become a better bugtomologist. It's a humorous term fully owned by him.

Thanks to Bill's natural curiosity, he has allowed me to examine stomach and intestinal contents of hundreds of his fish over the years, resulting in the corroboration of many of my suspicions via very messy evidence. Josh Sweat, Bill's sidekick and our mutual friend, has also provided numerous valuable reports in phone calls long after midnight from Lake Michigan piers.

Lynn "Tiny" Ray, AKA "Captain Tiny," 38 year charter captain on Lake Michigan, provided invaluable insight into the problems and challenges created by ever-changing currents in the largest lakes, particularly Lake Michigan. John Emory, 50 year "inventor extraordinaire" of legendary fishing products, also provided astute big-water observations that are only possible after a lifetime of designing equipment that works in it.

Creation of the saltwater fishing portion of this work would have been much more difficult without the lifetime of observations by my friend, Bud Guidry, original Cajun descendant, saltwater fisherman and commercial shrimper for 40 years in Louisiana coastal waters; Ted Patlen, retired school teacher with 25 years of saltwater experience in Altlantic coastal waters; and longtime friend, Roger Mims, business man and certified casting instructor with 30 years of intertidal zone fishing experience from New York to Florida, Mexico, and Alaska.

The seasoned insights of Phil Castleman, Attorney at Law and raconteur extraordinaire, were a beacon of reality throughout the entire creation of the work. He repeatedly submitted large parts of the work to his circle of brilliant friends for validation and feedback. His resultant comments, which at times were almost weekly, and 70 years of freshwater and saltwater fishing experience, helped shape the character of several passages of the book.

No one gave me more moral support through thick and thin than Ronn Lucas Sr. Our Oregon-Michigan phone conversations must have numbered in the hundreds over the course of the work, most after midnight on my end. He was a customer of mine years ago who became a dear friend and eventually bought my hook-making business. The relationship became yet more special and continues to grow after the change of ownership.

Lastly, but very significantly, I thank my dear friend, John Russell, BS, Urban Planning, career journalist-photographer of 30 years, for the daunting accomplishment of editing the entire manuscript. The difficult experience further cemented our bonds of friendship.

Introduction

This book is loaded with extraordinary new fishing secrets, including the secret of how barometric pressure affects fish behavior. Fishermen have sought it for centuries, and it will change fishing forever. Its full explanation and benefits for fishermen are published now for the first time. You are soon to be a very smart fisherman, and likely a much more successful one.

The goal of this book is to give you the ability to accurately *predict* when fish will be biting or naturally feeding, and put you on the water when the odds are highest to catch the most fish. You'll discover how to predict exact days and times to go fishing for best results. If you can only fish on Saturday or Sunday, you'll learn how to predict which day will be better. You'll know when to go or when to stay home — because you'll know how to predict when "the bite is on," especially the *best* bites.

Expect to learn more *new* knowledge about fishing than you've ever learned from any other single source. It also gives a major competitive advantage to tournament fishermen, fishing guides, and charter captains during every trip on the water, including on rivers, lakes of all sizes, and saltwater shores. Every chapter contains powerful information that helps you make accurate predictions for a lifetime. Additionally, everything in the book works *worldwide.*

Much of the material will look familiar at first, but your natural world will never appear the same again because your observational skills will be deeply improved.

You'll learn how flowers can tell you when to go fishing, as will the 70 mile rule, and the 14 day limit, and how wind direction can guide you to the best fishing of the day. Age-old proverbs like "Wind from the east, fishing is least," and "Fishing is best just before a storm" are also demystified with practical explanations.

Nothing in fishing literature is as jam-packed with new information, concepts, and principles that will contribute as much to your growth as a successful fisherman. You'll be among the first to learn about "ableness" and the pressure rules — which make it possible for you to predict the exact days when fly hatches will occur, and days when they will not. They will greatly improve your fishing success, and dramatically reduce your travel costs and time lost on unproductive fishing trips.

Whether you're a fly fisherman, spin fisherman, or baitcaster, you'll be captivated by the vigorous bites caused by pie hatches and pie molts, and learn how to predict the exact day they will occur, and where. If you fish the saltwater intertidal zone, you'll discover the effects of barometric pressure and wind on fishing near shore. There is so much more.

Understanding the effects of barometric pressure on fish behavior will be one of the most enlightening experiences of your fishing lifetime. The explanation presented, and the extraordinary fishing benefits it provides, have been meticulously reviewed and approved by a platoon of science scholars before revealing them in these pages (See Acknowledgements). A science thread runs throughout the explanations, as well as the entire book, but the whole work is written in fishermen's language as a fishing book for fishing success for all fishermen at all education levels.

The first six chapters reveal the interplay of factors in nature that must be understood for predicting good bites. The knowledge is then applied repeatedly throughout the remainder of the book for maximum fishing success.

Sidebars scattered among the chapters contain information that may be too disruptive if included in the general text, but contribute to deeper understanding of the topics being addressed. Reading their contents is optional, but recommended.

Chapter 1

Good Bites

If you have not read the short introduction, I urge you to go back and read it. It will make a significant difference in your experience with the information ahead.

Success

The big mayflies hatched or fell as spinners on the river every evening that I said they would. The trout fed well on those evenings, and fishing was spectacular. The mayflies did not hatch or fall as spinners during the evenings when I said they would not, and the fishing was lousy. This went on for weeks. As expected, the fishing was good when fish were responding to food. The bite really turned on when their food became available, and I was accurately predicting when that would happen. My predictions were perfect for the entire hatch season of the giant Michigan mayflies on the Boardman River near Traverse City, Michigan, in the year 2005. The same prediction results occurred during the next season in 2006.

My friends were becoming believers because they were doing the fishing while I was simply making the predictions from my home, twelve miles from the river. I had decided to risk my reputation by openly making

1

the predictions, yet not visit the river. I depended on my friends and a few patrons of the local fly fishing shop to report their observations and fishing results, which they did.

The predictions were flawless; and were the final proof that the bite could be accurately predicted for any lake or stream on the planet. I knew when the fish would bite. I knew when to go fishing, and when to stay home. This success was no fluke — it was based upon simple principles that every fisherman can master.

A Timing Problem

This story began a few years earlier when my life was a fire drill during the time that my wife, Laura, and I were raising our five children. I couldn't go fishing very often, but I still wanted to eat fish on a regular basis. My schedule was so tight that, if I wanted to eat more fish, I needed a way to catch more in fewer trips to the water. I couldn't afford to waste my time fishing if the fish weren't biting. I needed a way to catch more fish every time I went out. It quickly became clear that I needed to go fishing when fish were present in big numbers and the bite was on. (Sidebar #1: **The Bite Defined**)

Fortunately, I knew of a few times when fish were abundant and would bite like crazy. The best example was bluegills on their beds. I'd caught many limits of them over the years, but I'd also had to make many trips to local lakes to keep checking if they were on their beds or not. Timing was a problem. The same was true for pumpkinseed sunfish, and largemouth and smallmouth bass. Yellow perch and rainbow smelt would enter creeks and rivers in the spring too, and crappie entered the shallows, but as with the other species, timing of their appearance varied from year to year and was a problem. Fishing during spawning activities seemed like an obvious choice, but pinpointing the timing was frustrating. The strategy still required numerous trips to lakes or rivers that resulted in catching very little. I needed a better way to determine the timing. It took a while, and it came in stages, but I got it.

While I looked for a better way to predict spawning periods, many other instances of brisk bites came to mind. It seemed like the others all involved fish pouncing on abundant natural food. More importantly, the bites seemed to occur most intensely when the food appeared more suddenly. For example, when mayflies hatch in big numbers, fish vigorously binge on them shortly after they appear. The same thing happens with

The Bite Defined

In most instances throughout the book, "the bite" shall mean that fish are engaged in the act of natural feeding. At various times it shall also mean the act of a fish intentionally opening its mouth for the purpose of taking something into it, probably something it perceives as food. It doesn't always mean a fish's intent to swallow, although in most cases it seems reasonable to assume that that is the intent. It means that sometimes the fish are feeding, but at other times they only open their mouths as a spontaneous feeding reaction, such as when they are not actively feeding, but will strike at irresistible natural food, a lure or artificial bait. It can also include instances of a latent or unconscious feeding reaction such as is a common phenomenon in migrating salmon. They will strike a bait, fly, or lure, but are not actually feeding. It's much like someone who has quit smoking, but impulsively and mindlessly reaches for a cigarette. It's a conditioned reaction resulting from habit. The bite can also include instances of defending a nest, eggs, and offspring, when a bait or lure is presented too close to them and is attacked because it's deemed a threat.

caddisflies, stoneflies, and many other insects that suddenly appear in high concentrations. The fish attack them. The bugs trigger the bites. Minnows, crayfish, shrimp, scuds, and worms also trigger good bites, although the intensity of the bites can vary.

Most of these critters only appear in large numbers for short periods of time, maybe an hour per day, a few days in a certain month, or a few weeks per year. Each one is different because each occupies its own ecological niche. Fly fishermen are keenly aware of these occurrences and create flies that best exploit them by matching the particular fly or organism that's making the appearance. They "match the hatch." Spin fishermen and bait casters also do their best to present offerings that mimic the real thing. Everybody knows that you can catch more fish if you can fool a fish into believing that your bait is the same thing as the natural food that it's feeding on. Obviously there are many occasions when the bite can be fast and furious because of spawning or availability of food. The problem still remains, however, of being able to accurately predict when these events will happen.

Botanical Indicators

By the time I tackled this daunting problem, I had already solved another timing problem that gave me a clue for how to proceed: I have a hobby of picking wild mushrooms, and I know how to predict the exact day that the first morel mushrooms will appear each year in my spots. One of the most important factors in finding morel mushrooms is knowing when they will emerge each spring. Decades earlier I discovered a correlation between the emergence of the morels and the appearance of other plants at the same time. More specifically, certain ferns made a strong emergence in my yard and woodlot when the morels were at their peak abundance in woodlots miles away. I simply waited for the ferns to appear in my yard and woodlot before I ventured out for the morels. I always knew when to go, and I collected four to five thousand morels each year. The ferns were a perfect botanical indicator. After a few years, however, many more people had moved into the area, and squads of other mushroom pickers were harvesting the morels before I went out to look for them, so my personal harvest shrank because of the competition. Knowing when the peak of the morel crop occurred wasn't good enough anymore. I needed to know when they first emerged so I could start picking them on the very first day of emergence. I needed a good timing indicator so I could once again beat the competition.

Fortunately, within a couple years I identified a small yellow flower that blossomed about a day and a half before the first morels sprang up. The flower has been a flawless indicator that tells me exactly when they will emerge and can be picked. Now, no one beats me to the mushrooms; I always know when the first ones will appear, and I always get enough.

I fully expect my revelation about the little yellow flower to be happily exploited by mushroomers who read this book, and, if it's you, I wish you well. I've surely had more than my share, and I hope you enjoy them as much as I have. I've since discovered other wild mushrooms that are just as good, and I know exactly when they emerge too. If a small flower could be used to indicate the timing of mushroom emergence, it seemed reasonable to investigate whether or not similar indicators could be used to predict the timing of good bites.

Sure enough, several seasoned fishermen friends soon gave me examples of flowers being used to indicate good bites. Roger Mims, who grew up on New York's Long Island, said savvy fishermen there knew it was time to catch weakfish when the local French lilacs burst into bloom. Kenny Scott, of Jackson, Michigan, said southern Michigan anglers head to the Detroit River for a good walleye bite when the purple lilacs bloom in his area. Dan Hanna, of Williamsburg, Michigan, told me his uncle kept a lifetime fishing log and knew it was time to go after whitefish when the wild strawberries bloomed in a certain place near his home. He was known to bring home boatloads of whitefish, for decades. "Blue lilies" are used to indicate a great bite associated with Pale Morning Dun (PMD) hatches on a river in Colorado. There were several more. The anecdotes sounded promising.

Timing was still a problem, but I was now on a path that would reveal some answers. Further investigation provided some amazing discoveries.

Chapter 2

Natural Sequences

I was thrilled to learn that wildflowers could be used as indicators for good bites, that the correlations could be made and would be valid every year. I was so enthralled by the prospects that I became more interested in the knowledge than going fishing. Fishing would have to wait; I decided to spend at least a year observing, surveying, and recording every possible natural occurrence that could lead to correlations for good bites. One year turned into seven, but it was worth it.

Survey Sequences

The following year I carried out a huge survey of the natural occurrences that happen every year near my home in Williamsburg, Michigan. The survey period was for the entire year, from January through December, 2003. I also got scores of fishing reports from friends and others throughout the year that would help establish correlations. They kept me informed of when and where spawning and bites (and non-bites) were occurring for the entire period.

The survey hijacked my life. I drove a 58 mile circuit every-other-day for nearly the entire growing season — approximately six months. I recognized at the outset that wildflowers would probably be the most

7

useful indicators for good bites, so I bought every wildflower field guide I could find. I recorded data every other day for over 200 species of wildflowers and shrubs, daily climate data, foliation and defoliation data for dozens of deciduous woody species, water temperatures of two rivers, insect hatches and appearances, bird behavior, ripening of berries and other fruit, and much more.

I was determined to gather as much data as possible so I could make as many correlations as possible with good bites. I was consumed by it for the entire year. The data was so interesting that I continued to record key observations for the next six years. I still feel a compulsion to record some data on a continuing basis.

The data for just the first year filled a huge scroll of graph paper (1/4 inch squares) 3 feet high by 60 feet long, which I divided and rolled into three 20-foot scrolls.

The survey data made it abundantly clear that certain phenomena associated with living things happen at predictable times every year. For example, each wildflower species will first blossom at about the same time every year, depending on weather conditions. Those that first blossom in the spring will first blossom again the following spring, not in summer or fall, just in spring. Those that first blossom in the summer will only first blossom again the next summer, not in spring or fall, and so forth. They unfailingly appear and reappear in the same predictable sequence every year. What's important is that, on any particular plot of ground, the sequence never changes. Species number one will blossom first, then species number two, then species number three and so forth, and the sequence will not change from year to year if environmental conditions remain the same. You can bank on it. They are genetically programmed to appear at the same time every year. The key is when they first blossom, and that the sequence never changes. Weather extremes may cause a species not to blossom in a particular year, but it generally will not otherwise violate the sequence. This is a very important factor for timing good bites. Wildflowers are a great choice to use for indicators because a new species first blossoms quite frequently in most areas. Flowers of various trees and woody species are also very useful and dependable as botanical indicators in the spring.

Spawning sequences of various fish species are also vitally important. Just like the wildflower sequences, spawning sequences are very stable and predictable, especially in freshwater lakes and rivers. Extremely large lakes like the Great Lakes — Lake Michigan, Lake Superior etc — are sometimes deceptive and can appear to be exceptions because they act more like oceans. In lesser lakes, however, spawning sequences are reliable and predictable, worldwide. In one respect they are always the same: Every species is preceded and followed by the same two species of fish every year. The sequence never changes under normal conditions.

Timing the Spawn

Most healthy lakes will have many species of fish dwelling in them. Each healthy species, according to its own biological clock, always spawns near a certain time of the year. The timing is normally controlled by daily photoperiods (length of daylight and darkness) and water temperatures in favorable spawning areas of the lake. Every fish species prefers a unique water temperature range for spawning.

The table in Figure 2-1 contains a good example of the order in which a variety of fish species spawn every year in waters of the upper Great Lakes region. Each fish is named in the order that it spawns in the yearly sequence, from spring through fall.

The table reveals that several species can be spawning at the same time. Black crappie, pumpkinseeds, bluegills, and rock bass can bespawning simultaneously but in different sections of the same lake.

The table can also be somewhat deceiving. For example, largemouth and smallmouth bass appear to have almost identical spawning temperatures, and therefore spawning times. This is misleading because smallmouths spawn in deeper water, which remains cooler longer than does the shallow water preferred by largemouths. The shallow water warms up much sooner, so the largemouths will be on their beds sooner than the smallmouths. Largemouths are usually done spawning before smallmouths are on their beds. Persistent warm winds may cause warmer water to pile up in a favorite spawning area, however, and may cause both species to be on spawning beds at the same time, but at different depths, which would be quite unusual.

A few decades ago, a friend and I realized that bluegills spawned in local shallow lakes first because the water warmed up sooner than in the deeper lakes. We caught the spawning bluegills in those shallow lakes first, then, after the medium depth lakes warmed up a little more, we next caught the bluegills that began spawning in those. When the spawning activity tapered off in the medium depth lakes we then moved to the deepest lakes and caught the fish that were now spawning in those. Thereafter, we made an annual tour of following the temperature sequence, and therefore

Spawning Temperatures of a Variety of Fish in the Upper Great Lakes Region - Annual Spawning Sequence -		
Species	Temperature (deg F)	Notes
Burbot	33 - 35	often under ice - late winter
Northern Pike	40 - 52	
Walleye	42 - 52	typically 44-48 deg F
Yellow Perch	44	
Steelhead	45 - 55	peak of run for most strains
Rainbow Smelt	48 - 65	massing
White Crappie	60.8 - 68	
Largemouth Bass	62 - 65	shallow water
Smallmouth Bass	62 - 65	deeper water than largemouth
Carp	62.6	
Black Crappie	66 - 68	
Bluegills	67 - 76	
Pumpkinseed Sunfish	68 - 82	
Channel Catfish	75 - 85	
Lake Trout	57 - 48	cooling water in autumn
Brown Trout	48 - 44	cooling water in autumn
Lake Whitefish	46	cooling water in autumn

Temperatures obtained from:
W.B. Scott & E.J. Crossman, 1998, *Freshwater Fishes of Canada*,
Galt House Publications Ltd., Oakville, Ontario, Canada

Figure 2-1

the spawning sequence, from lake to lake just for the bluegills. We exploited the warming sequence from shallow lakes to deep lakes, and experienced many great bites because of it. I made detailed sketches and notations on lake maps, of the favorite spawning grounds, so we always knew where to fish during return trips. This is a proven sequence technique that you can use for chasing a good bite and catching most species of fish

Generally, spring spawners build nests and lay eggs when water is warming to their preferred temperature range; fall spawners build nests and lay eggs when water is cooling to their preferred temperature range.

Insect Sequences

Two other extremely important sequences are those of the (1) growth stages and (2) hatches of aquatic insects. It's probably accurate to assume that no sequences are more important to the freshwater angler. There are many aquatic insect species, but the most important ones include mayflies, caddisflies, stoneflies, and midges, not necessarily in that order. Many others are important, but these are the ones most familiar to anglers. They're important food sources for most fish species worldwide. They inhabit North America, South America, Asia, Europe, Greenland, Australia, New Zeeland, Africa, and even the arctic regions of the continents.

Again, just like the wildflowers and fish spawning sequences, the sequences of the growth stages and hatches of aquatic insects are very stable and predictable from year to year. For example, under normal circumstances, the hatching of each species of mayfly is preceded and followed by the hatching of the same two other species of mayflies every year; the hatching of each species of caddisfly is preceded and followed by the hatching of the same two other species of caddisflies each year, and so forth for each aquatic insect species across the globe.

It's common practice for savvy tackle shop owners to provide anglers, especially fly fishermen, with hatch charts that show when the various aquatic insects will hatch on local rivers and lakes. The charts list hatches in a rigid chronological order that remains the same from year to year. Each insect has a time of year that it prefers to hatch — spring, summer, fall, or winter — and it never changes. The best hatch charts are specific for just one lake or river because each water system harbors a unique roster of insects.

The insect species also have certain times of the day when they generally prefer to hatch and appear. Some species appear in the morning,

11

some at midday, and others in the evening or after dark. The time of day when each species hatches is also reliable and predictable. Each species will have its own unique time of day and time of year when it will hatch and appear, and it is genetically wired to repeat it year after year. This, too, is important information for timing a good bite.

Every fly fisherman knows that good bites happen when good hatches happen, but timing a good bite is still a problem because good hatches don't happen every day. Most seasoned fly fishermen have experienced good hatches and good bites, but they've also seen days when weather conditions seemed perfect for a good hatch, but nothing happened, and fishing was lousy. They saw no bugs and caught no fish; it just didn't make sense. Where were the bugs, and where were the fish?

These were wasted fishing trips because the fishermen didn't have the correct knowledge for predicting the hatch. Information in the next few chapters will help you know on which days those hatches and bites will happen. It'll explain why some days that look perfect for a good hatch are actually some of the worst days for fishing. You'll also learn why some of the worst looking days for hatches and fishing are actually some of the best. It'll help you discern when to go fishing or when to stay home.

Aquatic insects are members of a much larger group of organisms known as arthropods. All arthropods have an exoskeleton, which means they have no internal bones, just a hard outer shell. Crustaceans of all kinds, including shrimp, scuds, and crayfish are included in this group with the aquatic insects. Dragonflies, aquatic beetles, craneflies and many others are also included. You will soon learn that there are sequence traits shared by all arthropods that you can exploit to accurately predict good bites, often to the exact hour.

Sequences as Bite Indicators
The period during which a certain wildflower will blossom, or a certain fish will spawn, or a certain aquatic insect will hatch, will generally last for at least 10 days or longer, sometimes months, each year. They blossom, spawn, or hatch because of the stage of maturity they have reached shortly before they are due to appear, and then they undergo an additional small but final step of development caused by the surrounding environmental conditions that causes them to blossom, spawn or hatch as expected. It's our good luck that many of these occurrences happen at the same time. The key here is that the same environmental conditions are

responsible for the timing of all of them, and they will happen simultaneously again next year around the same time. The environmental conditions cause them to happen at the same time. It's very common for fish to be spawning in a lake while there are wildflowers blossoming nearby and insects are flying in the air. They are all responding to the same environmental conditions — the air is at a certain temperature, the water is at a certain temperature, the wind is from a certain direction, the sun is shining or not, the barometric pressure is at a certain level, the days and nights are a certain length (photoperiod), and the altitude above sea level is about the same. As the season advances, the environmental conditions will change and a new wildflower will blossom, a new fish species will spawn, and a new insect will hatch. The new events are caused by the new conditions, and so it goes for every species in every season.

My flower-flora-fauna surveys revealed when many good bites would occur. I found that the flowers and other natural things could be used as signs that tell me when those bites would happen. I discovered that the smelt would run up Shalda Creek when daffodils (not exactly a wildflower) blossomed on a nearby street, and bluegills would bed in nearby Long Lake when cow wheat first blossomed in my yard; the bluegills would also be spawning in Spider Lake when chickory first blossomed along the roadsides; huge trout in a section of the Boardman River would binge on giant hexagenia mayflies around the time that St. John's Wort first blossomed, and droves of smallmouth bass invaded the Elk River when the yellow blossoms of mossy stonecrop first burst forth. Perch could be found spawning in some local waters on the day when ruby throated hummingbirds returned for the season. It seemed like there was a natural indicator for just about every important bite that could happen, if I just looked closely enough.

I don't think I've discovered anything new in these correlations and indicators of a good bite. I've probably only rediscovered what Native Americans must have known and practiced for their survival through the ages. As hunter-gatherers they needed to know when fish were most plentiful and vulnerable. I doubt they would have packed their belongings, shelters, and families, and moved long distances based on hunches that fishing might be good. They must have known about reliable natural signs and indicators that told them their efforts would be rewarded in great measure. When the signs appeared, they reacted accordingly, and they expected to reap a bounty as they had for untold generations. Entire village populations would move, so they must have been very confident in their expectations. They couldn't afford to be wrong because starvation could be the price for failure.

Every sequence is worth a look, and might be a good indicator for a good bite. Some other sequences are: Ice-out on local lakes — ice melts off shallow lakes first, medium depth lakes next, and deepest lakes last; therefore, spawning sequences and insect hatches occur on the shallowest lakes first because they warm up first. Continued warming then causes spawning and hatching to occur in the medium depth lakes next and the deepest lakes last — the sequence never changes. River temperatures also have a sequence — they are usually warmest at the mouth and get progressively cooler upstream (rivers with dams are addressed later). Hence, insect hatches usually commence in the lowest, warmest reaches of a river first, then advance to the higher, cooler reaches as the season wears on and the headwaters become warmer. Birds: They arrive in a certain order every spring also. In my area, robins arrive first, then red-winged black birds, meadow larks, ruby throated hummingbirds, and so forth. I'm sure you recall that the swallows of Capistrano regularly return on the same day every year. There's also the ripening sequence of fruits, nuts, and berries — which ones ripen or drop first, second, or third and so forth? Stages of fruits in local orchards are another one. Consider also the precise seasonal changes of the location of stars and constellations, the angle of the sun, and the progression of emerging flower blossoms from bud to bloom, and leaves (foliation) every spring as they appear in the south first and then move to the far north. In autumn, aquatic weed beds die and collapse in northern waters first, and continue collapsing in all lakes for several months, the death advancing southward from northern latitudes to the deep south.

Sequences like these can be important to tournament fishermen who compete for money and prizes. They may not seem like much yet, but you'll soon understand how you can use them to significantly improve your chances of winning.

Evolution and Natural Selection

Fortunately for anglers, all natural sequences are a result of evolution. Evolution has shaped the genetics that control all the natural sequences of living organisms. The sequences have been formed by eons of environmental conditions and continuous natural selection. In almost all cases, because of natural selection, the sequences unfold in a predictable manner. Many sequences have a distinct starting point, then slowly build and accelerate to a peak, then slow down and taper off to an ending point. This happens regularly and is very handy for predicting good bites. Some of the best bites happen when fish spawning and insect hatches hit their peaks. Identifying correlations with wildflowers and other natural events can help you determine when those bites will occur.

The fish, insects, and other organisms forming the large population that's present during the peak of their appearances are thought to be the specimens best adapted for survival and reproduction in their environmental niche. **(Sidebar #2: Natural Selection)**

How Sequences Unfold

Fish spawning and insect hatch sequences, under normal conditions, are good examples of how the sequences unfold. A few individuals appear first, then the greater population appears, then the appearances diminish and taper to zero. Spawning periods for most species of fish will usually last at least one to three weeks, and sometimes for as long as several months. Aquatic insect hatch periods typically last for similar amounts of time, sometimes only a few days, but more often for several weeks, although the daily hatches will vary in volume as the season proceeds.

Consider the appearance of fish that arrive to spawn. Most often, on the first day of spawning only one or a couple fish may be present (which usually goes unnoticed). On the second day, perhaps one more or a few more will be present, but far more may be present in the next few days or weeks, and still more on subsequent days or weeks until the population of spawners reaches a peak for the season. After the peak is reached, spawning subsequently slows until no more fish will spawn for the season. Near the end, only one or two fish remain to complete the spawning event.

This kind of sequence can best be depicted by a typical bell curve as shown in Figure 2-2. The sequence is a succession of spawning that starts at zero, begins and rises slowly, accelerates to a peak of activity, then slows and diminishes in a manner that tapers to zero again. The annual sequence period may only last a week or two in a given location, or perhaps longer depending on the species and circumstances, but each species will be different.

Insect hatches unfold in much the same way as fish spawning sequences, although the population numbers are typically larger. The duration of the annual sequence will last from as little as a day to as long as several months, but most of the common annual aquatic insect hatch periods last at least one to three weeks.

Wildflower blossoms typically appear in a similar manner. Only one or a couple flowers will blossom on the first day. A few more may blossom on the second day or for the next few days, and far more may blossom on days thereafter, and still more on subsequent days until the blossoming reaches a peak. After the peak is reached, blossoming eventually tapers off until no more flowers will blossom for the season. Just like the spawning and insect hatch sequences, blossoming starts at zero, begins and rises slowly, accelerates to a peak, then slows and diminishes in a manner that

---

#2

Natural Selection

Natural selection is nature's way of selecting individuals that have better genetic chances for survival and can pass genetic traits to future generations. Natural selection works on traits that are inherited. The traits represent variations that give the organism genetic advantages or disadvantages that influence its degree of fitness for survival and reproduction in its unique environment. The variations occur randomly and are selected as a result of the complex conditions of life experienced by an organism. The variations are then tested by the environment in which an organism lives and reproduces. Some offspring inherit variations that are advantageous, but others do not. When offspring inherit traits that provide advantages, they pass them on to the next generation which increases the number of individuals with the advantages, as they are better suited to survive and reproduce. If the offspring inherit the traits with disadvantages, they are less fit to survive and reproduce. Therefore, the offspring with genetic disadvantages will become less numerous in the population and still less in subsequent generations and might eventually disappear. The net impact is survival of the fittest. The most-fit individuals will prosper, the unfit do not. Survival of species relies on the continuum of natural selection.

tapers to zero again. The
sequence may only last a
week or two, or as long as
an entire growing season
for that species, but each
species is different. Again,
this kind of sequence is
best depicted by a bell
curve as contained in Figure 2-2.

Typical Bell Curve

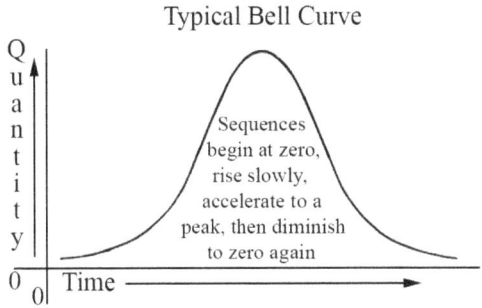

Figure 2-2

The duration of se-
quences — how many
days or weeks they last — is important for timing good bites. The dura-
tions are seldom the same length of time every year. A hatch period may
last 18 days one year, but only 14 days the following year. A spawning
period may last two weeks one year, but three and a half weeks the next.
They're a little different every year, but fortunately for us, they occur near
the same calendar dates year after year.

14 Day Limit

If statistics are kept for many years, each sequence will have an
average date when it can be expected to begin. It's rare indeed when a
sequence begins more than 14 days before or after its *expected date* —
termed here the *14 day limit*. Most will happen much closer to the expected date, usually within 10 days or less.

Rare exceptions to the *14 day limit* usually occur when average
water and/or air temperature is much warmer or colder than normal for
that time of year. The warmer or colder air is usually caused by events
like El Niño (warming of Pacific Ocean water) and/or large amounts of
dust blown into the atmosphere by volcanic eruptions that block out large
amounts of the sun's energy, making the atmosphere cooler. Water that
surrounds an island will also have a mitigating effect on sequences that
occur on the island. These circumstances may cause the sequences to shift
a few more days, or even a few weeks in extreme cases, but they will still
occur in the same order as in years past. They will also normally recur in
future years during the traditional time. A few wild plant species, e.g.,
dandelions, emerge and die off more than once per growing season, and
should not be relied upon for accurate predictions after their first emer-

gence and die off. Their subsequent emergences may create confusion in your records.

The reliability of many sequences is very helpful for predicting a period of days or weeks when good bites will occur, but your chances of picking the wrong day for fishing are still unacceptably high; and, what if there are no obvious sequences that can help you identify a good bite period? What then? How can you pinpoint the exact day and hour of a good bite when there is so much variation in the sequence periods?

Obviously you need to know how to use some sequences in a more revealing manner. You also need to know what causes a fish's food to appear (often quite suddenly) in quantities that cause a good bite. If you know when and where spawning sequences occur, and when and where the food will appear, you'll know when and where to go fishing, because fish will most often be there in a mood to strike or eat your offerings. **(Sidebar # 3: Fishing for Spawning Fish)**

Food is Key To Bites

Spawning events present great fishing opportunities, but they are usually unique and brief, and the spawning bite is not always about pursuing food. It's often about defending the nest, eggs, or offspring. At other times of the year, however, good fishing is almost always a function of fishes' interest in food. Fish are opportunists, and many exhibit a decided

---

#3
Fishing for Spawning Fish

There is much debate about the ethics of targeting fish while they are spawning. My position is that only you can decide whether your local standards of ethics, regulations, and statutes controlling such matters are reasonable and deserve your compliance. If the information in this book poses a threat to any fish species, I trust that concerned fishermen will act to create regulations that counter the threat. On balance, I perceive no redeeming benefits for withholding the information.

tendency to eat when abundant food presents itself. Food is almost always the basis for good bites during non-spawning periods. If you want good bites year-round, not just during short spawning periods, you must know when abundant food will appear to trigger them. Predicting the availability of food is the key to predicting the bites.

The 70 Mile Rule

If you fish waters more than 10 to 15 miles north or south from your home, or at different altitudes above sea level, the following story and sequence will have a weighty bearing on your future fishing excursions. If you are a traveling tournament fisherman, you'll find it extremely important and valuable by the time you finish this book.

I grew up in the countryside southeast of Muskegon, Michigan, almost exactly 140 miles south of where I currently live. I spent every spare minute of my boyhood fishing the local lakes, rivers and creeks nearby. I knew approximately when the crappies would spawn, when the steelhead would run, when the pike were in the backwaters, and similar facts about all the other fish that I desperately and always wanted to catch. I could hardly wait every year as calendar dates approached that often meant some kind of great fishing action would soon unfold. It was action that happened near the same dates, year after year. My fishing life seemed almost perfect. I felt like I knew when to go fishing, and I caught a lot of fish every year.

College, the Army, a new wife, and a new life 140 miles to the north took me away from those boyhood haunts. My new neighborhood, however, was rife with new places to fish. Ten rivers and dozens of lakes were within an hour and a half drive. The regional human population was also far smaller than where I grew up. It was an exciting new place in which to live because the fishing possibilities seemed spectacular. I was up north where all the good fishing was reputed to be. Naturally, I went fishing every chance I got. As hoped, I caught my share of fish from time to time, but I wasn't having the spectacular success like I had when I was a kid. Frankly, I was disappointed in the overall fishing situation because my boyhood knowledge didn't seem to apply here. The calendar dates didn't bring good fishing like they did in the old neighborhood. I kept in touch with my brothers and friends who still lived there, and they had great fishing as usual, but similar fishing wasn't happening at the same time in the area where I live now. It was downright puzzling. I hung out in the local tackle shops, but there were no loitering geniuses who could adequately explain why things were so different in the two locations. I was on my own.

About 30 years ago I heard a television weatherman share one of the most meaningful observations about nature that I've ever encountered. He was commenting about the brilliant colors of autumn foliage when the following gem slipped through his lips: "Autumn colors advance from north to south at a rate of about 70 miles every 10 days." It didn't mean much then, but I'm astounded by it now.

I remembered it and made efforts to verify it for many years, but more as a curiosity than a tenet of science. Only within the last few years have I realized the depth of its implications for predicting the bite.

My casual observations, spread over a couple decades, seem to affirm its validity. Colors in my area have never advanced southward at a rate of 70 miles every 10 days, but it's been close. They may have advanced about 65 miles in 11 days, or 80 miles in nine days, or some other rate, but the long term average has been about 70 miles every 10days. It's proven to be a relatively sound rate at my latitude (45 degrees North) and sea level (650 feet).

It eventually occurred to me that the statement could be re-phrased in the following manner: "The earth is entering the portion of its orbit that causes organisms to go dormant, from north to south, at a rate of 70 miles every 10 days." I refer to this as the "dormancy rate." Once stated in these new terms, it seemed reasonable to assume that when the dormant organisms showed renewed signs of life again in the spring, the renewed signs would advance in the opposite direction, from south to north at about the same rate. Indeed they do; life re-emerges and advances approximately 70 miles back to the north every 10 days. I refer to this as the "emergence rate." A practical rule for dormancy and emergence can now be stated:

The 70 Mile Rule:
Dormancy and emergence advance at about an average rate of 70 miles every 10 days in similar habitats at the same altitude, on the 45th parallel. (Applicable for up to about 1000 feet above sea level)

The average rates may differ somewhat in the subtropical and subarctic zones, but the 70 mile rate should be a useful starting point. (See Chapter 12, **Altitude Allowance** — and **Sidebar #26: Estimated Rates** for rates that may be slightly more helpful at your latitude.)

By sheer chance, I live almost directly on the 45th parallel, the latitude exactly halfway between the equator and the North Pole. The local trees and shrubs only have leaves for six months of the year, and are bare the other six months. It's the latitude in the Northern Hemisphere where this happens in equal measure at sea level. The same phenomena should occur on the 45th parallel in the Southern Hemisphere. My figures could be off by a day or two because of my altitude above sea level (altitude matters).

Living on the 45th parallel made the whole reasoning process easier.

We know the seasons change because the earth is tilted on its axis and it travels along a precise elliptical orbit around the sun. We also know the trip around the sun requires 12 months to complete. Dormancy lasts for six months at this latitude, which is the amount of time that it takes the earth to travel exactly halfway around its orbit. Upon completing that first half of the orbit, dormancy ends and new signs of life emerge and flourish for the next six months, which happens during the entirety of the second half of the orbit. The second half of the orbit requires the same travel time as the first half. Therefore, if the complete orbit is a precise ellipse, we can deduce that the second half of the orbit is a mirror image of the first half. If it's a mirror image, then the rate at which life emerges and moves from south to north in the spring, should be the same rate that dormancy moves from north to south in the fall. Indeed this appears to be the case, and I've used it very successfully in recent years to predict numerous spawning events, hatch events, and good bites. It's also very useful for predicting when botanical indicators (flower blossoms etc.) will first appear, sometimes weeks in advance.

I now understood why fishing events in my northern location always occurred about three weeks later than in my boyhood neighborhood, 140 miles away. If the rate of 70 miles every 10 days is applied, it would predict that those events would occur 20 days later in my northern neighborhood. That's about three weeks. Nice.

Knowledge about the sequences of dormancy from north to south, and emergence of life from south to north, gives you another powerful tool for predicting good bites, and especially for locating them. There is more on this in Chapter 12.

Thus far, the sequences addressed are those that occur as a result of seasonal climate changes. They are extremely valuable for identifying blocks of time during which good bites can be expected. Unfortunately, they can't always be used to accurately foretell the exact day and hour of a good bite. Better information is needed to precisely pinpoint the timing on a regular basis. For most good bites, that information is contained in just three additional concepts.

Fair Warning

This is an honest and fair warning: If you do not want to compromise the mystery and challenge that you enjoy from fishing, you should probably not read any further. The explanations shared in the following chapters are so revealing that you may lose much of your desire to go fishing because you know too much. They could torpedo the challenge for you. My apologies.

Chapter 3

Degree-Days

Eggs and Exoskeletons

The vast preponderance of food species eaten by fish begin life as an egg. The eggs range in size from microscopic to larger than tennis balls. Plankton, insects, crustaceans, and fish all begin as an egg. Algae and bacteria are notable exceptions, although algae emerge from spores that some argue is a form of egg. The fertilized egg of each species develops through many unique stages until it becomes an adult, propagates the species through more eggs, and eventually dies. The sequence is then repeated by every subsequent generation, each according to its own genetic code.

The first stage for salmon eggs, for example, is hatching to become tiny fish called "alevin." The egg sack is still attached to them and they use the yoke for nourishment. After the yoke has been fully absorbed and disappears, the small fish are known as fry. The fry then develop certain markings that define them as parr. When the parr lose the fry markings they are then called smolts. The smolts then develop into juvenile and adult fish. The adults then spawn more eggs. After they spawn and are near death, the spent salmon are known as kelts. As you can see, the original salmon egg developed and grew through many stages that are characteristic of the species.

Aquatic insects may be the most important freshwater fish food in the world, and there are many of them. Mayflies, stoneflies, and caddisflies are wonderful examples for discussion because they inhabit every continent except Antarctica. When their eggs hatch, the little critters that come out are known as a larva or nymphs. They're miniscule at first, but the manner in which they grow is extraordinary. They may look unremarkable to the untrained eye, but these little organisms are special because they have an *exoskeleton*. An exoskeleton is a hard outer structure or shell of the organism that gives it protection and structural support. Insects don't have bones for support; they have the exoskeleton, which performs the same function.

To eliminate confusion, the terms "nymphs" and "larva" are lumped together in this book and simply referred to as *immatures* (Sidebar #4: Nymph or Larva). Fortunately for fisherman, the exoskeleton is among the most important factors for good bites, and especially for predicting them.

Molting

As the exoskeleton develops on the insect's exterior surface, it becomes rigid and stops growing, even though the immature inside continues to grow and becomes larger. As the immature grows, it becomes restricted and probably somewhat compressed within the tight-fitting and constrictive exoskeleton. The immature becomes too large for the shell in which it's living. At some point the restriction of the shell becomes so great that the immature must escape from it or perish. Once again, a genetic code prevails and, from within, the shell separates from the immature and splits in a manner that allows the immature to slip out of it. The very nature of

#4
Nymph or Larva

Nymphs are actually the larva stage of many insects. They're unique because they *resemble the adult form,* but they're smaller and don't have wings that are fully developed. Conversely, the larvae of many other insects *do not resemble the adult form,* but appear more worm-like. They must pupate and metamorphose before they resemble the adult form. In both instances, however, the non-adult stages are all larva.

this step *requires* the immature to *become active* to slip out of it. It cannot slip out by remaining still. After the immature escapes the exoskeleton, a new exoskeleton is already forming over the entire surface area of the immature. This well-known process is called "molting." The abandoned hollow exoskeleton is called the "shuck." In most instances it looks almost exactly like the stage of the insect that just slipped out of it.

From the time they hatch out of the egg, most insects and crustaceans will grow a certain amount then molt. (Horseshoe crabs will molt several times while they're still in the egg!) They then grow a little more and molt again, and they do it again and again throughout their life cycle. Some insects may molt only a few times, but others may molt dozens of times before they reach adulthood, mate, and die. Every time an insect or crustacean molts, it is larger than it was the last time it molted. It's another step closer to being an adult. The step or stage between each molt is called an *instar*. If an insect molts seven times, for example, it has developed through seven instars. The instars are simply referred to as the first instar, the second instar, the third and so forth.

This sequence of growing and molting, over and over again, — from instar to instar —is the crucial mechanism that makes it possible to extensively predict good bites. This is very important for you to understand and remember: All aquatic insects and aquatic crustaceans molt numerous times throughout their lifetime. **(Sidebar #5: Molt or Hatch)**

A familiar example of molting is when you see mayflies, sometimes hundreds or more, suddenly appearing on the surface of a lake or stream. They usually pause for a few moments then fly away to nearby vegetation. Before they fly away, fish are typically eating them with vigor. A molt has just occurred, but a lot happened before you first noticed the insect's appearance.

Before the mayflies appeared on the surface of the water, they swam from the lake or stream bottom to reach the underside of the surface, but all of them were still in their old exoskeleton. When they reached the underside of the surface and made contact with it, their exoskeletons split open and the mayflies crawled out. In the process, they also struggled through the elastic and sticky surface film of the water, after which they finally rested on the upper surface of the film and the molt was complete (Surface film will be discussed in greater detail in Chapter 4. In this example, the molt occurred in the late stage of the insect's immature life, and produced a sub-adult instead of a bigger immature. The sub-adult stage is

Molt or Hatch

I use the word "hatch" loosely throughout the text to signify the most obvious sign of a molt that fishermen will see. They will see a new swarm or steady procession of one species of insect that is suddenly active, on or above the water's surface. This is commonly known as a "hatch." Contrary to common belief, however, insect hatches in the atmosphere aren't really hatches at all. Hatching denotes the presence of an egg, which is definitely not part of the proceedings underway. Insect "hatches" are the suddenly visible population of insects that just molted from an immature stage to an adult stage and emerged from the water to spend their remaining days on terrestrial earth. When I say "molt or hatch," I realize that using the word "hatch" is redundant, but I use it to keep you connected to the explanation. Molts are events that most fishermen never see, but hatches are evidence of molts that they see quite often. In my estimation, it's easier for you to relate to something if you've seen it before, and most fishermen have seen what we call insect "hatches." I also surmise that "hatches" are the only evidence of molts that most fishermen have ever seen. It's probably also valid to assert that a large percentage of fishermen have seen groups or clouds of insects and had no clue that the insects were there because of molting. Molting and hatching are not phenomena with which they are familiar. They'll become far better fishermen if they do become familiar with them. Generally, fly fishermen are quite knowledgeable in these matters and willing to share with those eager to learn more.

the next stage after the immature stage. Sub-adults look almost exactly like a full adult, no longer looking like the immature. The sub-adult will molt one time, after which it is then a full adult. Adults do not molt; they mate, lay eggs and die. The entire life cycle then begins anew.

As indicated in Chapter 2, if you can predict the appearance of food, you can predict good bites. Accurately predicting good bites, often to the hour, is possible because of molting. Until now, making accurate, consistent predictions about fly hatches, food appearances, and good bites has not been possible. You may get it right once in a while, but why can't you get it right every time, or almost every time? Would you stake your reputation on your ability to make correct predictions? Not likely. Who hasn't made the mistake of predicting today's fishing success based on how good the fishing was yesterday? Somehow it just didn't work out so well, even though the weather seemed even better today than yesterday. Sound familiar? What happened?

Most fishermen make their predictions based on casual educated guesses mixed with gut instinct and luck; and they're wrong most of the time. Sure, most will still catch fish some of the time, and some will still catch some fish most of the time, but fishing can become brutally hard work to catch those few fish. Many fishermen would probably stay home, at times, if they knew fishing was going to be more like work than play. It's supposed to be fun, and fishing is a lot more fun when a good bite is on. If you can predict those good bites, fishing will be a lot more fun over the long haul.

Also, consider children or spouses who now dislike fishing because they were first taken fishing on a day when fish wouldn't bite. The boredom nearly killed them. Getting them in a boat or waders again can be a challenge. The outcome couldn't be much worse, but it could have been much better if their guide (you?) knew how to predict a good bite.

Molting is a remarkable mechanism that has surrendered a trove of secrets for successful fishing over the years. Fishermen and scientists have had a basic working knowledge of molting for centuries, and many fishing techniques are based on it, especially in fly fishing. Every stage of molting of some insect or crustacean, for example, has had an artificial fly created that mimics it and attempts to exploit its "bite" possibilities. Even across continents, the catch phrase of the past couple decades has been "match the hatch," but there would be no hatches without molting. Knowledge of molting, and the secrets revealed by it have benefited fishermen everywhere; and it's utilized around the globe, every day. Still, the current state of knowledge of molting has done little for accurately and consistently predicting good bites. Fortunately, only a modest leap is required from the current state of knowledge to new knowledge that makes good predictions possible.

A basic understanding of molting unlocked some secrets, but some of the most elusive fishing secrets of the ages can now be unlocked by understanding the environmental conditions that *cause — or prevent —*

molting.

The result is simple: If, during the molting season, you know what causes a molt, you'll know some of the best times to go fishing. If you know what prevents a molt, or interferes with it, you'll know some of the best times to stay home.

Most of the food eaten by fish, besides other fish, is comprised of species with exoskeletons that molt. They include all arthropods, which includes all species of insects, spiders, centipedes and millipedes, and crustaceans like sowbugs, scuds, crabs, crayfish, and shrimp. There are many thousands of species.

Each species molts according to its own genetic code, but you do not need to know that code to predict a molt and a good bite. You just need to be confident that many individuals of a certain species should become active because of molting, and you must know which environmental conditions (mostly weather) will cause that molting activity to happen.

I repeat: two things must exist for predicting a molt, and hence a bite: (1) You must be confident that enough individuals of one species have developed and matured enough to molt on the day that you want to go fishing; (2) You need to know which weather conditions can cause the molt to occur.

This might seem like a lot to absorb, but things are much simpler than they seem at the moment.

Addressing the first of the two conditions: How can you possibly have confidence that enough individuals are ready to molt? If you can't see them or keep track of their development throughout the year, how can you know that they might be ready to molt? It seems ludicrous to think you could be confident about such a thing, but you can, and it's easy.
Here's how:

You can be certain that a large amount of molts will happen if you're fishing in a lake or stream that has plenty of fish in it, and they live there naturally. That's it.

The fact that many fish can live in that body of water is all you need to know to be confident that molting will happen whenever conditions are right. Fish populations would collapse if a broad spectrum of arthropods – aquatic insects and crustaceans – were not living in your lake or stream to populate the food web. If the fish are living there naturally, enough of the right food is there. Frequent molting is guaranteed because so many species of aquatic arthropods must be present to sustain healthy fish populations. Virtually hundreds of aquatic crustacean species and aquatic insect species are present in most healthy water systems. Their size can range from microscopic to several inches long. The population of individuals of each species can be staggering, sometimes thousands per cubic foot of bottom mud, and millions per acre. (**Sidebar #6: Aquatic Arthropods** and **Other Foods**)

#6
Aquatic Arthropods

List represents tens of thousands of species, their eggs, and their immatures worldwide — a substantial, reliable food base for fish

Alderflies	Fish flies	Stoneflies
Beetles	Fish lice	Water bugs
Blackflies	Mayflies	Various Plankton
Caddisflies	Midges	Crabs
Craneflies	Mosquitos	Crayfish
Damselflies	Snipe Flies	Scuds
Dragonflies	Soldier Flies	Shrimp

Other Foods
Only a few of these are reliable sources of nourishment for fish

Algae	Frogs	Slugs
Ants	Grasshoppers	Snails
Barnacles	Lampreys	Snakes
Bees	Leeches	Sowbugs
Birds	Mollusks	Spiders
Clams	Moths	Worms
Crickets	Rodents	
Ducklings	Salamanders	
Fish — eggs to	Seeds	
adult	Shrews	

(The lists in **Sidebar #6** are substantially constructed from information contained in W.B. Scott & E.J. Crossman, 1998, *Freshwater Fishes of Canada*, Galt House Publications Ltd., Oakville, Ontario, Canada)

Degree-Days

Addressing the second of the two conditions: You need to know which environmental conditions (weather) can cause a molt to occur, and cause a good bite.

There has never been anything in angling literature that offers definite information about the exact kind of weather that reliably causes molts or good bites to occur. On the other hand, the literature is peppered with anecdotal stories about how fishing seems to be better on overcast days, or sometimes good just before a storm, or better after bad weather clears out. There's no rhyme or reason mentioned in these anecdotes that you can use to predict when you should go fishing next.

Countless writers have described the weather on the day when they encountered good fishing. If they are to be believed, fishing was great during every imaginable good and bad weather condition. Conversely, they have also written that fishing was terrible during every good and bad weather condition imaginable. How can the same kind of weather produce both good and bad fishing? It's a paradox that doesn't seem to make sense. At the very least, it seems to eliminate the day's weather as the reason for molts or good bites. Well, things aren't always what they seem. Mother Nature has encrypted the answer to this mystery in a masterful way…

The answer is that hatches and bites are not completely dependent on the weather of the day. They are also dependent on the weather that occurred during each of the three to four days prior to the day when the hatches and bites occur. The deeper answer lies in what happens underwater during those prior days. It's the modern angler's great good fortune that most of the answers can be divined with a humble barometer. You'll learn those answers in chapters that follow.

To bolster your confidence even more, and propel your powers of predicting good bites to soaring new levels, you need to understand the *simple* agricultural concept of ***degree-days***. Understanding degree-days will help you know why the timing of molts and hatches of each species happens near the same calendar date, year after year. If you want to predict good bites in lakes and streams wherever you travel, understanding "degree-days" is critical for you. You will be pleased with yourself for taking the time to learn about it. It is interesting stuff, but you won't need to do much with it after you've read it. You just need to understand it. The explanation may temporarily cause you to think there's too much to keep track of, or that the task is impossible, but don't get snagged in that trap. I'll show you a simple way that nature keeps track of degree-day matters for you. Fishing should be fun, and understanding degree-days and the fascinating way to use it makes it more fun.

The simple premise of degree-days is:

All organisms must absorb a certain amount of heat in order to develop from one stage to the next, but the heat must be within a certain temperature range.

The temperature can't be too cold or too hot. If a plant or animal gets too cold it just won't grow. If a plant or animal gets too hot it becomes so stressed that it won't grow either. This makes perfect sense: You can't freeze a plant or animal and expect either to grow, nor can you boil them and expect them to grow. They can only grow if the temperature range is somewhere in between. Every plant and animal has a temperature range in which it grows and develops best. The minimum temperature needed for growth and development is called the ***threshold temperature*** — it's the temperature at which growth and development can begin. Threshold temperatures for some species are suspected to be as low as 32 degrees. The maximum temperature beyond which growth or development cannot continue is called the ***cutoff temperature*** — growth and development are cutoff and stop at that temperature because it's too hot. Cutoff temperatures are seldom a factor in the development of most organisms.

Let's use a hypothetical mayfly immature (nymph) to demonstrate the concept:

During winter when water temperature is too cold, the immature will not grow. As spring approaches and the days and nights get warmer, the water temperature also starts to get warmer, but we notice that the immature is still not growing or developing. It's not growing at 35 deg F, or at 45 deg F, or at 49 deg F; but, as the water reaches 50deg F, the immature begins to grow and develop. Notice that 50 deg F is the threshold temperature at which the immature begins to grow. After reaching 50 deg F, the water soon climbs to 51 deg F. The difference between the threshold temperature of 50 deg F and 51 deg F is one degree, but if that *one degree* difference is maintained for 24 hours, then the amount of heat accumulated during that 24 hour period is called *one degree-day*. The immature has absorbed *one degree-day* of heat in the 24 hour period because of the one

31

degree of higher temperature difference. If the water temperature climbed to 52 deg F (two degrees over the threshold temperature of 50 Deg F) and remained there for 24 hours, then there would be an accumulation of *two degree-days* of heat that the immature absorbs in the 24 hour period. If the temperature climbs to 56 deg F and stays there for 24 hours, then the immature will absorb *six degree-days* of heat in the 24 hour period, and so forth.

As the water continues to get warmer, and degree-days accumulate, the immature will continue to grow and molt as it gets too big for its exoskeleton; and it will grow and molt repeatedly as degree-days accumulate. The process will continue through adulthood and reproduction, and then the mayfly will die.

An exact number of degree-days are needed for the immature to develop from the egg to the first instar; then another exact number of degree-days are needed for it to develop from that first instar to the second instar, and so forth through every instar all the way through mature adulthood. For its entire life cycle, the immature always needs the same number of total degree-days to develop from egg to adult.

The mayflies and other aquatic insects, and all other arthropods, including shrimp, crabs, crayfish, and micro-crustaceans are genetically programmed to develop in this way; and it probably happens in every lake or stream where you have ever fished, or will fish.

The process and approximate timing of molting and hatching is guaranteed every year because of degree-day development. Degree-day heat is also guaranteed to occur at about the same rate every year because the earth's exposure to the sun is about the same every year. The exposure is always about the same because the earth always moves along its orbit in the same way throughout its annual orbital cycle. This also causes the average annual temperature, for any location on the planet, to stay within just a few degrees from year to year. The timing of molts and hatches is reliable because average weekly or monthly temperatures for most locations are also very close throughout most years.

A huge benefit of degree-day development for fishermen is that the great majority of immatures (instars), of a given species, are all at or near the same stage of development throughout their life cycle. They all grow up together in the same location, under the same conditions, and therefore at the same rate. Consequently, they all reach the same instar stages at roughly the same time. The happy result for fishermen is that an individual species will undergo a mass molt or hatch during the same approximate time period every year. For example, when one immature of one mayfly species molts, most of the other immatures of its species will also molt on or near the same date every year. Therefore, when one immature molts into adulthood, a majority of immatures of the same species will also molt into adulthood on or near the same dates as in previous years. Likewise, when it's time for pre-adult instars to molt, the entire population of that instar will molt during the same approximate time period as in previous years.

Remember that there can be hundreds to thousands of species of aquatic insects and crustaceans in most healthy bodies of water. Each of those many species will have immatures present that are at different stages of development for each species, each according to its own genetic program. They vary in size from microscopic to large enough to impale on a fishing hook. The population of each of the many species will also be present in numbers that can range from minimal to staggering. When the various populations of immatures of many species are combined in one body of water, they form a tremendous mix (aggregation) of immatures that can produce molting at almost all times of the year when degree-days can accumulate. In addition, the number of immatures that molt at any given time can be very high. The molting of one species can also overlap simultaneously with the molting of another species. Overlap of molting of more than one species is a common occurrence. Evidence of this is readily seen during some evenings on a trout stream: Several different species of mayflies or caddisflies may appear on the water at the same time or scattered throughout the evening hours.

Probabilities are high that immatures from more than one species, which will each be at different instar stages, will molt at or near the same time and same dates when conditions are right. For example, four species may be molting simultaneously: They could be a mayfly in its second instar, a caddisfly in its sixth instar, a stonefly in its fifth instar, and another mayfly in its new adult instar. This would be a *multi-stage, multi-species molt*. The angler, however, would only see the one mayfly species, the one in its new adult form that's resting on or flying above the water's surface. If enough of that species is molting, then a good hatch probably appears to be in progress, one that will provoke a good bite. To the angler's dismay, in this situation the fish may not feed on the species he can see. The unseen, underwater molting could be so significant that the fish may only be feeding on the species he can't see. For the fish, chasing escaping mayflies near the surface may require far more effort than feasting on the easier to catch, abundant prey near the bottom.

Recall that immatures *must become active* to crawl out of their old exoskeletons; they cannot escape them by remaining still. When multi-stage, multi-species molts occur, the immatures must become very active, which makes them more vulnerable to predation, at which time you can probably bet that the bite is on! Fish are opportunistic feeders, and they are triggered to feed when substantial food suddenly becomes available. Active, molting immatures are far more available as food than are comfortably concealed, inactive immatures. Their movement attracts the fish's attention. Multi-stage, multi-species molts create golden opportunities for fish to feed, especially if the immatures are not too small. Even small immatures, however, can trigger a good bite.

If the timing of insect hatches is a little early or late on the calendar from year to year, it's probably because the insects absorbed their required degree-days a little sooner or later than expected. There may have been a hotter-than-usual heat wave the week or month before the hatch's expected date, and more degree-days were accumulated during that time. If the required degree-days were accumulated early, then the hatch would occur early. It's also possible that a few extra degree-days could have accumulated during a heat wave or extended warm period that occurred during the previous summer or fall. That may also cause the hatch to occur a little earlier because development of immatures would be a little farther along. Extended cool periods would retard the accumulation of degree-days and therefore cause hatches to appear later on the calendar. Over the course of a year, however, environmental temperatures average out to about the same values as in previous years. This results in degree-day accumulation that's fairly consistent and repetitious from one year to the next.

Accumulation of degree-days is far more variable, however, when examined on a day to day basis. Daily weather conditions can present a bad-news/good-news situation.

The bad news is that every day brings varying amounts of degree-day development because weather conditions are so variable. The threshold temperature for any organism may only be exceeded for a few minutes or hours on some days. There is probably never a day when degree-days are a nice round number; it's likely they are always a difficult-to-use amount, a fraction of a full day or days. Plus, it's extremely difficult to determine threshold temperatures in the wild, and practically impossible for a fisherman to know how many degree-days are needed for any molt or hatch to occur. Another major problem is that fishermen never see the majority of molting that occurs. The overwhelming majority of it happens underwater out of view. Only the rarest fishermen would ever have an inkling that a molt is occurring unless an insect hatch is appearing on the water's surface or taking flight. They would probably never see nor be aware of crustaceans molting. No doubt, monitoring degree-days is far too cantankerous and impractical for fishermen to do.

The good news is that *plants* can tell you when the correct amount of degree-days has accumulated for certain molts and hatches to occur. They can *accurately* do the counting and monitoring of degree-days for you.

Just like insects and crustaceans, plants also develop from stage to stage because of temperature and degree-day accumulation. Their seeds need a certain minimum of degree-days to germinate, they need more degree-days to sprout stalks, leaves, and buds, and still more degree-days to flower, and even more degree-days to develop fruits and seeds for the next generation. Plants don't molt, but they do develop in stages that are reliably predictable and repetitive from year to year. **(Sidebar #7: Phenological Tracking)**

When insects and crustaceans are molting in a lake or stream, each species is doing it during a very specific time segment of the year, which is governed by their internal biological clocks. During that same time segment, the plants adjacent to the lake or stream have also reached a specific stage in their development according to their internal biological clocks. The exact same climate and weather has been influencing both the plants and the aquatic insects and crustaceans in their respective environments — same air temperature, same cloud cover, same barometric pressure, same wind, same sun and darkness, and so forth. The exposure isn't perfectly the same, but it's extremely close.

If you examine the numerous nearby plants when the molts or hatches are in progress, the plants will all be in various stages of development. The goal is to identify a plant that has reached a significant point in its development and has a feature you can easily identify every year. For example, is it flowering at the same time the insects are molting or hatching? Are its leaves the size of a mouse ear or a crow's foot? Are the catkins falling from the aspens, is thistle going to seed, are Jack-In-The-Pulpit

Phenological Tracking

Insects molting, fish spawning, flowers blooming, and butterflies migrating are all recurring biological events. They repeat every year and each has a relationship to weather. They are temperature dependent, which makes them ideal indicators for tracking each other's stages of development. For example, when Pennyroyal first blooms in your yard, largemouth bass may be spawning in a nearby lake. The first-day bloom of Ox Eye daisies may signal bass spawning in yet another lake. These relationships will generally hold true, year after year. Using plants as indicators for fish and insect behavior is a dependable and enjoyable way for fishermen to know what's happening in lakes and rivers many miles away, in the present and future.

These temperature-dependent recurring events are known as Phenological events. Phenology is the study of repeating biological events and their relationship to weather.

I've intentionally avoided discussion of specific chemical processes occurring during the molting process. This is a fishing book, not a chemistry course. Suffice it to say that hormones are responsible for the multitude of *physical* changes that occur to the exoskeleton and other properties of insects during the molting and hatching processes; likewise for crustaceans. We are primarily concerned with how the non-chemical elements of nature — like pressure, temperature, and light — influence the behavior of insects and crustaceans, and ultimately the fish we are trying to catch. We can't keep track of chemical reactions, but we can keep track of things that keep track of the chemical reactions for us; things like natural sequences (phenological events) and weather events that allow us to predict the time and place when unseen chemical processes produce a bounty of food for the fishes we seek.

berries turning red? The possibilities are many. If the hatching period lasts 10 days, two weeks, or a month during the growing season, there is always a plant that has developed to a stage that coincides with the time period of that hatch or molt, or close to it. The plant may reach the stage a week earlier than the hatch, but that's to your benefit. You will always know that the hatch (and the bite) happens about a week after the plant reaches the stage you've identified. The plant's stage becomes a botanical indicator you can depend on for good fishing.

Large agricultural universities and corporations around the globe have spent vast amounts of money on studies that rely on the "degree-day" concept. Their scientists use it as a primary tool for predicting when grains will ripen, when fruit trees will flower, when hybrid test crops will reach critical stages of development, when insect pests will be most vulnerable to pesticide treatment, and much more. Their controlled laboratory conditions have proven degree-days as a reliable scientific concept. It's a critical tool for developing and protecting the crops that feed the human race. University and corporate investments are huge because the concept is accurate and reliable, and the benefits are incalculable. If the world's smartest scientists are using the degree-days concept to predict natural events, fishermen should be using it too.

Plant Indicators and Precursors

The trick is to identify highly obvious plant stages that appear during the same time period that the most visible stages of the insects appear. The best plants, whether wildflowers, shrubs, or trees, are those that are plentiful and easy to locate. If you live on a lake or stream the task is easier because you can immediately correlate it to what the fish or insects are doing. For most fishermen, however, it's impractical to select plants near the edge of a lake or stream because it requires too much traveling back and forth to check them throughout the year.

The most convenient plants to use are those growing naturally in your yard or along the roadside near your home. Choose them where you live and travel most. Correlate the plant stages with your fishing experiences and observations, and visits to boat launches whereby you question other anglers at the end of the day, and with fishing reports obtained from local tackle shops or friends. As you identify the botanical *indicators* that correlate with fish activity and the activity of their food, and the fishing reports about specific species, you'll soon become a more successful fisherman. You'll have a powerful tool for identifying periods when good bites will occur. You'll have a form of biological calendar that gives you reliable predictions every year. The dates of the events change every year, sometimes by as much as a couple weeks, and rarely more, but the order in which the events occur will remain the same because degree-days makes it so. No matter how widely the weather differs every year, the order always remains the same. When the botanical indicator is present, the hatch or fishing event that you've associated with it will also be present, year after year.

This system allows you to know what's happening — and what's going to happen in your lake or stream of choice. As you identify the plants and their stages that are good indicators for good bite periods, you'll find it handy to identify other plants and some of their significant stages that occur *before* the real indicators appear. This would give you an indicator that is a **precursor** for the first plant. In other words, the precursor tells you to "get ready, keep your eyes open because the real indicator will be appearing soon." The precursor gives you advance notice that good fishing will be occurring soon and you won't want to miss the real indicator for it.

Delayed Molting

When an aquatic insect (or crustacean) absorbs degree-day heat throughout the year, it absorbs a different amount every day, depending on the water temperature. Additionally, its probability of acquiring the exact degree-days, at the exact preferred time for hatching or molting, are certainly remote. Theoretically, when it has absorbed the amount of degree-days necessary to molt, it should then molt, but it probably almost never does at that instant. Instead, for example, if the molt is from immature to adult fly, the hatch almost always occurs at the insect's preferred time of day. Why doesn't it hatch at the moment it acquired the necessary amount of degree-days? Why does it almost always wait until a preferred time of day to hatch or molt?

It's reasonable to assume that the insect will fulfill its degree-day requirement before the exact moment that it wants to hatch, and not at the same instant of hatching. It's likely that it receives the necessary degree-days perhaps many hours before, and, in many instances, several days before it finally hatches during its preferred hatching time. Therefore, if the insect receives the degree-days early, it seems logical to assume that it can delay its own hatching, sometimes for days. This might cause us to think that the insect has an internal controller or delay mechanism that can delay hatching even after it has received the necessary degree-days; and, perhaps it can adjust the timing of its hatch to coincide with its preferred time of day. (I've been unable to find studies that establish whether early instars also molt at preferred times or not, but it seems more logical that they do than don't.)

At first glance, a delay mechanism might sound like a good explanation for how the delay appears to be manipulated, but I don't believe it is. A better explanation is that there is no manipulation of the delay time. The flexible *delay time* may just be incidental to what's actually happening.

State of Ableness

I offer the following as a replacement hypothesis:

After the insect or crustacean has received its necessary degree-days, it does not actively or consciously delay molting or hatching. Hatching at the preferred time of day is genetically programmed and will occur without manipulation. Instead, the insect has simply developed to the point of being in a state of being able to molt or hatch; and each additional day improves the maturity, strength, and suitability of all factors that make it able to molt or hatch in a healthy, timely manner. It's in a *state of ableness* to molt or hatch, which may last for just a few hours or several days, depending on the species; and it can molt or hatch at any time during the hours or days that it's in the state of ableness, depending on weather conditions, which then trigger the molt or hatch.

The insect will be prompted to molt or hatch when either of two things happen: (1) environmental (weather) conditions are favorable, in which case it will molt or hatch at its next opportunity during its preferred time of day, or (2) the state of ableness is about to expire, which means the insect must molt or hatch no matter what the conditions are or it will perish.

The latter occurs because too much time has passed (several days?) during which favorable conditions have *not occurred* for molting or hatching — for example, during flood conditions. If possible, however, it will still happen at the preferred time of day. Favorable environmental conditions can cause the insect to molt or hatch during the earlier hours or days of the state of ableness; unfavorable conditions will delay molting or hatching until the latter days or hours of the state of ableness. Either will happen sometime during the state of ableness. Fortunately, the day, and often the hour can be predicted. A better understanding of these concepts will give you a far better understanding of when natural bites will occur.

The duration of the state of ableness is generally shorter near the equator than toward the poles because the accumulation of degree-days happens faster in the lower latitudes where more heat is present.

Also, the duration of the state of ableness can vary for a given species, for example: If an insect normally has a four-day state of ableness, the four days can be reduced to three days, depending on the rate of heat absorption. In other words, if a species absorbs an abnormally high amount of degree-day heat in a very short period of time, it will shorten the duration of its state of ableness and it will molt or hatch sooner. Conversely, the four days can be stretched to five days or longer if the water becomes overly cool for a prolonged period and the insect is unable to absorb enough degree-day heat to be fully mature and able in four days.

As a fisherman, you only need to know what the environmental conditions are so you can predict the day during which the molt or hatch will occur. Those conditions are explained in more detail in chapter 6.

A state of ableness is a much simpler evolutionary accomplishment for an insect to achieve than is a complicated delay mechanism. It also fits elegantly with all the explanations of barometric pressure and weather influences discussed later. **(Sidebar #8: Ockham's Razor)**

#8
Ockham's Razor

There is a principle in science called Ockham's Razor which holds that a theory with the fewest assumptions and postulations, and which offers the simplest explanation in comparison to other more complicated explanations, is probably the most correct. In that vein I contend that the simplicity of a state of ableness is a much preferred explanation over the complexity of a molting delay mechanism.

Biological Clocks

An insect's preferred time of day for hatching is set by its biological clock, which is controlled by the amount of daylight in a given day — the photoperiod.

It's well known that insects dwelling on the planet's surface are commonly sensitive to light-dark cycles ands light cues. If there is no light-dark cycle, controlled experiments have shown that some of them will die waiting for a cycle to occur before they'll emerge.

Further discussion on light-dark cycles, and the controls associated with them would require a deep trip into the studies of biological clocks and circadian rhythms. That's not necessary for this work, although a few brief comments about them are helpful, and scattered throughout the book.
(Sidebar #9: Photoperiods)

It's believed that all living organisms have an internal, master biological clock. It keeps track of the passage of time and cyclical changes in the environment, and helps the organism adapt and deal with them.

Part of the biological clock is the mechanism called the circadian clock, which controls circadian rhythms. Circadian rhythms are the things that organisms regularly do on a daily basis at certain times during a 24 hour day. Sleeping, hatching, photosynthesis, flowering, and habitual feeding times are all examples of circadian rhythms. The organism regulates itself to conduct such activities at certain times every day. The biological clock and circadian rhythms are generally not influenced by changes in temperature, which makes them very dependable, despite wide fluctuations in daily and seasonal temperatures. Biological clocks are the timing mechanisms that make degree-days work for the fisherman. All of the natural sequences of insects, plants, birds, molting, spawning, and hatching discussed so far, happen at the proper time because of biological clocks and circadian rhythms. They are crucial timing mechanisms that make the prediction of good bites possible — to the hour in many cases. Fishermen just need to capitalize on them.

Predicting the hour of good bites isn't that difficult, but predicting the *day* that good bites will occur has been far more difficult, until now. Choosing the right day is the fisherman's challenge. Knowing how to use a proper fishing barometer can repeatedly put you there on the right day. This work is likely to revolutionize the features that fishermen will demand in a new generation of fishing barometers. They currently don't exist, but hopefully they soon will.

In the rivers near my home, the giant Michigan mayfly, hexagenia limbata (aka hexes, hex flies, or just hex), normally hatches during dusk and first darkness in late June and early July. It's a dependable insect, and its appearance is anticipated at about 10 p.m. every evening by fishermen up and down the local rivers. I've spent hundreds of evenings, over several decades, enjoying the fishing they provide. In all those years, I've personally observed only one hex hatch that occurred at an unexpected

#9

Photoperiods

The length of daylight during each 24 hour day is called the photoperiod. The length of the photoperiod changes every day, and is longest in June and shortest in December. For any given calendar date, however, the photoperiod is almost exactly the same as it was on the same date the year before, and will be almost exactly the same a year later. There are only a few seconds difference.

For example, the length of daylight on July 4, 2002, was 15hours 29 minutes; on July 4, 2003 it was 15 hours 29 minutes; and on July 4, 2004 it was 15 hours 28 minutes. Any difference is just a matter of seconds per year, not minutes or hours. The precise rate that the earth spins on its axis is responsible for the precise length of the photoperiods every day. The fact that photoperiods are so exact on any given date makes photoperiods and calendar dates interchangeable, which makes it practical for fishermen to just keep records with dates, and disregard photoperiods.

Certain things happen on certain dates because the photoperiod on that date is the right length. Photoperiods are indirectly included and implied, even if only the dates are recorded. Biological clocks and circadian rhythms in all species are precisely tuned to the gradual daily changes of the length of the photoperiod, and the clocks make all the necessary daily adjustments. The clocks and rhythms are very dependable, which helps all fishermen who are trying to predict good bites.

time — 2:30 one afternoon. I also have friends who've seen hex hatches at unusual times — one at 3:30 a.m. and another at dawn. It's probably a safe bet that we've all missed more than a few hatches that occurred at skewed times. High water, muddy water, heavy cloud cover, and ill-defined light/dark cycles associated with frequent storm systems may possibly cause the insect to delay its molt or hatch well past its preferred time, resulting in *skewed hatch time*s. Sustained extreme environmental conditions may blur the cues responsible for hatches that occur at preferred times. Interviews with veteran river guides over the years reveal that hatches they've witnessed at skewed times have occurred shortly after high water crested following a period of bad weather. The hatches appeared after the water level began falling. More discussion of these conditions is contained in Chapters 6 and 7.

Apparently we have more to learn about degree-days and biological clocks before we can perfectly predict the hour when every hatch will occur. On the other hand, the vast majority of hatches always occur near the expected time of day. With few exceptions, the internal clocks of all living organisms regulate their behavior and keep them on a highly accurate and dependable schedule. Those dependable schedules are very handy for predicting good bites and the likely prospect of fishing success.

The concept of degree-days brings a higher degree of understanding about the development and behavior of many organisms, especially those which are important to fishermen. It gives us a measurement system that allows us to be confident about the correlations we can make between plants, aquatic fish food, and the feeding behavior of fish. It validates a method we can use to predict time periods when good bites will occur, year after year. We know we can trust it.

Chapter 4

Surface Film
Death Trap

During recent centuries, seasoned fishermen have developed a growing suspicion that barometric pressure is somehow linked to fish behavior. They've noticed patterns in fish behavior that sometimes correlate with the weather, but thus far, the behavior patterns have proved impossible to decipher. That changes with this book.

Current belief, although faulty, is generally limited to thinking that fishing is best during cloudy, inclement weather, which frequently occurs during periods of low barometric pressure; and fishing is worst during sunny, "bluebird" days and clear nights that occur during periods of high barometric pressure. They're both right, and wrong, because some of the best and worst fishing can occur in almost any type of weather.

Over the years a few rare, and highly disciplined fishermen have kept detailed records of their catches and numerous factors that they felt were associated with those catches. The factors include location, water depth and clarity, current speed, suspended depths of the target fish, underwater structure, water temperature, air temperature, wind direction, cloud cover, precipitation, barometric pressure, moon phase, major and minor tide times, tackle and baits used, boat speed, methods of presentation or retrieve, time of day or night, and the date, and more. No doubt, fishing situations exist in which any of these factors can be important for success.

The reason fishermen keep track of these factors is that they hope to identify one or more of them as reliable, repeatable indicators that will tell them when or how they can catch more fish. They're looking for something that will help them be more successful. They're not satisfied with how many fish they're currently able to catch. They want to be better, and able to catch more. I've heard plenty of unsuccessful fishermen say they are just happy to be out of the house and on the water trying to catch a fish. I'm sure that's true. They say it doesn't matter if they catch a fish or not, they're just as happy either way. I'm sure that's *not* true. If it were true they wouldn't be using their rod to try to catch something. They're seeking a bigger thrill. No doubt they would be happier if they were catching something. I'm also sure they'd be even happier if they could catch lots of fish every time they were out trying.

Indirect Effects of Barometric Pressure

Of all the factors that fishermen keep track of, barometric pressure has probably given them the least return for their effort. No two days of records of fish behavior and barometric pressure readings are ever the same. No matter how long they have kept records, dependable patterns of behavior never seem to emerge from the data. Once in a while they appear to form a vague relationship, but they don't seem to repeat in a dependable manner. Reliable patterns based on barometric pressure have remained insanely elusive. Money to study the matter is also elusive. Universities and corporations don't spend research money on it because, for recreational fishing, the potential profits or other benefits don't justify the expense. Despite the dismal payoff, however, it seems that the collective instincts of many fishermen keep them thinking that a fuller understanding of barometric pressure and its influence on fish behavior can somehow improve their catch. They are correct!

Personally, I don't believe barometric pressure has any direct effect on fish behavior, because there is no evidence that supports it, but the *indirect effects* are dramatic. Barometric pressure has a *direct effect on the food that fish eat — the insects and crustaceans — not on the fish*. It can cause the food to appear or not appear. The food then causes a behavioral response in the fish, all the way from the smallest minnows to the largest predators. It's the availability of food that affects the behavior of fish. *Fish respond to the food, not the barometric pressure.* Fish occasionally appear to be responding to the pressure, but the effect is *indirect*. Barometric pressure works both ways; it can *cause* food to appear, and it can *prevent* food from appearing. Put another way, it can appear to cause a good bite, and likewise appear to kill a bite for days. Fish are opportunistic feeders; they feed when food presents itself, especially if it's abundant, and they can become highly stimulated and activated by the sudden appearance of it. Barometric pressure plays a *major role* in when that food will appear or not appear. When the food shows up, so do the fish. Barometric pressure is one of the primary indicators that will help you determine when much of the fish's food will show up *or not*. Again, it's the food that controls the fish's behavior, not the barometric pressure.

Nature has done a pretty good job of encrypting the mysteries of barometric pressure, but I offer explanations in the coming chapters that help to decipher those mysteries in a dependable fashion. The explanations have been responsible for a couple hundred perfect predictions for good bites during the five years prior to finishing this book. My goal is to give you a commanding knowledge of pressure that will give you a huge fishing advantage for the remainder of your days on the water. You'll be capable of catching many more fish, and the notes in your fishing log will be far less bewildering.

Coffee, Surface Film and Surface Tension
About 25 to 30 years ago I read an article about making coffee in an elk hunting camp high in the mountains of Colorado. The author mentioned that the coffee came to a boil sooner at high altitude (Sidebar #10: Boiling Water). I thoroughly enjoyed the novelty of that comment because of all the science it brought with it. I guess that's why I remembered it, but I didn't realize its importance for fishing until about two decades later. Two decades! Now you know how intellectually slow I am, so you should have plenty of confidence that you can think and understand things at least as well as I can, and probably better.

My infatuation with the coffee statement happened instantly. I knew the coffee boiled sooner because the atmospheric (barometric) pressure is lower at higher altitudes. The pressure is lower because the atmosphere up there isn't as deep from top to bottom, (the bottom of the atmosphere where it meets the ground up there is thousands of feet above sea level) and air is always thinner at higher altitudes. This means that the air weighs less up there; it doesn't have as much weight as it would at sea level. The lighter weight of it doesn't push down as hard on the surface of liquid coffee, so the surface of the hot coffee doesn't have to push back against the atmosphere as hard to bubble and boil. At sea level, however, the atmosphere is deeper and therefore heavier, so its increased weight pushes down harder on the surface of the liquid coffee, requiring the hot coffee to push harder against it to bubble and boil. The effect is much like someone holding their hand over your mouth. If their hand pressure is light — like *low* barometric pressure, you can still talk and force air out of your mouth and probably even spit. If, however, the hand pressure is heavy — like *high* barometric pressure, you wouldn't be able to talk nor could you force air out of your mouth, nor spit without a great struggle. The effect is the

#10

Boiling Water

The following figures are valid for standard temperatures at the cited altitudes. Notice that standard barometric pressure is about 1in.Hg less per thousand feet of higher altitude.

Altitude	Boiling Temperature of water (degrees Fahrenheit)	Approximate Barometric Pressure (in.Hg)
sea level	212.0	29.92
2000 feet	199.9	27.82
5000 feet	181.9	24.9
7000 feet	169.7	23.09
10,000 feet	151.3	20.58

From: National Oceanic and Atmospheric Administration and National Institute of Standards and Technology, U.S. Dept of Commerce same on all liquids. Lake water and river water behave exactly the same way.

The lesson here is that the changes in atmospheric pressure can change the properties of the surface layer of water where you go fishing. The *surface layer* is best known as the ***surface film.*** It's only one molecule thick, but it's the interface layer between the water below it and the air above. It's what you see as you look out over the water. It's the reflective surface layer that acts like a mirror on every lake, stream, and pond. Nothing above it or below it acts in the same manner.

The lower barometric pressure normally present at high altitudes reduces the ***surface tension*** of the liquid coffee, which allows the coffee to boil sooner, and boil at a lower temperature. Surface tension is the force that holds the liquid surface of the coffee together. It causes the surface molecules to bind together and form a thin surface film on top of the liquid. The film is much like a thin sheet of sticky plastic or rubber. Low surface tension causes the film to be weak, so it won't hold together very well, which means the coffee bubbles can break through it a lot easier. They can break through with very little resistance. Low barometric pressure is the condition that permits the coffee to boil sooner.

At lower altitudes, however, the situation is different. The atmosphere is deeper and denser (thicker), so it's heavier and pushes down on the coffee with more weight or pressure. In other words, the air pressure (barometric pressure) is higher, which increases the surface tension of the liquid and makes the surface film much stronger. The stronger surface film prevents the coffee from boiling sooner because the bubbles can't form and break through it as easily. High barometric pressure creates the conditions that keep the coffee from boiling sooner.

Twenty years later, because of the coffee statement, I had an epiphany moment and realized that weather systems with low barometric pressure would reduce the tension of the surface film of lake and river water. This would allow hatching mayflies to struggle through the water's surface film more easily, and their chances for survival would be improved.

Most of us are familiar with the simple science experiment whereby a sewing needle is carefully lowered onto the surface of water in a drinking glass. The solid steel needle appears to float on the surface of the water. The surface tension of the water and surface film keep it atop the water, but the surface of the water appears slightly curved near the needle. The weight of the needle pushes down on the water's surface and warps the surface shape. The surface remains tough and unbroken, however, and won't let the needle break through and sink to the bottom of the glass. The water doesn't separate under the weight of the needle because the surface tension is too strong. The strong tension holds the film together, which makes it act like a strong sheet of plastic or layer of elastic skin. The surface film on a river or lake acts the same way and has the same properties. It presents a formidable barrier for hatching insects to penetrate and struggle through when they hatch. High barometric pressure makes the surface tension much stronger, which *makes the surface film much stronger* and very difficult for insects to penetrate and climb through. Low barometric pressure has the opposite effect; it dramatically weakens the surface tension, which *makes the surface film weaker* and much easier for insects to penetrate and climb through. These conditions are represented in Figure 4-1.

A good example of the strength and tenacity of surface films is when a fruit fly or ant plops into your cool beverage on a hot, bright summer

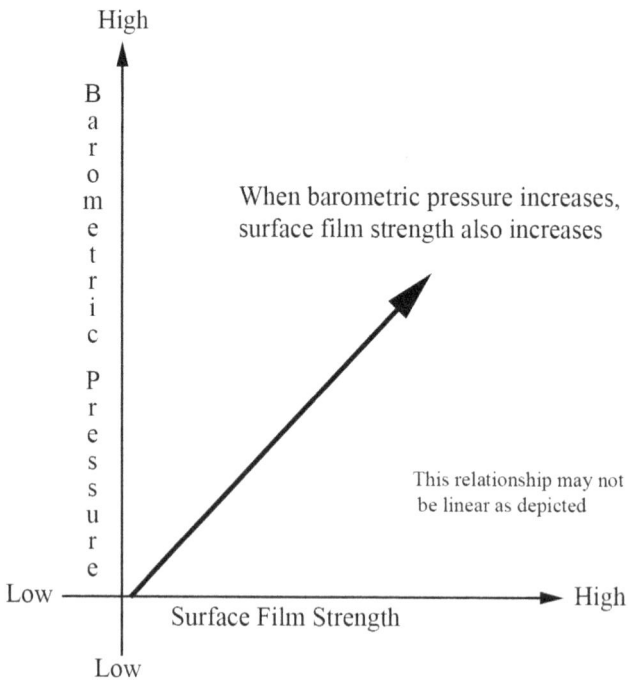

Figure 4-1

50

day. The insect is instantly captured in the surface film and cannot escape. It can barely move. Even moderately larger insects sometimes cannot extract themselves from the grip of the film. A herculean effort is required to pull itself free. The hot, bright day tells you that barometric pressure is high, therefore the surface tension on your drink is also high and strong, which in turn makes the surface film very strong, like a tough, sticky sheet of rubber or taffy. The binding forces of the film are too strong, and constitute a situation that is a life or death struggle for the insect. I'm sure you can recall finding a dead insect stuck in the film of your drink at some point in your life.

For the average insect, the surface film is a deadly threshold that can trap it and prevent it from flying off to mate. High barometric pressure is a culprit that makes the surface film such a dangerous threat and frequent death trap. It creates a surface film condition that is detrimental to the survival and reproduction of aquatic insects. Another force called *capillary force* makes escape even more difficult for the insect, but there's no need to explain it further here.

An insect has a far better chance if it falls into your drink on a muggy, overcast day. The weather indicates that the barometric pressure may be lower, which causes weaker surface tension and a much weaker surface film. The insect may be able to wiggle and slowly propel itself while partially submerged in the surface of the drink. It actually may have a decent chance of swimming through the drink to the edge of the glass and pulling itself to safety. The surface film will be weaker and far less of a death trap because the barometric pressure is low. Likewise, the weak surface film condition resulting from low barometric pressure allows hatching aquatic insects to penetrate the film and crawl up through it much easier. They don't get hung up in it and perish. They can escape through it and fly away to mate and lay eggs with little impedance. Low barometric pressure creates very favorable conditions for survival and reproduction of aquatic insects. The strength of the surface film varies depending on how high or low the barometric pressure becomes.

Water Temperature Affects Surface Film

Water temperature also affects the strength of the surface film. The surface film is weaker when water is warmer, but stronger when water is colder. Large, rapid swings in water temperature, however, are usually rare events and generally not a worrisome factor in surface film strength.

As mentioned in Chapter 2, molts and hatches typically occur when the water temperature range is right for the species. The strength of the surface film fluctuates very little because of the temperature, and its range fluctuates very little for specific hatches. Barometric pressure remains the major cause of fluctuations in film strength from day to day. Interestingly, as summer nears its end, many of the smallest and weakest aquatic insects remain to hatch — when the water is warmest and surface films are generally weakest due to the elevated water temperature. It appears feasible that they have naturally selected to emerge at perhaps the only time during the year when they have enough strength to struggle through the surface film.

If high barometric pressure is detrimental to the survival and reproduction of aquatic insects, but low barometric pressure favors their survival and reproduction, it seems logical that the insects may be genetically programmed to take advantage of low barometric pressure conditions. Eons of natural selection should have produced insects that will molt and hatch when conditions are most favorable, and that would be when barometric pressure is low. It would likely give them the best chance to survive until they can reproduce. This genetic adaptation would be very advantageous. My observations convince me that this adaptation has occurred and is a dominant trait in aquatic insects and aquatic crustaceans.

A Pressure Hypothesis

It all seems rather obvious now, but it took me several years to develop the following hypothesis and muster the necessary explanations and field observations to support it. Some of the details may not sport the correct scientific jargon, but that's intentional because I've tried to stick to plain English. On the other hand, I've endeavored to base the hypothesis on the strictest scientific principles as we know them today. I've also tried to include an unbroken chain of logical steps, each step based on the step before it that depicts the path I used to arrive at my conclusions. They can be checked for correctness by all interested parties. I'm keenly aware that the hypothesis, in addition to requiring a logical explanation, must elegantly explain and accommodate all known conditions and circumstances in nature that it might bear upon. I believe it meets those criteria. You can use it to reliably predict molts and hatches that cause good bites to occur, to the day, and to the hour in many cases.

The hypothesis:

Aquatic insects and aquatic crustaceans are genetically predisposed to molt and hatch during lower pressure conditions. They will also molt and hatch during higher pressure conditions, but the risks of mortality are higher.

I'm also convinced that constant natural selection has produced insects strong enough to successfully struggle through strong surface films during high barometric pressure periods. It's likely, however, that only the most mature and fully developed insects can do it most successfully. This is explained further in the discussion about the state of ableness.

As you will learn later, it's inevitable that hatches will also occur during high barometric pressure periods. Unfortunately, catastrophic insect population losses can occur during these periods under certain conditions, affecting the bite for years to come.

Humidity Requirement

Another question about insect survival nagged me for years. Like all fly fishermen will do from time to time, I occasionally collected mayfly samples and put them in my fly box for later identification. By the time I arrived back home the insects were dead. They always perished in the box. I later learned that adult mayflies survive best if atmospheric humidity is high. They need a moist atmosphere in order to survive. They will die if the air is too dry.

Two significant factors that make them susceptible to moisture loss are that their wings are gossamer thin, and the cross-section of their bodies is small. Osmotic pressure and respiration alone can cause a substantial amount of moisture loss. Even though their exoskeleton is a good barrier against moisture loss, it apparently has its limits. They need moisture from high humidity to stay alive. Dry air will kill them, and it won't take long. The dead mayflies in my fly box were certainly a testament to that. It appears that the exceedingly dry hair and feathers on the flies in my crowded fly box absorbed so much moisture, including the respiration from the mayflies, that the insects never had a chance.

The humidity requirement rocked me somewhat. It provoked a question that I was unable to answer for years.

My question was, "How can a mayfly possibly know that the atmosphere above the water is humid, and that it should hatch as soon as possible because the humidity is suddenly favorable in the world above?" The insect has spent its entire lifetime soaking at the bottom of a lake or river from the time it was just an egg to the present, just prior to hatching into adulthood. It has always been completely submerged and wet! How can it possibly know that humidity is even present in the dry world above that it has never known, or how much humidity up there is the right amount? Well, it doesn't know, and never will. Nor do any other aquatic insects or crustaceans.

If a mayfly or other aquatic arthropod can't determine if it's humid outside, how can it synchronize its molting and hatching to coincide with the correct humidity or pressure conditions that it needs in the atmosphere above? The answer lies within the state of ableness, which is explained further in the next chapter.

Chapter 5

The Pressure Rules

Recall that the state of ableness is the condition wherein an aquatic insect has developed to the point of being able to molt or hatch. The condition, depending on the insect species and its latitude/altitude, may last for just hours or several days or more. The insect is capable of molting or hatching at any time while in the state of ableness.

State of Ableness Details

Biological clocks aside, molts and hatches and the day they occur during the state of ableness are largely dependent on environmental conditions. They are particularly dependent on barometric pressure, both high and low. Water pressure is another major factor, and easily understood, and given detailed treatment near the end of this chapter. **(Sidebar # 11: A Human Hatch?)**

When aquatic insects finally reach the state of ableness, they become highly sensitive and *responsive to barometric pressure changes and water pressure changes* in their environment. Some of the insect's new physical changes, the ones developed for molting, are the reason.

This is the critical period for fishermen. During this period or state

#11

A Human Hatch?

Several years ago a national television network reported a dramatic rise or spike in birth rates in hospitals located in the direct paths of ongoing hurricanes. No explanation was offered for the spike in births, although stress was easily inferred as a cause.

I suggest that barometric pressure may be a significant contributing factor. Barometric pressure is exceedingly low near the eye of a hurricane or typhoon, but becomes progressively higher as the distance from the eye increases. The extreme low pressure near the eye should affect the mother's tissues in a pronounced way.

Pregnant women carrying full-term babies, and near-full-term babies, are themselves in a state that resembles the state of ableness. They are ready and able to give birth to babies that can survive and thrive without extraordinary care after birth. Some can be born as early as six weeks premature without extraordinary care. For each woman, all of the tissues, membranes, and fluids associated with her fetus are at or near their fullest necessary development that can produce a normal birth. Such pregnancies can be considered to be within a normal range that's ripe for birth. Naturally, each additional day of pregnancy improves the maturity, strength, and suitability of all factors required for a timely, healthy birth.

Perhaps the best known and most dramatic event that occurs prior to birth is that known as the "water break." When a woman's "water" breaks, birth of the baby usually follows within minutes or hours. What has actually happened is that the membrane that is the amniotic sac, which is filled with "waters" and surrounds the fetus and placenta, has burst. The waters then immediately drain out through the birth canal, usually wetting the expectant mother's clothing. She then knows that birth is imminent.

Obviously there is a direct, unobstructed path between...
See the continued, entire text of this sidebar in **Appendix A.**

of ableness, whether it lasts for hours or days, the insects behave in a predictable manner that can't be changed. They are slaves to the genetic codes working within them. They are under the uncontrollable influence of a cascade of internal processes that will cause them to molt or hatch. New hormone secretions override life functions and cause the physical changes necessary for molting.

It's extremely important to understand that some of the immature's development processes continue throughout the remaining hours or days of the state of ableness, which make the insect more mature and stronger on each succeeding day. It is stronger on the last day of the state of ableness than it is on the first day. On the last day it has more physical strength to overcome high pressure against its exoskeleton than it has on the first day.

The insect may not hatch on the first day because it doesn't yet have the strength to overcome the pressure bearing on its exoskeleton. For the same reason, it may not hatch on the second day or the third day, but by the fourth day it's finally strong enough to escape the exoskeleton and also emerge through a strong surface film. Conversely, if barometric pressure is low, or water pressure becomes low, which makes the total amount of pressure low, the insect doesn't need as much strength to pull free of its exoskeleton and can hatch earlier within the state of ableness. Its physical strength and the total amount of pressure it must overcome will determine when the molt/hatch will occur. It seems safe to assume that the insect will hatch as early as it can during the state of ableness. This also seems valid for crustaceans. The total amount of pressure, which is simply atmospheric pressure and water pressure added together, is explained in detail later in this chapter under the heading **Total-Pressure.**

Summarily, during the state of ableness, the insect or crustacean will behave in a *predictable* manner that is hugely influenced by the combination of barometric pressure and water pressure (hydrostatic pressure).

Molting

Aquatic insect species don't all molt in identical fashion. Some go through more steps than others, and some use varying but similar means to separate themselves from the restrictions of the exoskeleton when the right moment arrives. Despite these differences, however, they all have much in common that works to the fisherman's advantage. Ultimately, they all accomplish the same thing; they molt or hatch.

One of the key processes that occur to all insects during the state of ableness is that of separating themselves from the exoskeleton. Remember that the exoskeleton serves as the insect's bone structure; its muscles are all attached to it. It's a very tight-fitting part of its body structure. To say it's tight-fitting is an understatement. To molt out of it, the insect must completely detach from all connections to it. Even after it's detached, the insect is still confined within its tight, form-fitting shape. It's much like a tree branch that has been dipped in molten plastic that has hardened, and then trying to slip the branch out of the plastic's tight-fitting grip. Extracting it from the hardened plastic would be extremely difficult, if not impossible.

Secretions produced by the insect initiate processes that use some of the tissue from the old exoskeleton to create the beginnings of a new exoskeleton. During these processes the old exoskeleton becomes separated from the new one. The insect develops a very thin and flexible new exoskeleton, but is still residing within the confines of the old one. It's possible that a small amount of gas or gases are produced during the separation process, and at least some of the gas remains in the space or interface region between the immature and its old exoskeleton. It's also possible that a lubricant is produced that coats the insect and helps facilitate its escape from the exoskeleton. It's also possible that the process creates softer, compressible tissue on the surface of one or both of the exoskeletons, which would allow the insect to pull free when needed. Perhaps more than one of these possibilities is present, or another process altogether that accomplishes the same result. Fortunately for the fisherman, the old exoskeleton still fits pretty snuggly before the insect gets out of it.

To separate itself completely, the insect undergoes *strong contractions and body movements* to pull itself free from all points within the exoskeleton. Any gas, lubricant, or soft tissue occupying or bordering the space between the immature and old exoskeleton, aids the process by creating mechanical properties within the space that allow it to behave like a less than perfect vacuum. A perfect vacuum would cause the old exoskeleton to constrict tightly against the immature and prevent it from pulling free, whereas a less than perfect vacuum (partial vacuum) limits the constriction and allows the immature more wiggle room to pull free. The contractions happen dorsally, abdominally, and in the legs. Contractions also make the insect very active and conspicuous. Imagine the commotion created when the entire molting or hatching population begins having multiple contractions. It must be a spastic circus, and a siren call for the fish. Scientists know that fish's lateral lines are extremely sensitive to vibrations, so the vibrations caused by the contractions and movements of hundreds or thousands of insects must be like a clanging dinner bell to them. This is likely how molts cause good bites (See "buggy" scent, pp 119). If you can time the molt you can time the bite. Fish are atuned to it.

During the state of ableness, but after separation from the exoskeleton, insects use gases (air?) obtained through their gills, or other respiratory means, to create pressure that causes their body or parts of their body to swell up. As the swelling increases from the building pressure, the insect's swollen body and higher pressure push against the exoskeleton and cause the exoskeleton to expand slightly. The slight expansion may only be measurable in microns, but some expansion occurs nonetheless. It only makes sense that, if there is swelling, the swelling must have a place(s) where it has swelled *to*. The swelling is occurring within the insect that is encapsulated by the tight-fitting exoskeleton, which means the exoskeleton must expand slightly to allow the swelling of the insect to occur. The swelling would also expand into the slip-space between the insect and the old exoskeleton and compress any gas or soft tissue in or lining the slip-space. If the exoskeleton can't expand, then the insect can't swell much either. One can't happen very well without the other. It's likely that some swelling also occurs inwardly in some parts of the insect. At some point the swelling may stop, but the pressure continues to build according to the insect's genetic controls. The growing pressure eventually causes the old exoskeleton to split open along the top midline of the head and/or thorax region. If pressurized gases are trapped in the slip-space, they would escape when the exoskeleton splits. This would relieve pressure around the insect and allow it to more easily crawl out through the split. As far as I've been able to ascertain, all aquatic insects molt or hatch in processes that substantially resemble this one, as do aquatic crustaceans.

It's somewhat comparable to what happens in a bicycle tire. The insect inside its exoskeleton is very much like an inner tube inside a bicycle tire. As pressurized air is pumped into the inner tube, the tube expands and applies pressure against the stiff tire. As more pressurized air is pumped in, the inner tube keeps expanding and applying more pressure on the tire, which causes the tire to slightly stretch and expand to its rigid, physical limit. When the tire reaches its physical limit, it cannot expand any farther. When still more pressurized air is pumped into the tube, the pressure eventually becomes so great that the tube causes the rigid tire to "blow out" at its weakest point. If the tire is always a particular brand, and always has a uniformly weak seam in one spot, then it will always blow out in the same spot if the internal air pressure is roughly the same. In similar fashion, insects and crustaceans also "blow out" of their exoskeletons, but the timing is better controlled. (Sidebar #12: Internal Pressures)

Insects can regulate the swelling and pressure so that the completion of the process normally occurs at the insects' preferred time of day for hatching. They have an ability to slow the process down or speed it up by a few minutes or hours on any day during the state of ableness. They can molt or hatch on any day during the state of ableness, but almost always do so at their preferred time of day.

Molting at the preferred time probably occurs in a manner similar to the following scenario:

#12
Internal Pressures

Insects and crustaceans have several forms of internal pressure that bear on the molting process: Hemolymph (blood) pressure, osmotic pressures, and tissue elasticity.

Pressure from the swelling causes the exoskeleton to *expand slightly* to its maximum size (elastic limit), but not enough to cause a split just before the preferred time arrives. When the preferred time arrives, the insect then initiates a final increase of swelling and pressure that causes the exoskeleton to split and allows the insect to struggle out. Again, the insect becomes very active and conspicuous as it struggles out.

Aquatic crustaceans, like crayfish, shrimp, crabs, and many others, undergo similar processes to molt. Unlike Insects, however, crustaceans take on water instead of air, and pressurize it to aid the split.

Also like the insects, crustaceans undergo strong contractions and body movements that help to separate themselves from the exoskeleton. Considering that enormous amounts of smaller and micro crustaceans can be present at times, it's probable that their heightened activity can cause the same commotion and response in fish that insects do. When they molt, baitfish will descend on them because their populations are so great. When the bait fish descend on them, the predator fish are close behind. Some species of crustaceans, for example, crayfish and freshwater shrimp, are large enough that they are eaten directly by predator fish.

Exoskeleton Properties

Several properties of the exoskeleton play vital roles during the molting process. They link the insects and crustaceans to barometric pressure and water pressure in a manner that makes the organisms responsive to pressure.

The organisms need a system for sensing the force of the pressure so they can molt or hatch when the surface film is weakest, and humidity is high, giving them the highest chances for survival.

Barometric pressure and water pressure are *mechanical forces*; which means they act on an immature in a mechanical manner. Their mechanical force is applied against the immature's exoskeleton first. The exoskeleton has several mechanical properties that make it responsive to the mechanical force of the pressure. When the exoskeleton responds to the pressure, its response affects the immature inside in a controlling manner.

Below is a brief look at four mechanical properties of the exoskeleton that convey the pressure directly to the immature's body.

A primary mechanical property of the exoskeleton is its stiffness or *rigidity*. Most of the exoskeleton acts like a strong, rigid suit of armor that's in direct contact with, or is part of, the surfaces of the insect dwelling inside. The old exoskeleton loses its proximity to life support systems, so it may have lower moisture content, perhaps causing it to become more rigid than the new exoskeleton. The new exoskeleton continues to have the fluids and softer compounds of life in closer proximity to it, which may keep it slightly softer and more flexible than the old exoskeleton. The difference in rigidity of the two exoskeletons may aid the molting process in that it may ensure that the drier, old exoskeleton would rupture before the moister, new exoskeleton would.

Another property is its *elasticity*. A small amount, at least, is present in almost every material. Exoskeletons are generally regarded to have no elasticity, but there are situations that suggest otherwise (See Radical Pressure from Waves in Chapter 7). They either have some elasticity or are part of a system that behaves in an elastic manner. Elasticity allows the exoskeleton or the system that it's part of, to slightly expand and contract, at least in some places. The expansion and contraction is probably more pronounced near the insect's joints and mouthparts, and possibly along the seam where it splits, where tissue is more flexible, highlighting the fact that tissue has *flexibility*.

Tissue in the joints and mouthparts must have flexibility, which would allow those parts to move. Therefore, it seems reasonable to assume that if pressure is applied against the flexible tissue, the pressure can make the tissue bend, warp, distort, or move in the direction that the pressure is pushing, or relax in the direction toward which the pressure has been reduced. The areas of flexibility that are present in various parts of the exoskeleton may be enough to allow any expansion and contraction that the insect may need during a molt. The exoskeleton would become a device similar to an air-tight paper bag. The bag can have air blown into it to expand, or have air let out of it so it can collapse or contract, at least in some places.

Plasticity may be another key property of the exoskeleton. Plasticity means it can stretch to a longer length without retracting back to its original dimension, and do it without being damaged. The most obvious example occurs immediately after the critter crawls out of the exoskeleton: Before an insect molts and sheds its exoskeleton, it has already developed a very thin, *new* exoskeleton that protects it after it emerges from the old one. At emergence, the insect is quickly and noticeably larger than the exoskeleton from which it crawled out just moments earlier. How can it be so much larger almost immediately after crawling out? Obviously the insect must have been significantly *compressed* while still residing in the old exoskeleton. When it emerged it subsequently *expanded* to its larger size. It was able to expand its new exoskeleton in all directions from every point. The expansion may be due to the new exoskeleton *stretching* to its larger size, or simply *expanding* to fill a space much like fluid filling a bag — the bag providing a certain volume available for the expansion. It expands or stretches to a larger size in a matter of seconds and stays that size, or perhaps may get even larger without damage. Whatever the case may be, there is some capability for expansion somewhere in the lifetime and structure of the exoskeleton. Plasticity must certainly be considered a possibility.

Insects and Crustaceans Become Barometers
The various physical properties of the exoskeleton make it act very much like a straightjacket. Its degrees of rigidity, elasticity, flexibility, and plasticity all work together to make it slightly *variable* in size. At the very

least, it can slightly change the volume that it encloses. The range of the *variability* is slight, and may only be a distance of the thickness of a human hair, or more, or less, but it is variable nonetheless. Like a straightjacket, the exoskeleton can be caused to constrict and tighten against the insect, at least in some places, and it can be caused to loosen, which relieves the constriction against the insect.

Tightening and loosening of the exoskeleton is exactly what happens with changes in barometric pressure and water pressure. The insect feels every little bit of pressure change because the exoskeleton responds to the changes with slight changes in its size (in places?). When barometric pressure goes up, it pushes on the exoskeleton with more force, which forces the exoskeleton tighter against the insect's body, like a straightjacket getting tighter. When barometric pressure goes down, less force pushes on the exoskeleton, so it acts like a straightjacket getting looser.

Fishermen in wading boots are quite familiar with the straightjacket effect. When they wade into water that gets progressively deeper and deeper, the water pressure squeezes their waders tighter and tighter around their ankles and calves. The boots constrict very tightly, which can cause significant discomfort and circulation loss. The circulation loss frequently causes cold feet. As the fishermen step progressively backward out of the deeper water and into shallower water, their waders become looser and looser around their ankles and calves, effectively removing the constriction and relieving the discomfort. Barometric pressure *and* water pressure *combine* to cause this effect on a fisherman's calves and ankles. Pressure is pressure, it's all the same, whether from the water or the air, or from both.

An increase or decrease of pressure (tightening and loosening) exerted by the exoskeleton may also occur in a more *indirect* manner.

During the state of ableness, when an immature has mostly separated itself from the exoskeleton and is waiting to emerge, the old exoskeleton is actually a complete envelope around the immature, but it's mostly separated and sealed off from the immature. This creates a condition in which there are now two separate surfaces facing each other; the outside surface of the immature is facing the inside surface of the old exoskeleton. Much of both separate surfaces can slide past each other or move away from or toward each other. Also, the process of separation creates a very thin layer of *empty space*, or *slip space*, between the two surfaces in some places. See **Sidebar #13: Empty Space or Soft Tissue** for an alternative concept that replaces the empty space with soft tissue. Both concepts will work for this discussion.

If a change in external pressure pushes on or relieves pressure against the old exoskeleton, the sealed space between the two surfaces would act like a slight vacuum chamber. This is remarkable because the space would behave exactly like the vacuum chamber in common aneroid barometers found in many people's homes. The geometry of the insect's vacuum chamber is just shaped differently. In this case, *the insect has effectively created and become its own barometer.* It can detect and react to barometric pressure because, at this point during its brief state of ableness, t*he insect itself has transformed into a natural barometer or pressure gauge.* The effect should be similar with aquatic crustaceans.

Household aneroid barometers have a hollow, thin-metal vacuum chamber, with *no elasticity*, but plenty of *flexibility* to respond to pressure fluctuations. If the common barometer's sealed metal chamber is flexible enough to respond to changes in barometric pressure, surely the less-rigid and perhaps compressible exoskeleton can respond as well. The push-pull effect of the insect's vacuum chamber would transfer the full effect of

---

#13

Empty Space or Soft Tissue

The empty space between the surfaces of the exoskeletons may not be an empty space, but instead a space occupied by tissue from the old and new exoskeletons that possess a gradient or range of hardness that varies from soft to hard. Such soft tissue would be compressible over a short range. If the old and new exoskeletons are interfaced with slightly compressible tissue between them, then that same tissue could also decompress. Alternatively, the soft tissue, like the empty space with gas, would still provide the "barometer-like" mechanical elements (compressibility and relaxation) required for responding to barometric and hydrostatic pressure changes.

external pressure changes against the insect.

Both possibilities — empty space with gas, or soft tissue — can serve as models that explain that the insect's physical, mechanical properties make it capable of behaving like a natural barometer or pressure gauge.

Barometric Pressure Effects During Molting

When barometric pressure is high, the high pressure causes the exoskeleton to press more tightly against the insect and constrict at all points around it — the exoskeleton adjusts slightly. The higher force of constriction makes it more difficult for the insect to swell inside the exoskeleton. Thus, the swelling will take more time. The higher constricting force also holds the exoskeleton together with more force at the seam where it must split. The elevated constrictive force then prevents the exoskeleton from splitting as easily. Splitting then requires even more pressure from the inside. Such increased pressure requires more time to develop. The constriction also tightens the fit around the head and legs. This makes it more difficult for the insect to separate itself from the exoskeleton, even with strong contractions. Thus, under the influence of high pressure, the separation will take more time and more effort. The constriction may also have the effect of retarding internal chemical processes because the passageways (cellular, lymphatic, and capillary passageways) through which the compounds flow may be smaller due to the constriction, which restricts their flow. The restricted flow would cause the chemical or biological processes to take more time. If similar constriction can cause circulation loss in a fisherman's ankles and calves, it seems reasonable that a similar effect would be inflicted upon the insect. It therefore appears that the *molting processes are impeded and slowed by high barometric pressure*, including, to a small degree, their biological clocks.

When barometric pressure is low, the lower pressure causes the exoskeleton to press less tightly against the insect. It relieves some constriction of the exoskeleton at all possible points because the pressure pushes on it with less force; the exoskeleton adjusts or expands slightly. The lower force of constriction makes it easier for the insect to swell inside the exoskeleton and allows the swelling to happen in less time. The lower constricting force of lower barometric pressure also holds the exoskeleton together with less force at the seam where it must split to escape, which permits it to split more easily. Splitting then requires even less pressure from the inside, hence the pressure needed for splitting develops in less time. The reduced constriction also loosens the fit around the head and legs. This makes it easier for the insect to separate itself from the exoskeleton with strong contractions. Therefore the separation requires less effort and less time.

The reduced constriction may also have the effect of causing internal chemical processes to take less time because the passageways through which the compounds flow may be larger and less restricted. Less process time would be required because the compounds arrive sooner where they're needed. If reduced constriction improves circulation in a fisherman's ankles and calves, it seems reasonable that a similar effect would happen within the insect. It therefore appears that the *molting processes are aided and accelerated by low barometric pressure*, including, to a small degree, biological clocks. **(Sidebar #14: Water Pressure)**

How is it possible for an immature aquatic insect or crustacean to feel the changing *barometric* pressure when it's in the water at the bottom of a lake or stream? A critical part of the answer is that the critter dwells at a *constant level* somewhere near or in the bottom, whether in the sand or mud below, or on the rocks or vegetation above. Every aquatic insect has a preferred habitat (niche) in which it thrives best. When it enters that habitat it usually stays close to it. It stays there until its genes drive it to relocate. When it's living in its preferred habitat, it's usually at a nearly constant depth below the surface. If it lives in the mud, it may move about on short excursions to feed or improve the conditions that make it safe, but it doesn't usually go far either up or down (vertically). It stays near its selected depth and location in the mud. If it lives under a rock, it will usually stay under that rock, or the rock next to it or one nearby. Each species

---

#14

Water Pressure

The term "water pressure," as used in these pages, is better known in scientific circles as hydrostatic pressure. Not all fishermen are inclined toward the physical sciences, however, so I have chosen to use "water pressure" in the general text for easier understanding by all.

has been naturally selected to maintain its residence in its preferred habitat and stay close to it for the best chances of survival.

Consider a mayfly immature living under a rock in a typical river. Let's say that the immature's position under the rock is exactly two feet under the water's surface. In other words, the *water column* or *water level* is exactly *two feet deep* and the immature lives at the bottom of it. Like most rivers, the water level is usually stable, but can slowly drop during dry periods, or rise and fall at radically different rates due to runoff from rain, snow melt, or flow releases from dams.

A key feature of the river water is its weight. Its weight is what puts pressure on the immature. When the water level is stable at two feet deep, its pressure on the immature is also stable, it doesn't change, it's constant. The immature under the rock experiences a *constant pressure* from the water while it's living at its *constant level* under the rock. The *constant pressure* at two feet deep is the *normal pressure* of the water on the immature. The pressure of the water never changes if it remains exactly two feet deep. If the water level drops, however, the pressure of the water on the immature will be less because there is less weight from the water that's pushing down on it. The pressure from the water will be *less than normal* because the water is now less than two feet deep. Conversely, if the water level *rises*, the water pressure on the immature rises because there is more weight from the water pushing down on it. The pressure from the water will be *greater than normal* when the water is deeper than two feet.

Normal water pressure for any immature is simply the weight of the water that the immature is normally living under. An immature normally living under three inches of water experiences the weight of three inches of water as its normal pressure; if it normally lives under three feet of water, then it experiences the weight of three feet of water as its normal pressure; if it normally lives under 30 feet of water, then it experiences the weight of 30 feet of water as its normal pressure.

Normal pressure is that which results from the stable water level or depth, no matter how far the bottom is located below the surface. Each bottom depth has its own normal pressure, all due to the normal, stable water level above it. For example, the inclining slope of a lake bottom near shore has a different, but normal pressure for each point along the slope. Naturally, normal pressure is lower in shallow water, but higher in deeper water. Insects that dwell at different depths each experience a different water pressure, but the respective pressure is normal for each of them if the water level over them remains constant, no matter how deep or shallow they dwell. Natural selection has equipped each insect with its own special strength to cope with its unique normal pressure.

When the immature is in the state of ableness for molting, the normal pressure of the water applies normal pressure to the exoskeleton which allows the molting process to proceed at a normal rate for that insect (This assumes that temperature and barometric pressure are constant). If the water level drops, however, the water pressure that's pushing on the exoskeleton is reduced — and the straightjacket loosens — which allows the molting process to speed up. If the water level only drops a little bit, the molting process only speeds up a little bit. If the level drops a lot, the molting process speeds up a lot.

Conversely, if the water level rises, the water pressure that's pushing on the exoskeleton is increased — and tightens the straightjacket — which causes the molting process to slow down. If the water level only rises a little bit, the molting process only slows down a little bit. If the level rises a lot, the molting process slows down a lot.

Total-Pressure

Barometric pressure causes the exact same effects as water pressure. The difference, of course, is that the effects of barometric pressure are caused by the weight of the atmosphere, not the weight of water. Just like water, however, the atmosphere exerts pressure because it has weight. At sea level, the atmosphere is over one hundred thousand feet high and weighs about 14.7 pounds per square inch (@ 59 Deg F). A one-inch square column of water of the same weight would be approximately 34 feet high.

Most fishermen are aware that barometric pressure is constantly changing because the weight of the atmosphere (air) is constantly changing. The weight constantly changes because the temperature of the air keeps changing which makes the air heavier or lighter. Cold air is heavier, warm air is lighter. Mixing and layering of cold, heavier air, with warm, lighter air happens constantly in all weather systems. Therefore, barometric pressure readings constantly move up or down because the weight of the atmosphere keeps going up or down due to temperature changes.

The barometer seldom settles on one value and stays there for long. The values change because the air temperature is always changing and the atmosphere is constantly moving. Barometers are sensitive and change quickly to indicate the *changing* and *current* atmospheric pressure of weather systems that move through the area. Constant barometric pressure changes are beneficial for fishermen. The *pressure changes* cause significant food spikes that trigger good bites.

Water pressure and barometric pressure combine to create the total-pressure on all aquatic insect immatures. They are the only significant external pressures that the immatures will experience in their lifetime. Aquatic immatures are affected by both the barometric pressure and water pressure at the same time, *all the time*.

Let's again consider the mayfly immature living under the rock exactly two feet under the water's surface. The immature is subject to the constant, normal pressure of the water. If the water pressure does not change, and remains constant, it's reasonable to assume that the processes within the immature are also not changed by it. With respect to the unchanged water pressure alone, those processes remain on a normal course of development. Everything is normal and constant.

Everything changes, however, when the changing weight of the atmosphere — the barometric pressure — is added to the water pressure. The two pressures, or weights, are stacked one on top of the other; they are added together. The insect experiences the direct weight or pressure of the water, plus the direct weight or pressure of the atmosphere, *both added together*. The effect is that of two separate weights stacked on top of each other; the weight of the water *plus* the weight of the atmosphere that's resting on top of the water. Total weight or ***total-pressure*** is caused by the combined weight of the *two separate weights* — water plus atmosphere. If either the weight of the water or the weight of the atmosphere changes by a certain amount, then the total weight (total-pressure) also changes by that same amount.

Insects (and other organisms) only feel the total-pressure, the combined pressure of the water and the atmosphere; and *the effects on the insect are always caused by the total-pressure, not just water pressure separately or barometric pressure separately.* The "cause and effect" of total-pressure, especially during the state of ableness, is clear and direct:

If water pressure or barometric pressure (or both) *increases* and causes total- pressure to *increase*, then molts and hatches will be impeded and slowed down.

If water pressure or barometric pressure (or both) *decreases* and causes total-pressure to *decrease*, then molts and hatches will be aided and accelerated.

The rules for total-pressure effects on the molting and hatching of aquatic insects, (and aquatic crustaceans) during the state of ableness, can now be stated in final form; there are only two. Water temperature is assumed to be stable for both rules:

High Pressure Rule:
When total-pressure increases or is high, it hinders the molting processes and slows them down, which results in molts and hatches occurring later during the state of ableness.

This rule means: Molting and hatching will be suppressed when total-pressure starts to increase. They will remain suppressed, possibly for several days, depending on how high the total-pressure becomes. After the short suppression period, molting and hatching will begin and occur daily and cause good bites daily through the remaining high pressure period and through the downward total-pressure trend that immediately follows. When total-pressure begins to trend downward, molts and hatches are then subject to the **Low Pressure Rule**. Good bites will occur on all days that molts and hatches occur.

Low Pressure Rule:
When total-pressure decreases or is low, molting processes are aided by it and speed up, which results in molts and hatches occurring earlier during the state of ableness.

This rule means: When total-pressure is trending downward and stays down, molting and hatching will generally occur on the first day of the downward total-pressure trend and continue to occur daily and cause good bites daily until total-pressure begins to increase. When total-pressure begins to increase, conditions are once again subject to the **High Pressure Rule**, and the entire cycle will repeat. Good bites will occur on all days that molts and hatches occur.

Barometric Pressure Measurement
The earlier, separate discussions about water pressure and barometric pressure are now combined in a much more useful discussion about total-pressure. Understanding the effects of total-pressure on aquatic in-

sects, especially *changes* in total-pressure, is the key to predicting molts, hatches, and subsequent good bites.

The two pressure rules are truly intimate bedfellows. One or the other is always operational or giving way to the other. To understand them better, however, some basic knowledge about pressure measurement is required.

Pressure is usually represented as a certain amount of weight per square area, for example: pounds per square inch, or newtons per square meter. Water pressure and atmospheric pressure are always expressed in these terms — pounds per square inch (psi), etc.

Barometric pressure, however, has traditionally been expressed a little differently. In the United States, the most common expression of barometric pressure is usually just a number, like 29.92. It's a number that might be used by a TV weatherman who might say, "The barometer is currently sitting at 29.92," or, "at 29.92 and falling," or "at 29.92 and rising." What he means is that the current pressure or weight of the atmosphere will support a column of mercury that's 29.92 inches high in a standard mercury barometer. When he says it's rising or falling, he means the pressure has increased or decreased since the last time it was recorded. He's informing you of the direction in which the barometric pressure is moving, either higher or lower. He's letting you know that the pressure is exhibiting a trend in its movement to a higher or lower level.

Most official barometric pressure readings, such as those observed at local airports, are posted every hour and available on numerous websites. This makes a trend easy to see, whether it's rising or falling. For example, if the current pressure is 29.92, but it was 29.94 an hour ago, then the pressure has fallen two points and reflects a downward trend, and is referred to as "falling." Conversely, if the current pressure is 29.92, but it was 29.90 an hour ago, then the pressure has risen two points and reflects an upward trend, and is referred to as "rising."

In the examples above, you'll notice that I omitted any references to inches of mercury, or any type of units of pressure; I simply cited the numbers. For the sake of easier reading, this practice is continued throughout the book and, unless stated otherwise, "inches of mercury" is the implied unit of measurement. (Sidebar #15: Pressure Points: Barometric Pressure and Water Level Equivalents)

If you prefer a barometer with different units of measurement such as millibars, kilopascals, or hectopascals, that's perfectly fine. It's only important that it's reasonably accurate at all times and you can tell if the pressure trend is up, down, or steady. The principles revealed will work well for any measurement system you choose.

You can get the information you need from standard barometers, but their inadequacies will quickly become apparent in the next chapter. Fishing barometers with all the right features will surely come to market to meet the need. When they become available they will be addressed at **www.PredictingTheBite.com**.

#15

Pressure Points:
Barometric Pressure
and Water Level Equivalents

Throughout this book, barometric pressure is expressed as a number, for example, 29.92. The units are "inches of mercury (in. Hg)." The number is always limited to two decimal places, which means the decimal places are an expression of one-hundredths of an inch. As the decimal amount changes, each one-hundredth of an inch of change is referred to as a "point." For example, if the number changes from 29.92 to 29.96, it has changed by an amount of four one-hundredths, or four points; if the number changes from 29.92 to 30.21, it has changed by 29 points, and so forth. It doesn't matter if the change is an increase or decrease; it's still a matter of points. It provides a handy way to describe changes in the weight of the atmosphere, and a way to know how much it changes total-pressure. If barometric pressure changes by 20 points, then we know that total-pressure has also changed by 20 points.

It would be equally handy to use points for describing.....

See the continued, entire text of this sidebar, complete with calculations in **Appendix B**

Chapter 6

Putting It All Together

The high pressure rule and low pressure rule, and the state of ableness all work together in an elegant manner. They're also perfectly compatible with the kind of weather and environmental conditions that aquatic insects need in order to survive. Understanding them gives you a powerful tool for predicting good bites. This chapter brings them all together in a manner that gives you a strong command and instinct for how they work where you go fishing. You'll have a far greater ability to interpret what you see at your ol' fishing hole, and know when you should be there for a good bite. The times you choose to go fishing will be greatly enhanced if you apply what you learn here.

A Short Review

Recall that the state of ableness is the condition wherein an aquatic insect or aquatic crustacean has developed to the point of being able to molt or hatch. The condition may last for just hours or several days or more. The insect or crustacean can molt or hatch at any time that it's in this state, depending on the weather; but, their molts and hatches and the day they occur are particularly dependent on the water temperature and total-pressure that each day brings.

At this juncture it's important to review the chronological sequences that aquatic insects go through during their life cycle until they reach the time of year when they will hatch as adults. The following sequence is more descriptive of the life cycle of mayflies, but it's generalized enough to apply in some way to most other aquatic arthropods — the insects and crustaceans

Briefly: The insects develop and hatch from eggs, then grow and molt many times through numerous instars during a long period before they become adults. They finally reach their last instar as an immature and hatch out of it as some form of sub-adult or adult. They are transformed from immatures into winged sub-adult or adult insects. The winged sub-adults/adults then escape their watery environment by flying or crawling into the terrestrial world above. The entire annual population (generation) of the species will hatch in this manner during the coming days or weeks. This all happens during a life cycle that has a predetermined length.

Natural selection has genetically programmed each individual insect to live exactly as long as others of its species. For example, many species are genetically programmed to live 365 days, exactly one year. One year is a common lifespan in the temperate latitudes of both the Northern and Southern Hemisphere. Some species live longer, some live less, but lifespan is overwhelmingly the same within the same species. If a species lives longer, it's usually a multiple of years, not a fraction of years. If it lives less than a year, it may produce multiple generations each year. No matter how long it lives, however, the adult stage typically makes its appearances over a period of several days, weeks, or months. Many environmental factors, and no doubt, genetic mutations, have come to bear on the species over the eons and caused its hatches to span extended periods. The process continues today, and it all starts with an egg.

Development of Immatures

The entire *adult* population of a single species doesn't hatch on the same day because they don't all hatch as *immatures* from their eggs on the same day. Mating flights and egg laying are typically carried out over a period of weeks, so the age of most eggs are varied, and the ages usually vary by days and weeks. Mating flights and egg laying will normally occur every day in favorable weather conditions, but not during unfavorable conditions.

Every egg, in some way, settles into its environment in a slightly different spot and circumstance than other eggs. Even if the eggs are of different ages, or of the same age, their different environmental experiences will cause many of the immatures to emerge from the eggs sooner or later than expected. Widely varied weather conditions and natural selection have created an extremely high probability that tiny immatures are emerging from the eggs almost every day; and they continue to emerge from the eggs every day for a length of time that roughly matches the adult hatching period at the other end of their life cycle. It's best for fishermen to assume that immatures will be hatching from eggs everyday. There will be exceptions, but probably not many. As they grow, each immature will have a slightly different pressure and temperature experience; and slightly different degree-day development.

Daily egg hatches, spread over a period of weeks, is an evolutionary survival strategy. It is nature's way of avoiding catastrophic losses that could lead to a mass extinction of the species. Nature avoids those catastrophes by spreading the risk of loss over as much time as possible. Longer time periods ensure that some eggs, in varying levels of maturity, will survive to propagate the species. The longer time periods are limited to the duration that offers optimum survival in a given niche.

A result of immatures hatching from eggs everyday is that the ages of the immatures are also different for each day. The ones that hatched on the first day will be the first to mature because they're the oldest; the ones that hatched on the second day will reach maturity next because they're the next oldest, and so forth for the third day, and fourth day, and every consecutive day throughout the egg-hatching period.

Each daily batch of immatures will grow, develop, and molt through every instar.

Near the end of every instar, the immatures continue to develop until they reach a state of being able to molt (the state of ableness). When they reach the threshold of the state of ableness, they also acquire barometer-like properties and become slavishly responsive to total-pressure. Fishermen should assume that immatures of all instar stages of most species, if not all species, enter ableness every day during the seasonal hatch period, with few exceptions. They remain in the state of ableness until they have enough strength to overcome the conditions presented by total-pressure, and then they molt. At the end of their final immature instar, they strengthen one last time in the state of ableness and molt/emerge out of their exoskeleton as a transformed, winged sub-adult or adult insect.

They are now terrestrial, not aquatic. When they're terrestrial, the state of ableness is no longer as powerfully influenced by pressure because water pressure is no longer a component of total-pressure. Without water pressure, total-pressure is extremely low, and will remain extremely low because it will never be any higher than simple barometric pressure. The winged sub-adults or adults face no more lethal challenges related to pressure, for example, a strong surface film. If the species produces sub-adults, they will easily molt one more time to become full adults. Full adults mate, lay eggs, and die, and the cycle begins anew.

On the first day that the insects are mature enough to be in the state of ableness, they will only possess minimal strength to molt or hatch, and can only molt or hatch if total-pressure is relatively low (low pressure rule). If total-pressure is high on that first day, the immatures won't have enough strength to overcome the effects of it, particularly because of the strong, straight-jacket effect of their exoskeleton. Without enough strength to overcome the high total-pressure conditions, they will remain in the state of ableness longer. They will stay in it for another day or two or three, (or more?) until they have developed enough additional strength to overcome the conditions caused by the high total-pressure (high pressure rule) — there may be unrecognized factors in this process, but this model/paradigm has produced consistently dependable results. When the insects finally acquire enough strength, their biological clocks cause them to molt or hatch during the very next preferred time of day or night. Exceptions to hatching at preferred times can occur when rapid, drastic increases in total-pressure occur, such as when floodwater raises the water level, which can cause skewed hatch times (Chapter 4).

Although this is only an instinctive guess, it's probably not too unreasonable to expect that molts of the earliest instars also occur at the insects preferred time of day or night. I've uncovered no evidence that suggests otherwise. The early immatures would also enter a state of ableness that includes barometer-like properties for each molt. If the earlier molts do occur at the same preferred time, a fisherman who understands the pressure rules and the state of ableness would enjoy a significant fishing advantage. He would know when a molt and good bite should occur, even though there would be no hatch to be seen above the water's surface.

Similar molting processes occur for aquatic crustaceans. Aquatic crustaceans, however, have had no evolutionary need to develop a mechanism that deals with the deadly dangers of surface films. On the other hand, they still molt out of their exoskeletons and develop barometer-like properties that are inherent in their molting process.

Little is known about the circadian (daily) rhythms of many fresh-water crustaceans, but it's likely they have a survival strategy that involves activity at certain times of the day or night. Whatever that strategy might be, it probably overlaps the time when its barometer-like properties occur — when the crustacean is responsive to changes in total-pressure. That responsiveness very likely interferes with normal survival strategy and makes them vulnerable to predation, which means the responsiveness will cause good bites. There's an old fishing proverb that states, "Fishing goes dead for three days after a cold front goes through." There are hidden issues in the proverb that bear greatly on this topic. Those issues will be explored further in Chapter 9. There is implication in the proverb that supports the notion that crustaceans molt during the same environmental circumstances that cause aquatic insects to molt.

Terms Used

From this point forward through the book, when reference is made to insects that are molting, but not appearing above water as adults or sub-adults, they will be referred to as "*molters.*" Insects that appear above water as sub-adults or adults as a result of freshly molting or "hatching," will hereafter be referred to as "*hatchers.*"

Molters and hatchers can be lumped together as a group and simply referred to as "*emergers.*" Traditionally, especially among fly fishermen, emergers have only been regarded as the hatchers that are in the act of emerging out of their last (or next to last) immature exoskeletons as transformed, winged sub-adults or adults. It's puzzling that no term has been used in popular fishing literature that refers to an insect as it emerges from all of its earlier immature instars. Fortunately, *emerging* accurately describes what occurs during molts of all instar stages, not just the last immature one. Therefore, "emergers" will occasionally be used to mean both molters and hatchers, inclusively. "Emergers" will also mean newly molted crustaceans.

Adult mayflies that return to a lake or stream for a mating flight and ovipositing of eggs into the water are called "*spinners.*" After mating in the air the spinners will fall to the water's surface, sometimes with a slight spinning rotation, and the overall event as applied to the group is called a "*spinner fall.*" They die soon after they fall, often within an hour or so.

Also, from this point forward, for the sake of brevity and ease of use, the term "state of ableness" will be interchangeably used with its abbreviated form, "*ableness*." I'm sure you will understand it when you see it.

It's now time to put all the concepts into practice.

A Series of Examples

The following examples will help explain how to predict hatches and the natural bites that they trigger. The key task is to determine on which day during ableness that molts and hatches will occur. Those are the days when most natural bites will occur.

There are many factors responsible for hatches and bites, but most of them take care of themselves and generally don't need to be considered when making daily predictions. On the other hand, each can be important from time to time, for example: pH balance, dissolved oxygen, light penetration level, light intensity, turbidity, pollutants, and current speed. For most practical purposes, however, water temperature and total-pressure are usually the most important, and often the only factors that need to be considered when predicting molts and hatches. You will be able to successfully predict a majority of good bites based on temperature and total-pressure alone.

Let's consider a mayfly that has a state of ableness of four days, which seems to work well in many areas of northern latitudes of the United States.

During its next molt, the mayfly will hatch in late evening from an immature to a winged sub-adult that flies off the water of a local river impoundment. Remember, depending on the weather, the mayfly can hatch on any of the four days that it's in ableness. Our task is to determine during which day of ableness that molts and hatches will occur. It's fairly easy most of the time. Temperature and total-pressure are the controlling factors, but temperature is assumed to be optimal and not a factor for most of this example, with the exception of two cold fronts. Therefore, most predictions will be made solely on the basis of total-pressure, and a majority of those predictions will be based only on barometric pressure.

In the charts that follow, I've indicated total-pressure to be either high (Hi) or low (Lo), which helps keep the explanations as simple as possible. The goal is to develop your instincts for high and low pressure affects on hatches and bites. Hi and Lo work well to train those instincts.

(If you are curious about the definition of high barometric pressure, or standard barometric pressure at your altitude,see **Sidebar #16: Standard Barometric Pressure**.)

#16
Standard Barometric Pressure

Scientists have established standard barometric pressure* at sea level at 29.92 in.-Hg (inches of mercury) when air temperature at sea level is 59 degrees Fahrenheit. Barometric pressure is constantly changing at all locations on the planet, so this is a long-term average number. Because it's at sea level, however, it's naturally the highest average pressure on the planet, with rare unimportant exceptions like Death Valley (no fish). All other average annual pressures are lower than 29.92 in.-Hg if they are measured above sea level.

Pressures greater than 29.92 occur more frequently in winter because air is much colder, denser, and heavier then, so it exerts greater average pressure than during warmer seasons. Pressures are lower during the warmer seasons because the air is then less dense, which makes it lighter.

If 29.92 is the highest average pressure, it seems reasonable to surmise that it figured prominently in the evolution of the state of ableness. It would be the highest average annual pressure that aquatic arthropods have needed to overcome for molting at altitudes near sea level. Arthropods would have naturally selected to handle conditions associated with this highest average pressure, or perished.

Arthropods inhabiting higher altitudes may have naturally selected to cope only with the highest average barometric pressure at their resident altitude, which would be less demanding than the higher pressure at sea level. The result may be that populations at higher altitudes have naturally selected with less strength than their counterparts at lower altitudes. Their reduced strength may...

See the continued, entire text of this sidebar in **Appendix C**

The examples are structured in a manner that addresses a broad spectrum of environmental conditions that affect molts, hatches, and bites. They are somewhat simplistic, but the proper lessons are conveyed with detailed explanations in most instances. There are numerous situations with added discussion. *You may find it helpful to make a* **photocopy** *of each chart for easier reference while reading this chapter.* Still further discussion is provided in chapters that follow.

Figure 6-1 illustrates the mayfly's daily hatches as they occur, or do not occur, during a 14 day period. Low pressure is regarded to be 15 to 20 points less than high pressure, which is often enough to cause extra hatching, depending on the species. It's treated as enough in the chart because it's what appears to occur in some species where I live. A pressure reduction of fifteen to 20 points represents a moderate or shallow low pressure that has a moderate effect on hatching and molting. It's probably safe to assume that moderate low pressure seldom causes a radical result. For example, it does not cause hatches or molts to occur extremely early in the state of ableness, which reduces the probability of blanket hatches. It's about enough to cause the early appearance of emergers by only one day for insects that have a four day state of ableness. Moderate low pressure generally results in moderate hatches and spinner falls. **(Sidebar #15: Pressure Points: Barometric Pressure and Water Level Equivalents)**

Deep low pressure causes hatching and molting much earlier in the state of ableness, and frequently what appear to be heavier hatches, and will be discussed in Figure 6-3.

A slightly different range of pressures may be more applicable in the waters where you fish. The presure range may be smaller for all hatching and molting events as altitude increases due to atmospheric dynamics and possible differences in arthropods' strength at increasing altitudes. **(Sidebar #17: High Water at Different Altitudes)**

Water level is treated as static and unchanged for most situations discussed in the example. Lastly, you'll notice and repeatedly be reminded that immatures are entering the first day of the state of ableness during every one of the 14 days in the hatch charts, which is probably normal; an exception — large waves — is discussed in Chapter 7.

Figure 6-1
As indicated in Figure 6-1, no prediction can be made for DAY 1

80

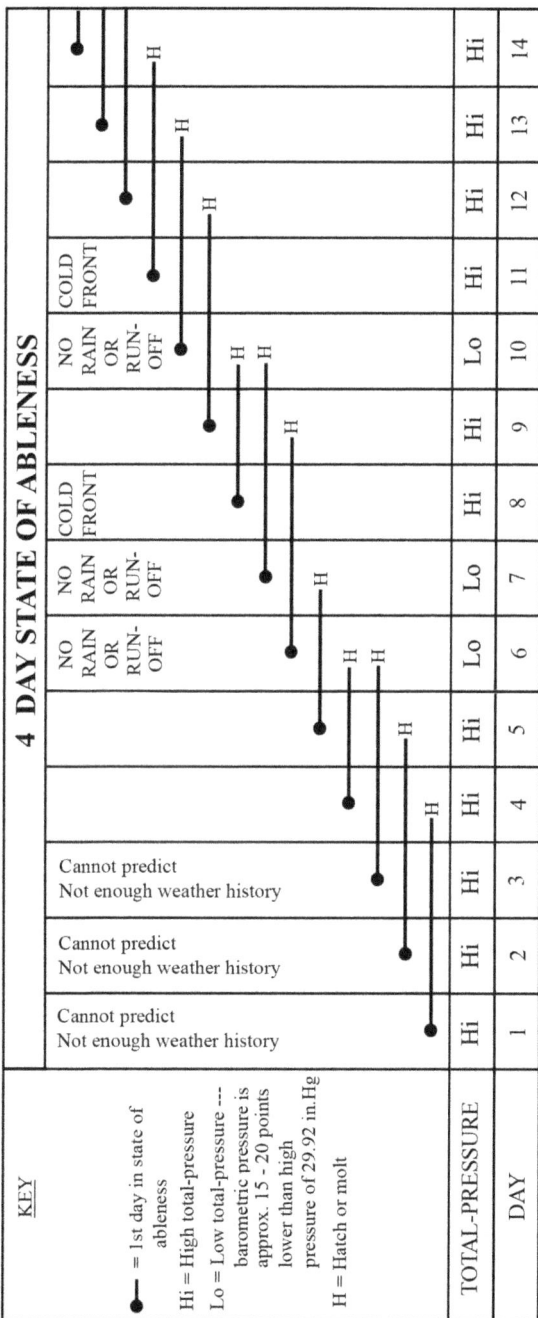

4 DAY STATE OF ABLENESS

DAY	Weather / State	TOTAL-PRESSURE
1	Cannot predict — Not enough weather history	Hi
2	Cannot predict — Not enough weather history	Hi
3	Cannot predict — Not enough weather history	Hi
4		Hi
5		Hi
6	NO RAIN OR RUN-OFF	Lo
7	NO RAIN OR RUN-OFF	Lo
8	COLD FRONT	Hi
9		Hi
10	NO RAIN OR RUN-OFF	Lo
11	COLD FRONT	Hi
12		Hi
13		Hi
14		Hi

KEY

— = 1st day in state of ableness

Hi = High total-pressure

Lo = Low total-pressure --- barometric pressure is approx. 15 - 20 points lower than high pressure of 29.92 in.Hg

● =

H = Hatch or molt

Figure 6-1

81

because there is no weather history for the three days that precede it. At a minimum, you must know the barometric pressure history for those three prior days. Without it, it's impossible to know if a hatch or molt will occur, and therefore if a good bite will occur. Nonetheless, the chart does convey two valuable bits of information for DAY 1: (1) Immatures have entered their first day of ableness and (2) Total-pressure is high (Hi).

The situation is the same for DAY 2 and DAY 3. Predictions can't be made for hatches or good bites on those days because at least three days of prior barometric pressure history are needed to do so, but it's not available. Once again, though, more immatures have entered their first days in the state of ableness on DAY 2 and DAY 3, and total-pressure has remained high for three consecutive days.

It's possible that hatches could occur on DAY 1, DAY 2, and DAY 3, but they just can't be predicted, due to the lack of barometric pressure history, but this changes on DAY 4.

We can now predict with near certainty that there will be a hatch on DAY 4. This mayfly has a four-day state of ableness and we know that some immatures have been in ableness at least four days (from DAY 1). We know they've been in ableness for four days because pressure has been high for three days, which prevented them from hatching sooner. It has kept them in ableness longer (high pressure rule). We also know that four days in ableness allows them to achieve maximum maturity and strength, which they now have, so they are now able to hatch or molt in both high and low total-pressure conditions. No extraordinary total-pressure conditions are expected, so a hatch should occur, and indeed it does. The hatch on DAY 4 is comprised of flies that were immatures on DAY 1, but they matured and strengthened through the entire 4 day state of ableness and hatched on the fourth day (see the horizontal line that extends from DAY 1 through DAY 4). Once again, more immatures enter their first day of ableness on DAY 4.

It was possible to make hatch-molt predictions for DAY 4 because the barometric pressure history (total-pressure history) was available for the three days that preceded it.

It's also possible to make hatch-molt predictions for DAY 5 because the barometric pressure history is available for the three days preceding it. The total-pressure history for DAY 5 is also a duplicate of the history that preceded DAY 4. DAY 5 is a repeat of DAY 4, which also means that immatures that have been in ableness for four days will be the ones that hatch on DAY 5. Therefore, the immatures that entered ableness on day 2 are the ones that hatch on DAY 5. Once again, more immatures enter their first day of ableness on DAY 5.

DAY 5 teaches a critical lesson: During the seasonal hatch period, when total-pressure remains high and steady for several days, hatches will commence on or near the last day of ableness and repeat on each day thereafter as long as the pressure stays steady and high (high pressure rule). If total-pressure stayed high on DAY 6 and DAY 7, hatches would continue to occur with no change in the pattern. Most importantly, this type of pattern allows you to predict the hatches and time of day that they occur, and predict the good bites that result. If the weather forecast calls for continued nice weather (high pressure), you can expect good bites at the same time on each successive day while the weather holds. It's a pattern you can use to predict good bites to the hour. You will know when to go, and when to stay home.

DAY 6 is an exciting day because it could produce a natural bite that is especially good.

Recall that changes in total-pressure in Figure 6-1 are solely because of changes in barometric pressure. Total-pressure has gone low (Lo) because barometric pressure has gone low. Therefore, lower barometric pressure on DAY 6 has caused an extra hatch to occur.

The immatures that went into ableness on DAY 3 have now hatched on DAY 6. They were kept in ableness by three days of high pressure. On DAY 6, the fourth day in ableness, they were at full strength and would hatch regardless of the total-pressure, except perhaps in high flood conditions.

The immatures that went into ableness on DAY 4 have also hatched on DAY 6, which has doubled the volume of the day's hatch. Doubling the size of the hatch is likely to cause a markedly vigorous bite. The immatures from DAY 4 were able to hatch after three days in ableness instead of four because total-pressure dropped on DAY 6. Three days in ableness gave them enough strength to hatch in the low pressure conditions. They didn't need more maturity and strength that would be gained from another day, a fourth day, in ableness. The low pressure conditions induced them to hatch a day early.

DAY 6 is the kind of day that fishermen dream about. There will be a hatch and a good bite regardless of the total-pressure conditions, and it's extremely predictable. It's a classic set of conditions that every fisherman should learn to recognize. Good hatches and bites should almost always occur when a low total-pressure trend replaces two or more days of steady, high total-pressure. The good bite will happen on the day that the pressure trend heads downward because it will cause a sharp rise in available food.

Once again, more immatures enter their first day of ableness on DAY 6.

Another hatch occurs on DAY 7. Low total-pressure on DAY 7 is exactly the same as on DAY 6, but the hatch on DAY 7 is only half as large as the day before. The total hatch is smaller because only the immatures that went into ableness on DAY 5 have achieved enough strength to hatch on DAY 7. Total-pressure has not gone low enough to cause a hatch of the immatures that went into ableness on DAY 6. The immatures that entered ableness on DAY 4 might have been available to hatch on DAY 7, but they hatched on DAY 6, a day early, because of the low total-pressure on DAY 6. Thus, only one batch of immatures with enough strength, the ones from DAY 5, are hatching on DAY 7. Nonetheless, one nice hatch will produce a nice bite; and the bite on DAY 7 is predictable if you can be certain that total-pressure will remain low. Large weather systems with low barometric pressure can frequently influence the total-pressure for a couple days or more. Rain and runoff can become factors in your predictions when big systems dump water in your fishing hole. (Sidebar #15: Pressure Points and Equivalents)

Comparing the hatches of DAY6 and DAY 7 is interesting because both days have the same environmental conditions, but the hatches are significantly different. The cause of that difference is that both days have a different three-day history. The total-pressure history of the prior three days was different for each day, and caused significantly different hatch results.

This is a pattern that always holds true: The appearance and magnitude of a hatch or molt is always dependent on the total-pressure conditions that occur during the several days that precede the hatch or molt, and, most of the time, the conditions of the day on which they occur. Curiously, the last day *of* ableness (not the last day *in* ableness) is usually the least important with regard to causing a good bite. If an immature must stay in ableness to build strength until the very last possible day of ableness, it will generally hatch regardless of the total-pressure. It has the strength to hatch and will do so, despite most adverse pressure conditions.

Keeping track of barometric pressure conditions for several days in a row, on an hourly basis around the clock, is a daunting task. Most fishermen can't do it. They need a proper fishing barometer that can record and store barometric pressure data for several days before they go fishing. The need for these fishing barometers poses a great financial opportunity for equipment makers in the fishing industry. Pray they respond.

No hatch occurred on DAY 8 because high total-pressure is back. High pressure on DAY 8 has kept the immatures from DAY 6 in ableness for an additional day. The immatures from DAY 6 were exposed to low pressure during their first two days of ableness, but the immatures were also at their weakest strength during those two days. They were physically weak, and the moderate low pressure was not low enough to allow them to hatch by their second day in ableness. They needed a little more strength. They would have hatched on DAY 8 if the pressure remained low because they would have had enough strength by then because it was their third day in ableness. Pressure became high, however, and prevented them from hatching on DAY 8. The high pressure conditions demanded more strength, so they still didn't have enough. They were forced to remain in ableness until the fourth day. DAY 8 is a great day to stay home — no hatch, no bite.

DAY 8, however, provides an invaluable lesson: When total-pressure goes high or trends higher, immediately after a low pressure trend, hatches and bites are severely suppressed. In other words, on the day when high pressure replaces low pressure, hatches and bites will be dramatically reduced. This agrees very nicely with the high pressure rule. This is one of the rare instances when you only need to know the total-pressure history of just one day prior to the day that you want to go fishing. For example, if you want to go fishing today and you know that the pressure is high today, but it was low yesterday, it's probably best to stay home today.

Once again, more immatures enter their first day of ableness on DAY 8.

High total-pressure continues on DAY 9, but a hatch still occurs. This hatch is comprised of the immatures from DAY 6, which have been in ableness for four days and achieved maximum strength. Again, a good hatch likely produced a good bite — a very predictable bite because it occurred on the last day of ableness. Once again, more immatures enter their first day of ableness on DAY 9

Day 8 and DAY 9 provide another classic example of two contiguous days with the same total-pressure conditions, yet different hatch results. No doubt, back-to-back days like these have been a maddening cause of confusion among fishermen. Their fishing logs reflect identical barometric pressure, yet wide disparities in hatch and bite activity and the amount of fish they caught each day. It's even more maddening when compared to DAY 4 and DAY 5 which had identical conditions as DAY 8 and DAY 9, but hatches occurred on both days. Comparisons like these have made it easy for many anglers to conclude that barometric pressure had little or nothing to do with their fishing results of the day. Nothing could be further from the truth. The total-pressure history of the prior days bears profoundly on the natural bite on every day that a fisherman ventures forth.

Day 10 is another exciting day because it probably produces an especially good natural bite, much like the bite on DAY 6. Low total-pressure has returned and induced an extra hatch, effectively doubling the size of the hatch. Expressed in different but similar terms, the size of the hatch has been doubled due to a drop in barometric pressure. Double hatches frequently offer the fish a bounty of food that they are happy to pounce on.

Half of the hatch is comprised of the immatures that went into ableness on DAY 7 and were kept in ableness by high total-pressure on DAY 8 and DAY 9. They now have maximum strength for hatching on DAY 10. Also, much like the immatures from DAY 3 that hatched on DAY 6, the immatures from DAY 7 have more strength than needed because the pressure went low on the last day (fourth day) of ableness. They would have hatched regardless if pressure was high or low, except perhaps in high flood conditions. High flood conditions create very high total-pressure that can lead to mortality.

The other half of the hatch is comprised of the immatures that went into ableness on DAY 8. They only needed three days, instead of four, to gain the strength to hatch in the low pressure conditions on DAY 10. The low pressure induced them to hatch a day early. The immatures that entered ableness on DAY 9 still don't have enough strength to hatch on DAY 10. The moderate low pressure isn't low enough to induce a hatch to occur two days early; it's just enough to induce it to occur one day early. Once again, more immatures enter their first day of ableness on DAY 10.

DAY 10, like DAY 6, is the kind of day that fishermen hope for There will be a hatch and a good bite regardless of the total-pressure conditions, possibly a double-size hatch, and it's remarkably predictable. It's a classic set of conditions that every fisherman should learn to recognize. *Good hatches and bites should almost always occur when a low total-pressure trend replaces two or more days of steady, high total-pressure.* The good bite will happen on the day that the pressure trends downward because it will cause a sharp rise in available food. An exception would be if the downward trend occurs after the insect's preferred time of day for hatching, which would cause the hatch and bite to occur the next day. This all happens very fittingly in accordance with the low pressure rule.

DAY 11 is uneventful with no hatch. High total-pressure has moved in and abruptly replaced the low total-pressure of DAY 10. The immatures that entered ableness on DAY 9 were unable to hatch on DAY 10 because the pressure didn't go low enough to allow hatching so early in ableness. They also can't hatch on this DAY 11 because they've only been in ableness three days and still don't have enough strength to overcome the difficult high pressure conditions of the day. The high pressure conditions of DAY 11 causes them to remain in ableness for an additional day. The immatures that entered ableness on DAY 10 have also not spent enough time in ableness to overcome the high pressure conditions of DAY 11. Once again, more immatures enter their first day of ableness on DAY 11.

DAY 11 repeats and reinforces the lesson learned of DAY 8: *When total-pressure goes high or trends higher immediately after a low pressure trend, hatches and bites are severely suppressed.* In other words, on any particular day, after the time that high pressure replaces low pressure, hatches and bites will be dramatically reduced, all in accordance with the high pressure rule.

High total-pressure prevails again on DAY 12. At first glance, DAY 12 appears to be somewhat unremarkable, but it is the beginning of something remarkable indeed.

A single hatch occurs that is comprised of the immatures that went into ableness on DAY 9. They weren't strong enough to hatch in the moderate low pressure conditions of DAY 10, nor strong enough to hatch in the high pressure conditions of DAY 11. The total-pressure conditions of each day led to them staying in ableness for a full four days, whereupon they hatched on DAY 12. The remarkable aspect of DAY 12, however, is that it is the first high total-pressure day in a series of high total-pressure days that each has a hatch. A hatch occurs during the high total-pressure conditions of DAY 12, and also during the high total-pressure conditions of DAY 13 and DAY 14, and will continue to occur on all subsequent days thereafter if the total-pressure remains high. This is exactly the same pattern that developed on DAY 4, DAY 5, and DAY 6. The lesson is that hatches will regularly occur every day during high total-pressure conditions, but will only occur after high total-pressure has prevailed for at least two-to-three consecutive days, in most cases. This circumstance is examined further in Chapter 9 — Proverbs F and G.

Recall that one of the greatest challenges facing the insect during high pressure conditions is the strong surface film. It can be a death trap. The benefit of extra strength gained during each additional day in ableness is evident in this example. Temperature and total-pressure are the environmental factors most responsible for keeping the insect in ableness for the correct time needed to survive hatching in high pressure conditions.

It's all made possible by the barometer-like properties that the insect possesses during ableness. The properties act as a regulator that keeps the insect in ableness for the time necessary to acquire enough strength to molt or hatch in a broad spectrum of environmental conditions. The regulator also prevents the insect from staying in ableness unnecessarily. It permits the insect to molt or hatch when its odds are greatest for survival. If the insect lacks the strength to molt or hatch during the prevailing conditions, it unwittingly continues building more strength so it can molt or hatch on the next day at its preferred time, or the next day, or the next. It's a simple and effective strategy for survival. (The preferred time of day may shift slightly due to environmental conditions like cloud cover, temperature swings, water levels, or dirty water, depending on the species and time of year.)

Predicting hatches and good bites hinges on your awareness of conditions that cause immatures to molt out of ableness. Good predictions depend on knowing which conditions will terminate the immature's stay in ableness. Fortunately for anglers, the conditions are almost always limited to *total-pressure, temperature, and time.* These three factors are the basis for the occurrence of almost all natural bites, and very frequently where the bites will occur.

Figure 6-2
Figure 6-1 depicts mayfly hatches that result from changes in barometric pressure, but it omits the spinner falls that result from those hatches. In Figure 6-2, the spinner falls are included in the chart and noted with an "S." The hatched, adult mayflies of Figure 6-1 become spinners 48 hours

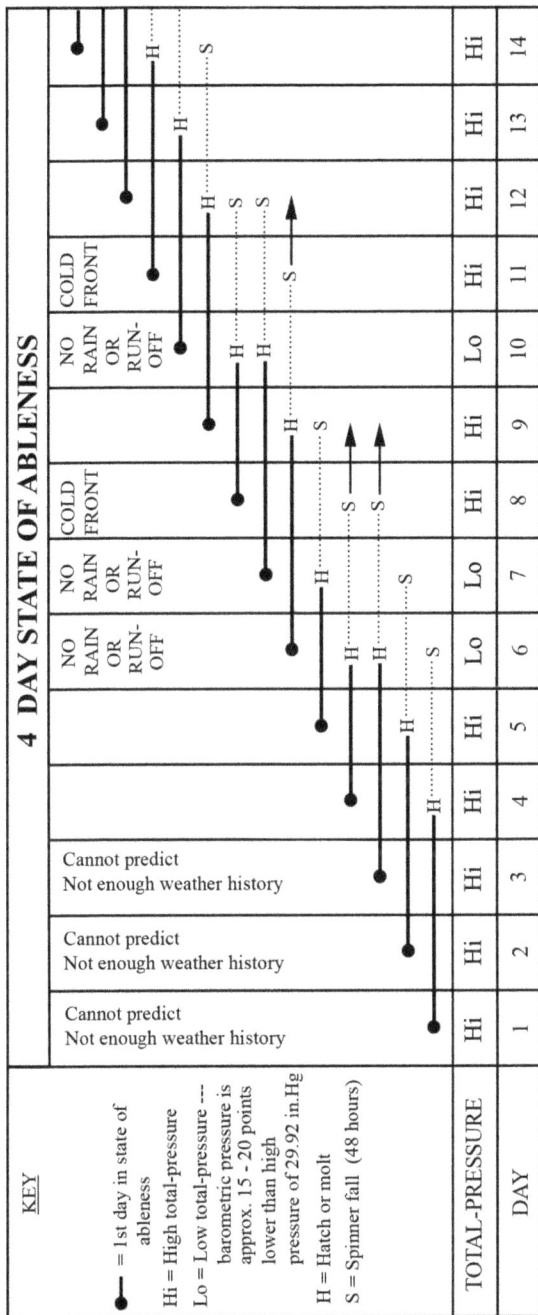

4 DAY STATE OF ABLENESS

KEY

● = 1st day in state of ableness
Hi = High total-pressure
Lo = Low total-pressure --- barometric pressure is approx. 15 - 20 points lower than high pressure of 29.92 in.Hg
H = Hatch or molt
S = Spinner fall (48 hours)

	DAY 1	DAY 2	DAY 3	DAY 4	DAY 5	DAY 6	DAY 7	DAY 8	DAY 9	DAY 10	DAY 11	DAY 12	DAY 13	DAY 14
Weather						NO RAIN OR RUN-OFF	NO RAIN OR RUN-OFF	COLD FRONT		NO RAIN OR RUN-OFF	COLD FRONT			
Note	Cannot predict — Not enough weather history	Cannot predict — Not enough weather history	Cannot predict — Not enough weather history											
TOTAL-PRESSURE	Hi	Hi	Hi	Hi	Hi	Lo	Lo	Hi	Hi	Lo	Hi	Hi	Hi	Hi

Figure 6-2

89

after they emerge from the water as adults. Therefore, in Figure 6-2, they are included 48 hours after they hatch. It's important to note that spinner falls also stimulate good bites, but not always.

Notice that spinners are the only insects available to stimulate a bite on DAY 8 and DAY 11 in Figure 6-2.

The spinners falling on DAY 8 are the insects that hatched on DAY 6, which was a double hatch. Naturally, the double hatch has produced a double spinner fall, making a good bite possible and easy to predict. A cold front is present on DAY 8 that could influence whether or not the spinners actually fall on this day. If the air is too cold it could cause the spinners to be too chilled to fly. If they don't fly on DAY 8, they will most likely fly on DAY 9 as indicated by the arrows in the chart. If they are delayed until DAY 9, it's possible that they may fly earlier than their preferred time of day. The magnitude and duration of the cold is a factor because of the small amount of degree-days that the mayfly must still absorb to accomplish its final flight and egg laying activities.

Under normal conditions the mayfly is genetically programmed to perform those activities within 48 hours, but the cold air has disrupted the normal flow of events. The cold has extended the mayfly's life, but death is near. As death approaches, the insect's physiological processes are breaking down. The biological clock is probably close to malfunctioning and screaming for the insect to complete its mating activities before it expires. The extended life may rob the biological clock of some of its ability to continue normal functions. The clock attempts to function as long as possible, but it, too, will finally succumb. When and if the clock falters, it can cause the spinner fall to occur before the preferred time of day, and therefore a bite at an unexpected time.

This could create an interesting situation on DAY 9. It's possible that the double spinner fall will occur earlier in the day than at the normally preferred time. There will also be a spinner fall and hatch that occur at the preferred time. The early, double spinner fall could trigger a good bite that leaves the fish with full stomachs. Fish could be fully gorged and off the bite when the normal spinner fall and hatch occur later. It's been my experience that the early spinner falls don't occur radically early, only about an hour or two.

If the air remains too cold for too long, the mayflies may simply perish in the terrestrial vegetation and no spinner fall or bite will occur.

If a spinner fall is sparse, smaller fish are usually the only ones that are stimulated to feed. If the spinner fall is highly populated, however, even the largest fish are stimulated to feed. An exception is when the water is muddy and off-color because it's carrying a heavy load of sediment. The turbid water obscures the spinners from the fishes' view and prevents them from knowing that a feast is drifting over their heads, so a good bite is unlikely to occur. It's simply a matter of the fish not knowing that the insects are there, because they can't see them or sense them. Remember, spinners are close to death, or dead, as they drift on the water's surface, so they don't create much commotion that signals their presence. The fish are simply unaware that they are silently drifting overhead when the water is muddy, so the probability of a good bite is low.

The same circumstances confronting the *double* spinner fall of DAY 8 also confront the single spinner fall on DAY 11. A single spinner fall will occur on DAY 11 unless the cold front delays it to occur the following day — on DAY 12 as indicated by the arrow. If the spinner fall occurs on DAY 12 it may occur an hour or two earlier than the normally expected time for the same reasons it did on DAY 9. An additional double spinner fall and hatch occur at the normal expected time on DAY 12. No doubt, the bite will be most intense during the double spinner fall and single hatch. That's when the most food is available and causing the most commotion that makes the fish aware of the opportunity to feed.

Spinner falls that are delayed by cold air deserve a closer look, along with the affects cold air has on hatches.

Assume that the cooler air of the cold fronts of DAY 8 and DAY 10 was cold enough that it actually delayed the spinner falls until the next day. The cooler air rapidly chilled the insects and made them too lethargic to fly.

The effect is rapid because the spinners are exposed directly to the air. The effect on insects underwater is far different; they don't feel the cooling effects of cold air until much later — after the water has slowly lost some of its heat into the air. The cold air will have a much more immediate effect on spinner falls than on hatches.

During short time spans, the temperature drop of the air is always far greater than the temperature drop of the water. This is due to radical differences of heat loss dynamics of air versus water. When fishing, you may feel a quick 20 degree change in the air temperature during a half hour period, but your lake/stream thermometer may show only a degree or two of change (or less!) in the water temperature over the same time period. It takes a relatively long time for the air temperature to change the water temperature. For this reason, cooler air does not immediately delay molts (hatches) and bites that occur underwater. If the cool air lingers long enough, however, it will then lower the water temperature which will be an additional factor that eventually delays hatches and bites.

Fishermen need to remain mindful that the cooler air of cold fronts is dense and heavy, which gives it the property of exerting higher pressure, or more correctly, higher barometric pressure, which creates higher total-pressure. It's the higher barometric pressure of these fronts that first causes the delays in hatches and good bites, not the temperature of the cold air. The underwater insects are affected by the increased total-pressure first, not the air temperature. Total-pressure changes happen instantaneously, whereas temperature changes happen gradually and slowly.

In summary, air temperature has a rapid and acute effect on spinner falls, but negligible immediate effect on hatches; and, total-pressure changes associated with all weather systems, including cold fronts and storm systems, always exert their influence on arthropods underwater long before temperature changes caused by the same systems.

Note that no rain has been included with the cold fronts in the examples so far. I did this to keep the explanations as simple as possible. In reality, cold fronts bring rain more often than not. Weak cold fronts may bring little or no measurable rain, moderate cold fronts may bring moderate rain that won't affect total-pressure very much; and strong cold fronts may bring torrential rains with dangerous winds, lightning, flooding, and significant changes in total-pressure.

The explanations for Figure 6-1 and Figure 6-2 are based on moderate total-pressure differences — in the range of 15 to 20 points. They're also based solely on changes in barometric pressure. Moderate total-pressure differences are typical throughout the year in most locations. Occasionally, however, barometric pressure will go very low and influence fishing for several days.

Figure 6-3
A single example of very low barometric pressure is depicted in Figure 6-3 for DAY 7, and will sufficiently convey the lesson. Figure 6-3 is exactly the same as Figure 6-1, except *low* (Lo) total-pressure on DAY 7 is replaced by *very low* (VLo) total-pressure. The difference between high pressure and very low pressure in the chart is 35 to 45 points.

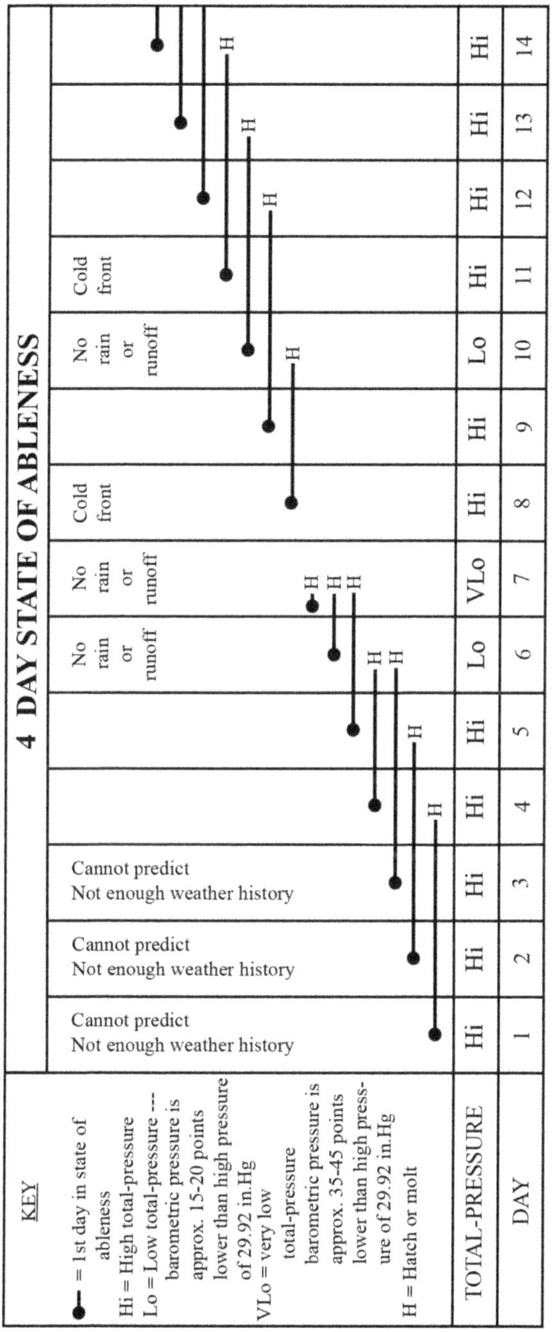

4 DAY STATE OF ABLENESS

KEY

● = 1st day in state of ableness
Hi = High total-pressure
Lo = Low total-pressure --- barometric pressure is approx. 15-20 points lower than high pressure of 29.92 in.Hg
VLo = very low total-pressure barometric pressure is approx. 35-45 points lower than high pressure of 29.92 in.Hg
H = Hatch or molt

Notes	DAY	TOTAL-PRESSURE
Cannot predict Not enough weather history	1	Hi
Cannot predict Not enough weather history	2	Hi
Cannot predict Not enough weather history	3	Hi
	4	Hi
	5	Hi
No rain or runoff	6	Lo
No rain or runoff	7	VLo
Cold front	8	Hi
	9	Hi
No rain or runoff	10	Lo
Cold front	11	Hi
	12	Hi
	13	Hi
	14	Hi

Figure 6-3

93

It's not unusual, although not common, to see natural pressure drops of over 100 points. Such large drops are generally associated with very large storm systems.

The glaring aspect of DAY 7 is the occurrence of three separate batches of immatures that hatch, which effectively triples the population of insects that hatch on this day. A deep drop in barometric pressure (VLo) induced a threefold increase in the hatch volume of the day. Basically, the very low pressure induced a triple hatch. This contrasts sharply with the single hatch induced on DAY 7 by the moderate drop in barometric pressure depicted in Figure 6-1. The very low pressure (VLo) caused a radical increase in the population of hatched insects.

The primary lesson of DAY 7 is that very low total-pressure can induce every insect in ableness to hatch. All fishermen should remember this lesson. Very low total-pressure eliminates almost every barrier to hatching that natural selection has prepared the insects to overcome. Every insect at every level of strength and maturity in ableness can hatch without difficulty if pressure goes low enough. Incubation of all insects in ableness terminates because they all have the necessary strength to hatch, and they do hatch in the favorable conditions of very low total-pressure. Imagine the frenzied natural bite that results when so much food becomes available. A triple hatch would certainly be cause for fish to feed heavily. Very low total-pressure events like this are fairly common in areas that experience large storms every year. Such events were influential in the formulation of the low pressure rule.

The next lesson is that there will not be another hatch or molt for at least three days. There is no hatch on DAY 8 nor on DAY 9; the next hatch is on DAY 10. However, the hatch on DAY 10 occurs as a result of total-pressure going low again.

The immatures that entered ableness on DAY 8 are finally strong enough to hatch on their third day in ableness because total-pressure is low. If total-pressure remained high, a hatch would likely not occur on DAY 10 because the high total-pressure would cause the immatures to remain in ableness to acquire yet more strength. If low pressure had not occurred on DAY 10, and high pressure instead prevailed every day from DAY 8 through DAY 10, the first hatch to occur after DAY 7 would be on DAY 11. There would be no hatch and no natural bite on DAY 8 through DAY 10. The natural bite (on the mayflies) would go dead for three whole days. Recall the famous fisherman's proverb, "Fishing goes dead for three days after a cold front goes through." Now you have an explanation for it. There is more on this proverb in Chapter 9. Notice in the charts that almost every time that low total-pressure or very low total-pressure occurs, the lower pressure induces an extra hatch or hatches to occur. As total-pressure goes lower, even more hatches are induced to occur.

The amount of extra hatches that occur are determined by the duration of the state of ableness. For example, if the duration of the state of ableness is four days, then low pressure can only cause an early hatch on three of the days, because a normal hatch will occur anyway on the fourth day if high pressure causes the immatures to remain in ableness that long. In like manner, if the state of ableness is three days, then low pressure can only cause an early hatch on two of the days, because a normal hatch will occur anyway on the third day if high pressure causes the immatures to remain in ableness for the entire three days. It also follows that if the state of ableness is two days, then low pressure can only cause an early hatch on one of the days because a normal hatch will occur anyway on the second day if high pressure causes the immatures to remain in ableness for two full days. Early hatches will not occur if the duration of ableness is only one day; they will simply occur every day during the insect's preferred time of year for hatching. Recall that ableness is generally shorter near the equator than toward the poles because of the faster accumulation of degree-days that occurs in the lower latitudes where there is more heat.

Observe on all charts that every one of the *extra* hatches is induced by low pressure, despite the length of the state of ablenes and all other circumstances. Every extra hatch occurred a day or two earlier than it would have if pressure had remained high. In other words, *all extra hatches occurred early*, and *they were all induced by low pressure*. Every extra hatch is a *pressure induced early hatch*, from which the acronym "*pie*" can be derived — **p**ressure **i**nduced **e**arly hatch. For the sake of easy reference throughout the remainder of this book, these additional early hatches will often be referred to as "*pie hatches.*" For example, in Figure 6-3 on DAY 6, there was a normal hatch plus a pie hatch; on DAY 7 three pie hatches occurred, and another pie hatch occurred on DAY 10 ("pie" is pronounced the same as if used in the term "apple pie").

Figure 6-4
Figure 6-3, omits the spinner falls that result from the hatches shown on the chart, but they are included in Figure 6-4 and noted with an "S."

95

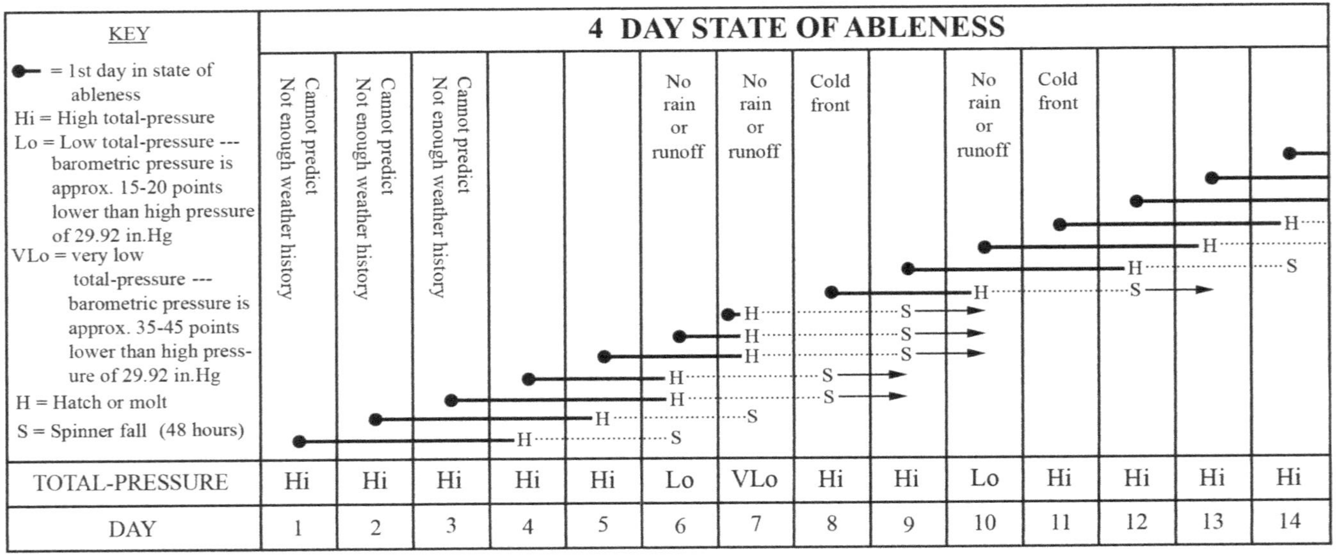

4 DAY STATE OF ABLENESS

KEY
▬● = 1st day in state of ableness
Hi = High total-pressure
Lo = Low total-pressure --- barometric pressure is approx. 15-20 points lower than high pressure of 29.92 in.Hg
VLo = very low total-pressure --- barometric pressure is approx. 35-45 points lower than high pressure of 29.92 in.Hg
H = Hatch or molt
S = Spinner fall (48 hours)

	1	2	3	4	5	6	7	8	9	10	11	12	13	14
Notes	Cannot predict Not enough weather history	Cannot predict Not enough weather history	Cannot predict Not enough weather history			No rain or runoff	No rain or runoff	Cold front		No rain or runoff	Cold front			
TOTAL-PRESSURE	Hi	Hi	Hi	Hi	Hi	Lo	VLo	Hi	Hi	Lo	Hi	Hi	Hi	Hi
DAY	1	2	3	4	5	6	7	8	9	10	11	12	13	14

Figure 6-4

96

Remember that these are adult mayflies that become spinners 48 hours after they emerge from the water as sub-adults. They are included on the chart 48 hours after they hatch.

It's noteworthy that the very low pressure of DAY 7 has no effect on the two spinner falls on DAY 8. However, a cold front is present on DAY 8 that could influence whether or not the spinners actually fall on this day. If the air is too cold it could cause the spinners to be too chilled to fly. If they don't fly on DAY 8, they will most likely fly on DAY 9 as indicated by the arrows in the chart. If they are delayed until DAY 9, the spinner fall possibilities are astonishing. The spinners from DAY 8 could fly earlier on DAY 9 than their preferred time of day, or they could combine with the three other spinner falls and create a single, extraordinary spinner fall comprised of five separate groups of spinners from five different hatches. This is very possible if the cold front shown on DAY 8 gives way to warmer air on DAY 9. The magnitude and duration of the cold is a factor because of the small amount of degree-days that the mayflies must still absorb to accomplish their final flight and egg laying activities. Depending on when the combination of five spinner falls occurs during the seasonal hatch period, the resulting spinner fall could range from modest to massive.

Figure 6-5

The bell curve of Figure 6-5 depicts the typical progression of hatch sizes, and therefore the size of spinner falls, as they occur during an insect's seasonal hatch period. When hatching first starts during the seasonal period, only a relatively few insects hatch during the first few days (**A**). Ideally, the population of each subsequent hatch then gets larger (**B**) and larger (**C**) until reaching a crescendo of larger hatches near the peak (**D**), midway through the seasonal hatch period. When hatches occur after the peak, they steadily diminish in size (**E**) and become increasingly smaller (**F**) and smaller (**G**) until all hatching of that species ceases for the season. A similar curve would also reflect the molting activities for all earlier instars of the immatures as well; and for many aquatic crustaceans.

The hatching could happen during a span of time in any part of the year, and could occur over a period of days, weeks, or months. Every species has its own preferred annual period for hatching. One species might hatch in April, another species in June, and yet another in August, but each species always hatches or molts near the same time of year, every year if

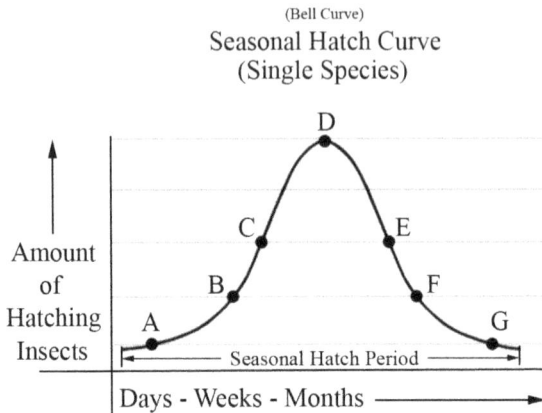

(Bell Curve)
Seasonal Hatch Curve
(Single Species)

Figure 6-5

its life cycle is 365 days. If its life cycle is longer it will continue to molt until it hatches in its final year of age.

Assume that DAY 7 in Figure 6-4 is point A on the bell curve in Figure 6-5. Any hatch occurring at **A** would be a small hatch, so the three small hatches occurring on DAY 7 isn't much to get excited about. The three combined hatches may only produce enough insects to cause a few small fish to feed — a minimal bite. The resulting spinner falls on DAY 9 would also be small and create a minimal bite.

If, however, DAY 7 is point **B** on the bell curve, the three hatches would each be much larger and create a combined hatch that would nearly equal individual hatches that occur near the peak of the season. It would create a tremendous natural bite, and probably excellent fishing. The resultant spinner falls on DAY 9 could also create equally good fishing.

If DAY 7 is point **D** on the bell curve, a veritable *blanket* hatch could occur. Each of the three hatches would be as large as an individual peak hatch. They would then combine to produce a hatch three times as large as any individual peak hatch. The huge combined hatch could look like a blizzard of insects. All fish would be feeding with abandon, a huge bite would occur, but fishing success would likely be dismal. There is simply too much food available and a fisherman's offering would be lost in the overwhelming mass of insects. Spinner falls on DAY 9 would also be overwhelming and create a huge bite, but fishing would be just as dismal as when the massive hatch occurred two days prior. There would be

98

simply too many naturals on the water, and the angler's offerings would disappear among the masses. See more about this bite and how to fish it in Chapter 8, section **Bites during Hatches of Larger Insects.**

The possibility of cold air delaying the two spinner falls from DAY 8 until DAY 9, creating five combined spinner falls on DAY 9 is illuminating. It helps you understand how much the combined spinner fall population can vary, and the perils they face, and how each change can affect the bite.

The insect populations, and the bite in each separate event, depend on when the hatches and resulting spinner falls occur on the bell curve. In other words, they depend on when they occur during the seasonal hatch period. If they occur near the beginning or end of the seasonal period, the population can be relatively small, creating low intensity bites — if any. If they occur near the peak of the seasonal period, the populations can be extremely large and create frenetic bites. Most of the best bites and fishing opportunities, however, will occur when hatches occur on the steeper slopes of the bell curve.

One of the greatest spectacles any fisherman can witness is the occurrence of many thousands, perhaps millions of hatching insects on the water and in flight during an event referred to as a ***blanket hatch***. It's called a blanket hatch because there are so many insects, figuratively speaking, that they appear to be touching each other wingtip-to-wingtip, and cover a large expanse of the water like a blanket from bank to bank. The bite usually rages during such hatches, but fishing is generally lousy because the fisherman's bait is swallowed into obscurity among the naturals. You may catch fish, and possibly a whopper, but the odds are against you. A consolation is the angler's unforgettable experience of wonderment at the spectacle of it.

It's unusual for blanket hatches to occur on the same water every year because the conditions conducive for them don't ordinarily occur every year. All the right conditions must occur in proper sequence. The conditions on DAY 7, and the conditions of the previous days leading up to DAY 7 will produce a massive amount of hatching insects if the conditions occur at the right time during the seasonal hatch period — near the upper portion of the bell curve. Also necessary is that the insects destined to hatch have not suffered a catastrophic population loss during recent years, especially in the last year. There must be a large population of surviving immatures that were produced by the generations of recent years.

Also, the absence of rain is a critical factor if a blanket hatch were to occur on DAY 7. Total-pressure remains very low on DAY 7 because there is no rain and runoff. Rain and runoff would cause the water level to rise, which would cause total-pressure to rise and hinder the molting processes (high pressure rule). The very low total-pressure, in the absence of rain and runoff, facilitated the triple pie hatch on the day.

Normally, very low barometric pressure is a feature of very large storm systems that are imbedded with heavy rain. Fortunately for fishermen, the very low barometric pressure of the large systems will often extend out in front of the storms by hundreds of miles. I've seen the pressure influence as far as 800 miles from the heavy rain that was coming with it. When the distance is that great, the pressure influence can precede the rain by several days, depending on the speed of the storm. Generally, the closer the approaching rain, the lower the barometric pressure.

Thus far throughout this chapter, the examples of variations in the occurrence or non-occurrence of hatches and spinner falls have been caused almost exclusively by changes in barometric pressure. Temperature changes have been a factor in the form of cold fronts, but barometric pressure has been the single-most contributing factor.

Water pressure is just as important as barometric pressure, although it doesn't fluctuate as often, or as much, most of the time. The next example gives it a closer look.

Figure 6-6

Figure 6-6 illustrates how water pressure, like barometric pressure, can radically change the occurrence of hatches and spinner falls.

Once again, a change is introduced: Rain and runoff are introduced on DAY 7, but the remainder of the chart is exactly the same as the chart in Figure 6-4; the only change is rain and runoff on DAY 7. The carry-over effects of the rain and runoff are shown on the days following DAY 7. Notice that total-pressure on DAY 7 is indicated as VLo-Hi. It means barometric pressure is still very low (VLo), but total-pressure is much higher (Hi) because the water level has risen six inches from heavy rain and runoff in the morning.

The introduction of heavy rain and high water has completely changed the hatch and bite situation. Previously, in Figure 6-4 when rain missed the area, the very low total-pressure caused a massive triple pie hatch and a furious bite. Now, however, the water has risen six inches

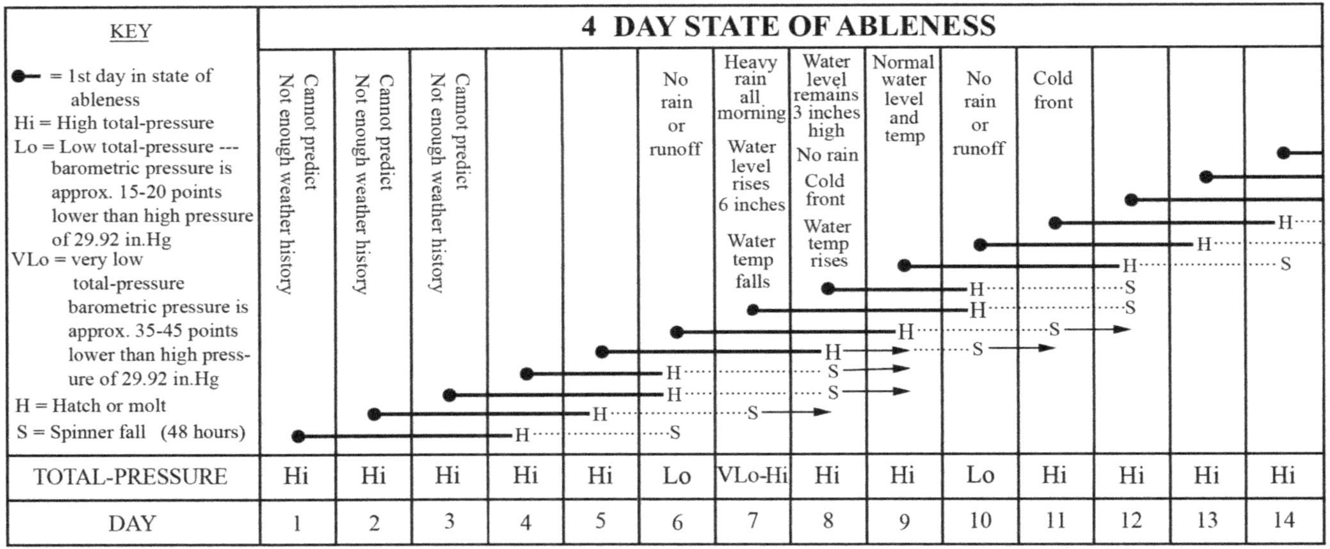

4 DAY STATE OF ABLENESS

KEY
● = 1st day in state of ableness
Hi = High total-pressure
Lo = Low total-pressure — barometric pressure is approx. 15-20 points lower than high pressure of 29.92 in.Hg
VLo = very low total-pressure barometric pressure is approx. 35-45 points lower than high pressure of 29.92 in.Hg
H = Hatch or molt
S = Spinner fall (48 hours)

DAY	1	2	3	4	5	6	7	8	9	10	11	12	13	14
TOTAL-PRESSURE	Hi	Hi	Hi	Hi	Hi	Lo	VLo-Hi	Hi	Hi	Lo	Hi	Hi	Hi	Hi

Day 1: Cannot predict / Not enough weather history
Day 2: Cannot predict / Not enough weather history
Day 3: Cannot predict / Not enough weather history

No rain or runoff (Days 5–6)
Heavy rain all morning / Water level rises 6 inches / Water temp falls (Day 7)
Water level remains 3 inches high / No rain / Cold front / Water temp rises (Day 8)
Normal water level and temp (Day 9)
No rain or runoff (Day 10)
Cold front (Day 11)
No rain or runoff (Days 13–14)

Figure 6-6

101

and there are no hatches on DAY 7. Why? The explanation is relatively straightforward and simple.

The barometric pressure (VLo) on DAY 7 is unchanged and remains at 35 to 45 points below normal. Even though the barometric pressure is low, it is overwhelmingly offset by the increased pressure of the water level that has risen six inches from rain and runoff.

Recall that 1.36 inches of water exerts the same amount of pressure as 10 points of barometric pressure (**Sidebar #15: Pressure Points: Barometric Pressure and Water Level Equivalents**). Therefore, the added pressure from six inches of rain and runoff is 44 points (6 in. ÷ 1.36 in./.1 in.-Hg = 4.41 in.-Hg = 4.41 in.-Hg x 100 points/in.-Hg = 44.1 points). If the barometric pressure is as much as 45 points lower than normal high pressure, then the 44 points of added pressure from rain and runoff effectively offsets and eliminates the very low barometric pressure effect on total-pressure. The net result is a return to normal high pressure, although it's one point lower, which is negligible (-45 points + 44 points = -1point).

So, even though barometric pressure is very low, the rain and runoff have created a state of high total-pressure that has radically interfered with molting and hatching.

Also, the heavy influx of cool rainwater and runoff lowered the water temperature which contributed to the interference. A small value of evaporative cooling, and cloud cover blocking the sun's heat may also have contributed to lower water temperature. The lower temperature of the rain/runoff interfered by causing the insects' metabolic processes to slow down (less degree-day absorption). The combination of higher total-pressure and cooler water has completely eliminated all hatching on DAY 7. This is consistent with an important phenomenon familiar to seasoned fishermen: *Hatches and natural bites seem to go dead during substantial rising and cresting of water levels.* An exception is when fish are spawning and laying eggs. Other fish, often the same species, are triggered to bite by the presence of the eggs, which they will often eat very selectively, despite water levels or conditions. This is common among anadromous fish like salmon and steelhead. Fish eggs are the trigger, not a molt or hatch of insects or crustaceans.

A lone spinner fall occurs on DAY 7, but it's unlikely to trigger a bite. The rain and runoff has probably dirtied the water, obscuring the majority of spinners from the fishes' view, so a significant bite has little chance to occur. It's also possible that the spinner population was decimated by the pummeling rain, so there would be far fewer to trigger a bite. It's also possible that the large volume of rain created a microclimate near the stream that is cooler than the surrounding countryside. The cooler microclimate may chill the spinners enough to cause them to shift their flight and fall to DAY 8, eliminating all chances for a natural bite on DAY 7.

Another high-water complication for fishermen is that fish often won't move into or hold in normal feeding lanes because it's suspected they need to seek refuge locations where the sudden increase of silt and dirt in the high water won't foul their gills. It's also thought that the new locations must provide relief and rest from the increased current caused by the heavy rain and runoff.

The primary lessons of DAY 7 are: (1) The bite can be furious when barometric pressure is very low and there is no rain or runoff. (2) Conversely, even though barometric pressure is very low, the moderating effect of heavy rain and runoff on total-pressure can kill the bite. (3) Pie hatches are eliminated when water levels rise fast and high enough, even if barometric pressure remains very low. (4) Total-pressure is most often the critical factor, but water temperature also influences the occurrence of molts and hatches. You must remain cognizant of both when predicting the bite.

DAY 8 is also revealing. The high water level has dropped three inches because the rain has stopped, but the level is still three inches higher than normal. High pressure and a cold front have settled in, although the water temperature has risen. These are conditions often present after a big storm.

It's possible that a bite could occur on DAY 8, but maybe not. Conditions after a storm can be difficult to interpret, so as an angler you must have practical expectations. Bites expected during the days after a storm can easily occur on the following day(s). The unexpected shift usually occurs because you aren't sure how much the water has risen or fallen, so you misjudge changes in the total-pressure.

High barometric pressure has moved in on DAY 8, but total-pressure is much higher than normal because the water level is still three inches higher than normal. Three inches higher means total-pressure is still approximately 22 points higher (3 inches ÷ 1.36 inches/10 points = 2.205 [10 points] = 22 points) than would occur from the return to high barometric pressure (Hi) and normal water depth.

The chart shows that immatures that entered ableness on DAY 5 will hatch on DAY 8, but the hatch could shift (arrow) to DAY 9. The water temperature dropped on DAY 7 which may have slowed development of the immatures in ableness. They may not have gained enough strength to hatch and need yet another day to build strength to overcome the 22 points of added pressure from the higher water level; so it could push the hatch and the bite into DAY 9. Still, the water temperature rose on DAY 8, which would aid development in ableness (degree-days absorption), and it's more likely that the hatch will occur on DAY 8, despite the higher water level. The water temperature could rise due to runoff over warm ground, or because much of the cold rain has drained out with the river current, which has enabled heat from solar radiation to raise the water temperature. Both of these possibilities are speculation, but they are the type of influences that can directly affect when bites occur. Sometimes the important factors are involved in less-than-obvious ways.

This all leads to another phenomenon known by seasoned fishermen, especially veteran steelhead and trout guides: *After the water level rises and crests, the bite begins to recur at some point when the water level is falling.* DAY 8 is a perfect example of this phenomenon because the water level has dropped three inches. A hatch and double spinner fall, and possibly a third spinner fall, likely occur and cause a moderate bite. However, the cold front that has moved in behind the rain, which is typical, may cause two of the spinner falls to shift into DAY 9.

Any bite on DAY 8 is likely to be moderate to light because the high water is probably turbid with sediment and detritus from the runoff, causing limited visibility in the water column. Limited visibility obscures the availability of food, so larger fish are less likely to be triggered to feed. As always, the size of the hatch and spinner falls, and intensity of the bite are dependent upon when they occur on the bell curve of the seasonal hatch period.

Figure 6-7

All examples analyzed so far have been of insects that have a four-day state of ableness. Figure 6-7 departs from the four-day state of ableness, and looks at insects with a three-day state of ableness.

The total-pressure conditions are exactly the same as those in Figure 6-3 and Figure 6-4, which includes the same very low pressure on DAY 7 The very low pressure is now combined with a three-day state of ableness which produces a modestly different result in hatches and spinner falls.

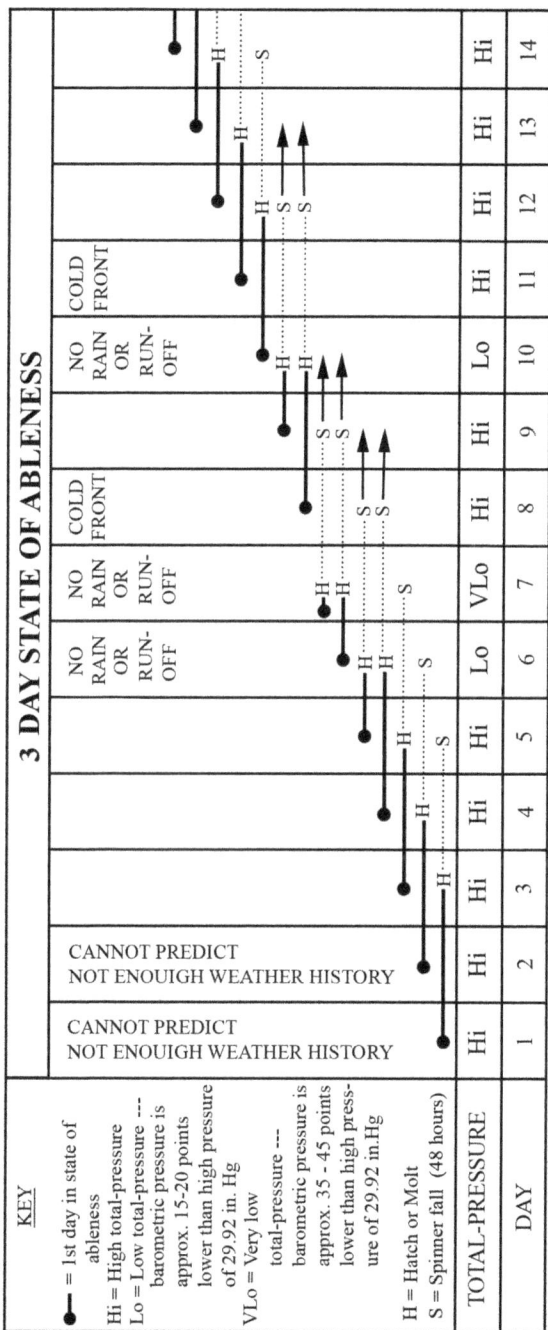

Figure 6-7

In briefest terms, the reduced number of days in the state of ableness (one less day) causes a proportionate reduction in pie hatches and their spinner falls. In other words, there's always one less pie hatch and one less spinner fall that will occur when compared with the hatches and spinner falls that would occur with a four-day state of ableness. The three-day state of ableness is likely to occur further from the poles, but not quite sub-tropically. Recall earlier assertions that the state of ableness is probably shorter in the lower latitudes because there is more heat for degree-day absorption. Cold fronts, if cold enough, could still delay spinner falls to occur a day later than expected — as indicated by the arrows.

A reliable pattern that appears in all the charts, despite the length of ableness, is that *hatches do not occur on a high pressure day that immediately follows a low pressure day*. This can also be seen in Figure 6-8, which is a chart with a two-day state of ableness. The pattern alerts the astute fisherman that fishing will be far more challenging on a high pressure day that follows a low pressure day. Depending on how low the pressure went on previous days, fishing could remain frustrating for a couple days as barometric pressure and total-pressure resume a high level.

Figure 6-8

Note in Figure 6-8 that the occurrences of pie hatches are reduced even further when ableness is reduced to two days. This is another revelation from the charts that renders a useful rule-of-thumb: *Pie hatches become fewer as the state of ableness becomes briefer.*

All the charts also show that hatches and bites begin to recur again after several days of steady high pressure. This pattern is well known to veteran freshwater fishermen around the world. It reinforces my claim in Chapter 4 that barometric pressure has no *direct* effect on fish behavior, but it can have dramatic *indirect* effects on their behavior. The direct effects are on the foods that fish eat. Fish respond to the food, not the barometric pressure.

I have not included a chart depicting insects with a one-day state of ableness because it would simply show insects hatching every day, and no pie hatches. It would also show spinner falls occurring every day except on the first day that cold air is present that has moved in with a cold front. The cold air would be unusual in the latitudes that have insects with a one-day state of ableness, which possibly occur almost exclusively in the

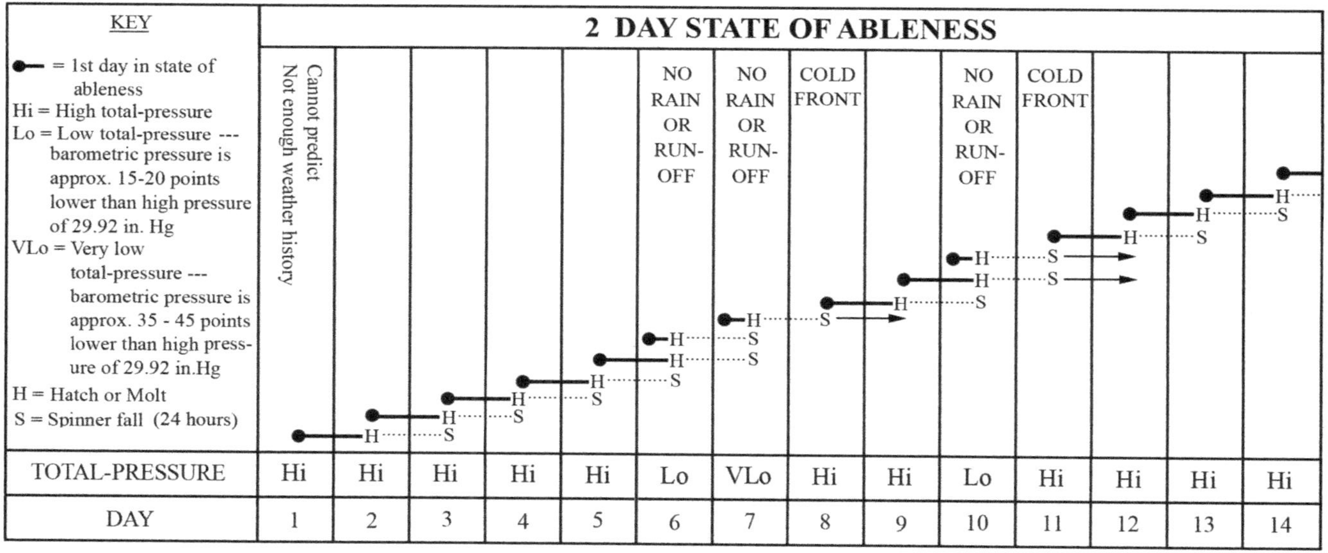

2 DAY STATE OF ABLENESS

KEY

● = 1st day in state of ableness

Hi = High total-pressure

Lo = Low total-pressure --- barometric pressure is approx. 15-20 points lower than high pressure of 29.92 in. Hg

VLo = Very low total-pressure --- barometric pressure is approx. 35 - 45 points lower than high pressure of 29.92 in.Hg

H = Hatch or Molt

S = Spinner fall (24 hours)

DAY	1	2	3	4	5	6	7	8	9	10	11	12	13	14
TOTAL-PRESSURE	Hi	Hi	Hi	Hi	Hi	Lo	VLo	Hi	Hi	Lo	Hi	Hi	Hi	Hi

Day 1: Cannot predict / Not enough weather history

Days 6, 7, 10: NO RAIN OR RUN-OFF

Days 8, 11: COLD FRONT

Figure 6-8

107

subtropical or tropical latitudes. Once again, evolution of the brief state of ableness can be attributed to the abundant, fast absorption of degree-day heat in the subtropical or tropical regions.

All of the preceding examples in the charts of hatches and spinner falls are idealized so you were able to get a quick understanding of the concepts at work. The high pressure and low pressure values were simply stated as Hi or Lo, but they didn't vary during the 24 hour periods. They remained the same or only changed at the stroke of midnight when a new day was presented on the charts. In reality, barometric pressure changes constantly; this is readily observed in hourly weather postings on websites of local airports. During stable weather the pressure may vary only a few points, but it varies nonetheless. Sometimes it will creep low enough to affect hatching and the bite with no noticeable change in the weather. Only regular, periodic pressure readings can reveal the trend and tell the tale. You can't always trust what you see in the sky.

Cold fronts in the charts also appeared to last exactly 24 hours, which is not the usual case. Cold air ushered in by a front usually lingers as a component of the high pressure system, sometimes for many days, until it's replaced by the next low pressure system. As a rule, high pressure systems and their cooler air survive far longer than low pressure systems and their warmer air.

The number and combinations of high and low pressure systems, with related temperature and rain influences, are limitless. Despite the infinite possibilities, however, you now have an understanding of the factors in play that cause good bites. Not only do you know the factors in play, but you can confidently interpret them to improve your fishing success. You can understand the hatch and bite events unfolding before your eyes on the water where you are fishing. Best of all, you can watch the weather and natural sequences and precisely predict when your fishing efforts will be rewarded beyond anything you could have previously imagined.

Your ability to predict bites is now greatly enhanced, but Mother Nature still presents some encrypted mysteries that will be unraveled in the following chapters. Not only will new mysteries be decrypted, but more of the details that you might have wished were in the charts will be addressed as well.

An entertaining observation that you can take away from this chapter is what it corroborates:

In a way, it supports all the thoughtful fishing logs compiled by countless fishermen over the centuries. Their logs show that fishing success is *good* and *bad* during almost every imaginable barometric pressure possibility and every weather condition. Unfortunately, none of the logs revealed obvious patterns and were seldom helpful. They have been extremely confusing and mysterious ever since the Italian physicist, Evangelista Torricelli, invented the first barometer in the year 1643 A.D.

The charts in this chapter also show that good and bad fishing can occur during almost every imaginable barometric pressure and weather condition. After hundreds of years, however, the mysteries are now stripped from the logs.

Chapter 7

Hatch Notes

This chapter contains a host of brief insights about hatches and molts that will help you refine your predictions for good bites.

Flooding and Training

In Chapter 6, advice was given to always assume immatures are entering the state of ableness every day during their seasonal hatch period. This is important advice that should be followed, but there are circumstances in which immatures do not go into ableness every day.

One circumstance is when heavy rain or runoff floods your lake or stream with cold water that sharply reduces water temperature, and the reduced temperature persists for several days. It would prevent immatures from absorbing enough degree-day heat to enter ableness. Depending on the severity of the cold, hatching could be delayed until water temperature recovers, or until immatures have spent an inordinately prolonged period in ableness so they have the strength to hatch. A heavy, flooding rain is usually an infrequent event that does not significantly change the duration of the seasonal hatch period.

A second circumstance involves a phenomenon called *"training."* It's a series of storms that follow each other through an area like boxcars attached to a locomotive. The storms can be mild or severe, but they inflict a similar effect on hatches, molts, and fishing. They are a series of low pressure fronts or systems that roll through an area at close intervals, dumping cold rain into lakes and rivers. The fronts are often spaced only a day or two, or three, apart. Sometimes the area will see training occurring repeatedly — perhaps two or three fronts will go through each week for several consecutive weeks. The recurring rains lower the water temperature and raise the water levels higher than normal, especially in streams. Lake levels are usually less affected. Average daily water temperatures also drop due to persistent cloudy skies that keep the moistened earth cooler, which keeps the water cooler. The cooler water causes sharply diminished degree-day absorption. Total-pressure remains high, perhaps extremely high because of the high water. The frequency of the storms makes it impossible for lakes and streams to recover between storm events, so total-pressure and temperature remain abnormal for extended periods. Once again, the immatures are unable to obtain enough degree-day heat to enter ableness at a normal rate.

A sharp reduction in degree-day absorption would also cause immatures to develop much slower while in the state of ableness. The slower development means that immatures would need to remain in ableness longer to obtain the same maturity and strength that they would normally achieve when the water is warmer. The net effect is the state of ableness would be longer when the water becomes too cold during the seasonal hatch period. For example, a four-day state of ableness would become a five-day or six-day state of ableness (or longer) if the water becomes too cold during the seasonal hatch period, especially when combined with higher total-pressure. The longer state of ableness and slower development would extend the time needed for *all* of the season's remaining immatures to mature and hatch. It then follows that the seasonal hatch period would extend far longer than normal.

I've seen training similar to this example that caused seasonal hatch periods to last three to four weeks longer than normal. I didn't realize what pie hatches were at the time, but I do recall that decent hatches were sporadic. Hatches that did occur were frequently a mere fraction of what I normally expected. They just dribbled until their hatch season was over. The smaller hatch sizes generally produced fewer enthusiastic bites, especially by larger fish. The reduced hatch sizes may indicate some mortality resulting from the training. Any mortality may be reflected as diminished hatch populations in following years.

A simple representation of the smaller hatch sizes and longer hatch period caused by storm training is depicted by the dotted line in Figure 7-1.

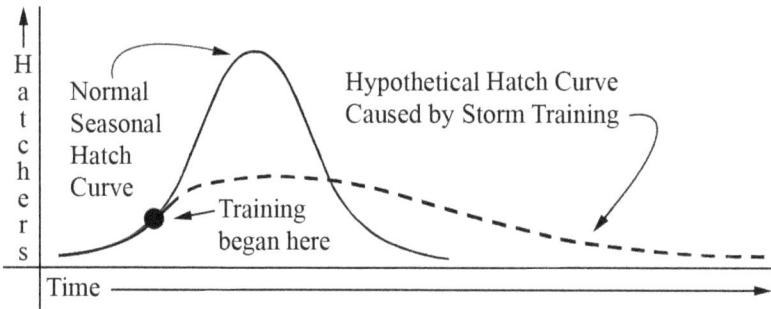

Figure 7-1

The same effect could happen to molters as depicted in the curve and dotted line of Figure 7-2, and would apply to every affected instar of all species.

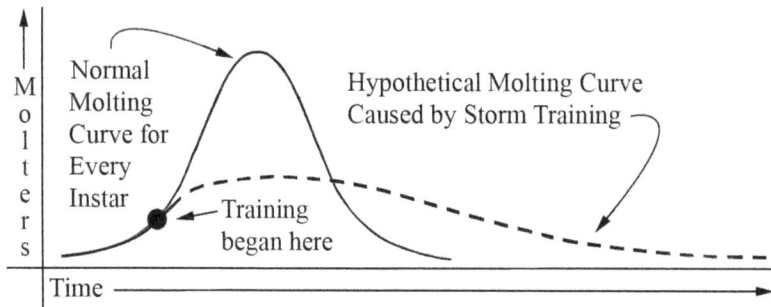

Figure 7-2

Whether caused by training or a single big storm, flood-level water always seems to have a detrimental effect on hatches, and probably molting too. I have asked countless fishermen if they have ever witnessed an aquatic insect hatch when water is at flood level, and none have. Nor have I. Even when floods persist at high levels for several days, none of the fishermen could recall seeing a hatch. They usually speculated that the high water washed the immatures downstream; it simply scrubbed them out because they were too weak to resist. I partly agree with that assessment, but total-pressure and colder water may be the more direct culprits.

I suspect there may be a point at which the water level becomes high enough that it creates total-pressure that is higher than most immatures can conquer. Total-pressure from the extreme high water may bind the immatures so tightly within their old exoskeleton that they cannot overcome the extreme total-pressure increase and escape. In addition, the colder water would slow their metabolism, making them slower to generate adequate internal pressures needed to overcome the extreme total-pressure in timely fashion. If they fail to overcome the extreme total-pressure, they might then be swept away because they are so weak or have perished, or they may somehow remain in place as forage for other organisms. Either way, it's possible we never see them again, and we remain unaware of any bite associated with the possibility of their unfortunate demise.

It's also possible that a few mutant individuals are able to overcome some of the higher pressures and emerge in what appears to be a very light hatch, although the volume of the hatch would likely be too low to cause a bite of any consequence.

I also suspect that high water at high altitudes suppresses hatches and molts to a greater degree than an equal amount of high water suppresses them at lower altitudes. (Sidebar #17: High Water at Different Altitudes)

Floodwater usually wreaks havoc on hatches, but it also has merit and can facilitate exciting bites that would not occur otherwise. This is addressed further in Chapter 8, section Floodwater Bites.

Drought and High Temperature

The opposite effects of training and big storms can occur during times of drought and high temperatures. Low water levels caused by drought can cause persistently low total-pressure. Also, low water heats up faster from solar radiation, so water temperature goes up, which causes faster accumulation of degree-day heat in the aquatic organisms. The faster heat absorption effectively shortens the state of ableness because insects and crustaceans achieve maturity and full strength in a shorter amount of time. When high temperatures and low total-pressure persist, more hatching occurs in a shorter length of time, the hatches become more condensed. The normal seasonal hatch period will also become shorter as illustrated in Figure 7-3. Hatches will also occur earlier on the calendar, including

17

High Water at Different Altitudes

A Little Case Study

High water at high altitudes may suppress hatches and molts to a greater degree than an equal amount of high water suppresses them at lower altitudes. The reason is because aquatic insects that have selectively adapted to conditions at higher altitudes may simply be weaker than insects that have similarly adapted to conditions at lower altitudes.

Insects dwelling at low altitudes need extra strength to overcome two critical conditions that are much more severe than they are at high altitude: (1) Far greater normal barometric pressure, which must be overcome during molting at all instar stages; and (2) Far greater surface tension that must be overcome when hatching.

Conversely, insects dwelling at high altitude face drastically lower normal barometric pressure, and far weaker surface films although cold water at high altitude would strengthen surface films somewhat. The normal conditions they face require far less strength to overcome than the strength needed by their counterparts at low altitude.

If insects at higher altitudes are generally always subject to conditions that require less strength, then it's probably reasonable to assume that they have adapted to the reduced selective pressures with less strength. They haven't needed more strength over the ages so they may not have naturally selected for it. If they haven't selected for it, they are probably more susceptible to adverse consequences when environmental conditions pose challenges that exceed the abilities of their strength. It follows that one of the biggest challenges may then be posed by high water.

When high water occurs at high altitude, inadequate strength of insects at that altitude should have the result of keeping....

See the continued, entire text of this sidebar in **Appendix D**

earlier onset of their seasonal hatch period instead of the normal start of the seasonal hatch period as shown at **X**.

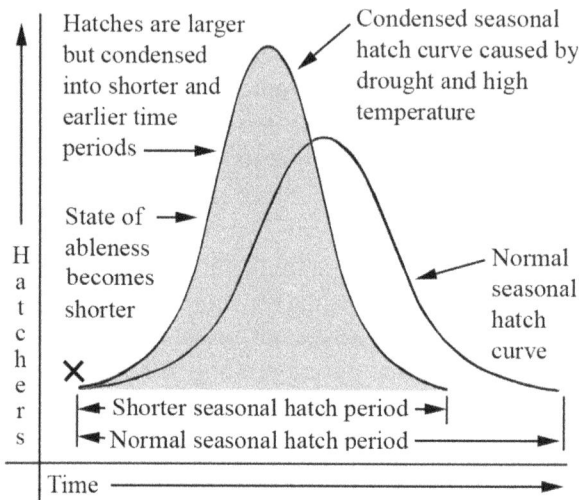

Figure 7-3

Simultaneous Multiple Molts & Hatches

The charts in Chapter 6 were limited to depicting the hatches and spinner falls of a single species of mayfly on a particular day. On most lakes and streams, however, it's fairly common to see several species hatching on a given day. Accordingly, it's not unusual to see several species appearing at the same time, perhaps three or four different mayflies. The simultaneous appearances could also be comprised of a combination of taxonomic orders; for example, mayflies, caddisflies, and stoneflies all appearing at the same time.

It's also possible that only one or several hatches could occur simultaneously in combination with other species that are only molting, but not hatching into adulthood. The molters would go unnoticed, but could be the most abundant species available as fish food. Also, if molts of different species occur at preferred times, various molts could occur at certain times throughout an entire day — morning, midday, and evening, and perhaps through the night; and many of the times may not be associated with a telltale hatch. The angler is far more likely to encounter hatching and molting of a plurality of species on an average day of fishing, instead of just a single species. All should be logged so they can be predicted accurately in following years.

Figure 7-4 illustrates some generic possibilities of combined hatches or molts, using seven bell curves.

In the first example, the curves represent a combination of hatches and molts on a particular day. Use the curves and their peaks to envision the following scenario:

Peak 1 is a caddisfly immature that is molting underwater, but the angler never sees it. Peak 2 is a mayfly that the angler sees hatching and flying off the water's surface. Peak 3 is a stonefly immature that is molting underwater, which the angler also does not see. A close examination of curve 2 reveals that at least three species of insects (curves 1, 3, 5) are molting or hatching at the same time (shaded in gray) that the mayflies of curve 2 are at their peak on the water.

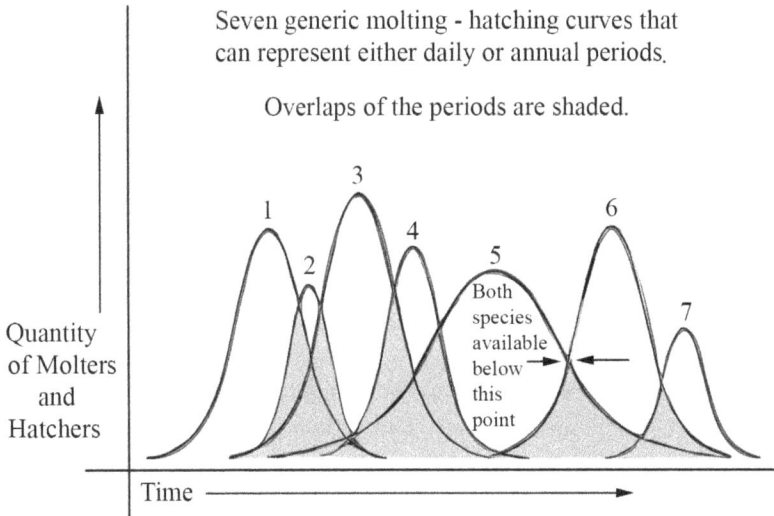

Figure 7-4

The angler only sees the mayflies as the primary fish food, but the underwater molters (caddisflies and stoneflies) are also very numerous when the mayflies are near the peak of their hatch time. The combination of mayflies and active caddisfly and stonefly immatures will probably cause a vigorous bite. Characteristically, comments about similar circumstances cited in fishing literature often say that fish will act opportunistically in this situation and feed on the largest, easiest-to-obtain prey. I generally agree. The fish will sort them out, and the angler must do the same. The angler may want to use a fine-mesh net or other device to facilitate identification of the organisms in play; and a smart angler will keep a good log of the experience. Best of all, if the angler has a working knowledge of the high and low pressure rules, and knowledge of the total-pressure and temperature changes and local sequences, he can confidently predict when to be on the water when this bite takes place. Then, it's angler against fish.

This sounds like a bit much to keep track of, but with a little practice most of it becomes second nature, and fishing becomes extremely more interesting. It's similar to finding your way home after moving to a new neighborhood; you instinctively learn the way home after just a couple trips along new, yet unfamiliar roads. Expect the same results after a few attempts at making predictions using total-pressure, temperature, and sequences. You'll soon develop instincts for the right times to go fishing. It's not nearly as difficult as learning to hit a baseball, or sewing a quilt. Believe in yourself and give it a go. It's not rocket science.

The concept of simultaneous hatches and molts is developed further where curve 5 intersects with curve 6 between the arrows. It's a point below which both species are available to feeding fish. Both sides of the intersection could be molters, hatchers, or either of the two. Such combinations occur numerous times in the chart, and each is depicted where the bell curves intersect. There can be few, or there can be many, but they will all be in various stages of development. This is exactly the type of situation every angler faces during every trip to the water. It's a multi-stage, multi-species example of molts and hatches first described in Chapter 3. It's a most practical circumstance. The population of each species may not be very high, but the combination of the two could cause a very nice bite.

The message of Figure 7-4 is that a significant amount of hatches and molts are sequentially occurring in many combinations, mostly unseen, and many are causing bites that are never seen; and most anglers are never aware of them, but the unseen activity may be the key element of most successful fishing trips.

The unseen activity by insects and crustaceans may be responsible for keeping most fish in a feeding mode for as long as the unseen activity lasts. All fishermen know that food activates fish to bite, that's why they use bait. It follows that the molting we can't see may raise fish's inclination to feed, even if the fish are not actively feeding. Their inclination may rise because so much food is readily available. It might also cause more spontaneity in their feeding because their inclination to feed becomes more acute, so their reaction to food may be only a hair-trigger away. Also, molting may release a higher level of "buggy" scent into the water; residue that may be clinging to the inside of ruptured exoskeletons and freshly exposed insect or crustacean bodies may get rinsed into the water column, alerting fish's olfactory senses that food is imminent.

We humans get that same inclination when driving through aromas wafting from a bakery or steakhouse, or when walking past a buffet table. It smells or looks so good that we want a bite, now. The impulse is spontaneous, but it has a tendency to linger. Our inclination to feed goes way up because food has instantly stimulated it.

In a nutshell, food appears to have the same effect on fish. They will bite better if they have a higher inclination to feed, which occurs when there is more food available from hatches and the unseen molts. When fish are in such a mode, a tantalizing, vulnerable offering from an angler may be all that's needed to trigger a bite from an individual fish, or several.

Fish's heightened inclination to feed, caused by hatches and the unseen molts, is probably responsible for better odds of successful fishing on most days, even if a little extra effort and ingenuity are needed for us to succeed. The unseen molts, particularly, would be a very important factor for successful fishing.

The absence of the inclination to feed, which could be caused by the absence of hatches and the unseen molts, may also be responsible for the very difficult fishing days that occur after a very low total-pressure system and its cold front pass through an area.

Pie Molts

The low total-pressure causes pie hatches that frequently remove much of the available food for days afterward, which may diminish the fish's inclination or tendency to feed. The diminished tendency for feeding would be diminished even further by the counterpart of pie hatches (Figure 6-3), which are "*pie molts*" — pressure induced early molts.

Pie molts are simply molts of the immatures that are too young to hatch into adults; they're the young molters, not the old hatchers. Pie molts could have a far greater effect on the bite than pie hatches. Pie hatches are well depicted in the charts of Chapter 6, but pie molts can be substituted directly in their place. It's all part of the same molting phenomena — some are hatchers, some are molters. All the same rules apply.

Pie hatches only involve one or a few species that are hatching during their limited seasonal hatch period. Pie molts, however, could involve the immatures of all the other species in the water, which could be dozens or hundreds of species or more. The immatures have many molts to accomplish before a final molt into adulthood. There could be immatures at every instar stage — first instar, second instar, third, etc. The multi-stage, multi-species, early molting possibilities are huge. Figure 7-4 depicts the possibility of only a few species molting simultaneously (overlaps), but far more species could molt simultaneously during a pie molt. Generally, for all species, every instar is vulnerable to a pie molt if the total-pressure is low enough and the critter has already entered ableness. Reason dictates that we should expect far more pie molts than pie hatches. The odds favor them overwhelmingly.

During the part of the year when most hatches are occurring, pie molts and pie hatches will occur simultaneously and can produce a temporary glut of food for the fish. The glut would usually be available for one or two days and cause a vigorous bite by fish of all sizes. Food may be so abundant that fish become engorged, and possibly too full to eat for awhile, which may be another reason that fishing becomes difficult for a couple days.

The down-side of pie molts and pie hatches is that normal hatches and molts won't occur again for up to several days afterward. Normal hatching and molting that created the visible hatches and so much unseen underwater activity is suddenly nonexistent for a day or two or three.

If the unseen activity is nonexistent for a few days, which means there is very little available food, then a major factor is missing that would normally put fish in a feeding mode. The lack of food may lower their inclination to feed because it's not present to constantly remind them of its availability. It then follows that their inclination to feed on something may no longer be a hair trigger away. If fish have a lower inclination to feed, they would then be more difficult to catch. This is certainly the case for a short time after low total-pressure is replaced by high total-pressure and cooler temperatures. Pie molts, therefore, probably play a far more significant role in the level of a fish's inclination to feed.

Barometric Pressure Trend Challenge

On average days with average weather, the average fisherman will usually expect to have an average day of successful fishing, and will usually get it. On average, catching fish is not too difficult. Average days on the water usually occur during steady, unremarkable weather. It's the kind of weather that sustains unseen underwater molting every day, which heightens fish's inclination to feed. I can only imagine that each molt occurring at a different preferred time of day acts as a pulse for renewal of a fish's inclination to feed; and each molt, depending on the size and population of the immatures, causes a different level of inclination in each fish.

If you want better than average fishing, and want to avoid fishing on days when the chances for success are remote, your knowledge of total-pressure, temperature, natural sequences, and a little bit about aquatic organisms will sway the odds in your favor. It will put you on the water at the right time. Natural sequences and botanical indicators will practically guarantee perfect timing for certain bites. Let the wildflowers, shrubs, trees, and other insects inform you when the timing is right. They will tell you that the right period of time has arrived for the respective bite to occur, after which you will have about a week or two to take advantage of the timing. They will help you identify good bites that repeat year after year; I've never seen it fail. Thereafter, your wits as an angler will determine whether you can convert a good bite into a good catch. Your fishing success with such bites in future years will be enhanced even more if you keep good logs that also include your tackle, techniques, and your degree of success.

A little practice will begin to provide you with a lifetime of amazingly accurate predictions of good bites. The accuracy of your predictions, however, will be critically dependent on knowing the history of the local barometric pressure for the previous three to four days. If those days have been unusually cold, up to six days would be better. Nevertheless, I've been able to make reliable predictions for several years based on barometric pressure readings recorded in one hour increments for three to four consecutive days. Readings spaced one hour apart have been adequate for revealing whether the pressure is trending up or down. Anything more than an hour is a handicap because, in many cases, the readings aren't available soon enough. Trends happen every day, and you must know how far they rise and fall. Some are slight and insignificant, while others are more pronounced.

It could be important to know if a new trend is developing before leaving the house so you know how to deal with it. If readings are only available every three or four hours it won't help much. It would require waiting too long to observe the makings of a trend. It could be especially important if you plan to drive an hour to meet friends and then kill a few more hours before going fishing with them.

If you're going on a weekend fishing trip, the trends will make a significant difference in the terminal tackle you'll need to take along. If the trend tells you not to expect significant hatches or molts, then you won't expect good natural bites; in which case you'll want to pack terminal tackle that triggers bites. There will be more on triggered bites in Chapter 8, section Triggered Bites.

For fishing locally I'm fortunate that I can get barometer readings from my local airport which posts them on a weather website, but it's still limited to three days of data. Many times it's not enough. I've made it work by making copies of it from the internet a couple days before I need them, then get copies for the final two days on fishing day. It would be so much handier to have a recording barometer with five or six days of data in my vehicle, boat, or fishing vest. So, again I beat the drum for clever engineers to produce an affordable recording barometer, a proper fishing barometer that enables anglers across the planet to be on the water when fishing can be most productive.

One of the most difficult challenges I've faced has been determining how long barometric pressure, and therefore total-pressure, must remain low in order to produce a pie hatch or pie molt. In other words, if the most prolific natural bites are produced by pie hatches and pie molts, and they are caused by low total-pressure, how long must the low total-pressure persist to cause the hatches, molts, and best bites to happen? How can the necessary duration be determined? (Don't let the next few paragraphs scare you. I will rescue you from the nightmarish picture they paint.)

The obvious solution is that you must be present on a lake or stream when pie hatches or pie molts occur during various low total-pressure events. These events are typically caused by low barometric pressure systems that are approaching or over-spreading the area. You also need to be there during the insect's preferred hatching time of the day. If the hatches or molts do not occur when just one hour of low total-pressure precedes them, or two hours, or seven hours, but occur if a minimum of eight hours of low total-pressure precedes them, then the answer, of course, is "about eight hours." You would know that "about eight hours" of low total-pressure is required to cause pie hatches and pie molts of certain species on this date and time.

The exasperating difficulty in this solution is that low barometric pressure systems typically move into an area too soon or too late to facilitate precise conclusions about pressure influence on hatches and molts. Another big problem is those same systems may occur only once, twice, or not at all during seasonal hatch periods that normally last only two-to-five weeks. The systems occur so infrequently that the chances of a precise duration of, say, eight hours occurring are extremely low. How many years would you have to wait for exactly eight hours of low total-pressure to occur so you finally learn the answer? Even if it does occur, the timing may be terrible because you could be required to stay at work that day, or in school, or deal with a host of other reasons that can cause you to miss the opportunity to observe its effects. It's information that can be difficult to acquire without help.

Yet another problem is that a hatch could occur, but you may be unsure as to whether it's a regular hatch, or combined with a pie hatch, or a pie hatch by itself; likewise for molts. Avoiding such confusion requires that you have knowledge of hatch sizes and total-pressure history from the days immediately preceding the one you're currently observing. Again, it can be difficult information to acquire

Local tackle stores, flyfishing shops, marinas, and fishing clubs can help local anglers conquer these problems and obtain this key information quite rapidly. If many anglers share their observations of hatches and barometric readings, then the burden and challenge is not borne by one person. When more anglers seek the answers together, they will all have it sooner. Some will go fishing when others can't, and some will watch the barometer and total-pressure when others can't; and someone can ramrod the effort and record the observations in a proper log. The cooperative effort will soon sprout big rewards.

If you are fortunate enough to learn a precise duration, it may only be applicable to the species hatching or molting on the day you acquired it. Conversely, you may have discovered that the duration is applicable across a broad spectrum of organisms in the waters where you fish. You may find that four hours, eight hours, or twelve hours is a very acceptable duration at all times and in most or all of the waters in which you fish near a certain latitude and elevation.

This is essentially what happened to me. My circle of friends fed me constant fishing reports and I asked as many questions about their outings as I thought their friendship would tolerate. The questions were about observations of natural phenomena they might have made while on the water: Was there a hatch? What hatched? What time did it occur? What was the date? Where did it occur? Was the bottom sandy, silty, or stony? What was the water temperature, etc? It didn't take long until most became savvy about what I would ask, and their observations became quite astute. Their eyes and ears were the lifeline of this book. Some of them have fed me hundreds of reports over the seven years of collecting data for this work. We have become far wiser fishermen and closer friends.

Here is where you get rescued: We also learned that pie hatches could reliably be expected to occur if low total-pressure persisted for the previous six to eight hours before a preferred hatching time of the day. It's still an uncertain number, but it is responsible for countless successful predictions of good bites that would occur during daily preferred hatching times. It's also responsible for scores of fishing outings that were not taken because hatches and bites were predicted not to occur, and it was later learned that they did not. The time may be shorter, perhaps two to five hours, maybe less, but I'm still gathering the necessary evidence. Remember, this is not a number needed to predict normal hatches and molts; it's only the number needed to predict *pie hatches* and *pie molts*, and the vigorous bites they can cause. I would be comfortable with six to eight hours, maybe a little less, in the temperate latitudes. There may be a shorter duration in the lower, warmer latitudes because of faster degree-day development.

Not only must low total-pressure be present before pie hatches and pie molts can occur, it seems logical that it must also persist during the species' preferred hatching time of day. If high total-pressure returns before the preferred hatching time, the increased pressure would hinder hatching (high pressure rule) and perhaps delay it until another day.

Radical Pressure from Waves

One natural event that radically lowers and raises total-pressure, but doesn't appear to cause pie hatches or pie molts, is the occurrence of large waves. Recall from Chapter 6, 1.36 inches of water exerts the same pressure as ten points of barometric pressure; and, a pie hatch can be caused by as little as 15-20 points of barometric pressure drop, or the equivalent water level drop of approximately 2-2¾ inches. A water level drop of 2¾ inches would occur with a wave that's only 5½ inches (2¾ inches x 2 = 5½ inches) from top of the wave crest to bottom of the wave trough.

Multiple pie hatches can be caused by as little as 40-60 points of barometric pressure drop, or the equivalent water level drop of approximately 5½-8 inches. A water level drop of 8 inches could occur with a wave of 16 inches from crest to trough.

Wave heights of 5½ inches occur almost daily on most inland lakes, and 16 inch waves are very common on larger lakes, depending on wind speed and distance of fetch across the lake.

Figure 7-5 illustrates waves being created by wind blowing across a lake, and moving some of the water to the leeward side of the lake. You can demonstrate this effect on your kitchen table by placing a single drop of water on the tabletop. The drop will appear symmetrical, but you can distort it by blowing on it at a low angle with your breath. Because of the small wind you create, the water in the upper part of the drop will shift away from you. If you blow hard enough you can move a large portion of the drop a substantial distance from its original position, perhaps a couple inches away. Winds blowing across a lake have the same effect. They move the water a substantial distance. When the water hits a shoreline, however, it can go nowhere but up, so it begins to pile up and get deeper along that shoreline. This is the effect illustrated in Figure 7-5 in shaded area A.

The piled-up water, however, is probably working another unheralded miracle of nature. Generally speaking, warmer water is topmost in lakes and gets blown around the most. It is the water that usually gets

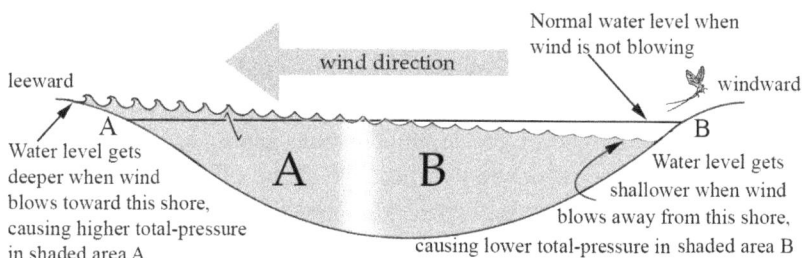

Figure 7-5

125

blown into shorelines and piles up. We already know that warm water accelerates degree-day absorption and causes hatches to occur sooner. So, the warmer, windblown water might be suspected to cause hatches to occur in the warm, turbulent, crashing waves, but they don't. The reason they don't can probably be attributed to the increase in total-pressure caused by the piled-up water. The increased water depth with its higher total-pressure would thwart the hatches, which probably prevents catastrophic mortality that the insects would suffer in the violence of breaking waves. It's another example supporting the notion that natural selection has favored aquatic insect molting during low total-pressure.

And behold, the lowest total-pressure spot on the lake is on the windward shoreline of region B where the water level has been lowered by the wind. The water is relatively flat with almost no wave action, so crashing waves and turbulence are not threats to insects that might hatch as a result of the lower total-pressure. The wind has actually created a safe place for insects to hatch or molt. Hatching or molting, however, is not guaranteed.

When warm water is blown away from a shore, it is replaced by cooler water from below (Explained further in Figure 10-5). If the cooler water at the bottom near shoreline B remains the same temperature or close to what it was before the warm water blew away, then water temperature will have little effect on hatching or molting; but if the water temperature becomes colder at the bottom where it covers the insects in their habitat, the colder temperature will hinder hatching and molting, despite lower total-pressure from the lower water level. Degree-day absorption becomes a factor. It's another simple instance of hatches and molts controlled by water temperature and lower total-pressure. The outcome and future predictions can only be discerned by good logs.

Despite the uncertainties, this is a valuable lesson for observant anglers: Keep your eye on windward shorelines of lakes and large reservoirs during prime hatch times. An ample duration of favorable total-pressure in area B will be dependent on how long the wind has blown in the right direction and on the history of barometric pressure that bears on the state of ableness. In summary, be aware that hatches and good bites in lakes and reservoirs can be wind-dependent because of the effect of wind on total-pressure. Wind effects on lakes are examined further in Chapter 10.

An interesting thing that probably happens when wave crests and troughs are occurring is that insects in ableness are compressing and decompressing with the passage of each crest and trough. Total-pressure increases and decreases intermittently every few seconds and the stress must be great when waves are large. A moderate wave height of only two feet can create a massive total-pressure swing of 176 points, yet the insects don't hatch. Somehow, their biological clocks prevail and they are able to delay hatching until the preferred time of day. It's a very impressive capability. Their exoskeleton structures are undergoing very high, trip-hammer-like strain without cracking open. Such high strain levels make me suspect that their structures have some elasticity that relieves the strain, even though conventional entomological wisdom holds that their exoskeletons have no elasticity. Consider how much repetitive strain could be caused by waves three feet high or larger; yikes!

Although this brief look at waves discounts their effects on hatches, waves are still responsible for good bites, which will be addressed further in Chapter 8.

Mystery Hatch

Occasionally you will encounter a hatch that, at first blush, seems to defy all conventions of angling wisdom, but you now have the tools to figure it out. Consider the following example:

One day, after a couple years of making almost flawless predictions, I assured a recent fishing acquaintance that there would be no hatch of giant Michigan mayflies (hexagenia limbata) in the Boardman River that evening. I based my predictions on recent rain and a lingering cold front, although we had had warm sun for several hours in the afternoon on this day. Still, he insisted on trying to catch a nice brown trout, and convinced me to go along. He would fish, but I was so convinced that no hatch would occur, and was so keen on just observing that I left my rod at home. He felt good that I was giving him every advantage. There was a noticeable chill in the air as dusk descended.

To my great chagrin, when hatch time arrived — about 10 p.m. — the center of the river soon populated with large drifting mayflies that were about five feet apart, although they appeared languid and very few were trying to fly off the water. It looked like a great hatch, even though the mayflies acted more like spinners than hatchers, and I was wholly at a loss to explain it at the moment. My new acquaintance was enjoying some wonderful fishing because the bite was on. I was thoroughly embarrassed.

About half way through the hatch, however, I noticed that the flies were not hatching in our stretch of the river. These flies are silt dwellers and always hatch near the silt beds along the margins of the stream, but they were nowhere near the silt beds. They were simply drifting in the middle of the river like a common foam line. Something unusual must have been happening upstream.

Near noon the next day I donned waders and struggled upstream through a nasty patch of swamp and discovered a shallow, silty backwater that was heavily littered with mayfly shucks (exoskeletons). The water was only about four-to-seven inches deep. I had forgotten my thermometer, but the water felt far warmer than the water in the mainstream of the river. It covered a couple acres and had a five-feet-wide, fast-flowing outlet into the main river. Obviously this was the source of the drifting mayflies. There was no sign of shucks upstream of this point. The mysterious hatch of the previous evening was soon explained.

Apparently the shallow water had absorbed an extraordinary amount of heat from the afternoon sun, and the warm water caused a good hatch in the backwater. Immediately upon hatching, however, the mayflies encountered the lingering cold air from the cold front, which inhibited their ability to fly. Lacking the ability to fly, they rode the backwater current through the outlet onto the mainstream of the river. The river current then corralled them to the middle of the stream where they continued to drift for hundreds of yards downstream. The combination of cold night air and cool river water continued to suppress their ability to fly, so all the fish downstream got an unexpected feast. Due to the unusual combination of environmental conditions, this hatch probably suffered very high mortality, depleting the hatch sizes in subsequent years.

Looking at the bright side of this story, my prediction of no hatch in the river was still valid, but with a twist. Although the river and backwater created an unusual situation, I was able to interpret and understand it with simple knowledge of total-pressure and temperature. A little knowledge of the mayfly's preferred habitat also helped. The experience sharpened my alertness for circumstances that are more extraordinary than I'm capable of conjuring in my ordinary imagination.

Some Insect Behavior Reduces Pressure

It's worth noting that the behavior of some insects has the effect of reducing the total-pressure they experience before they molt. For example late-instar stoneflies are known to crawl out of the water to molt as adults on land or on objects protruding from the water. As they crawl from deeper water toward the bank or shore, the water becomes shallower until they finally leave the water altogether. As the water becomes shallower with each step toward shore, total-pressure for the insect also becomes lower and lower with each step. Depending on how deep the water was where they began their migration, the reduction in total-pressure between there and the bank could be very large, and it could occur quite quickly, depending upon how fast they travel. It must surely have a very positive effect.

Hatching Synchronized with Humidity

Discovering that aquatic insects have temporary properties of a barometer helps to explain how they synchronize their hatches with periods of high humidity.

High humidity is a critical benefit of hatching when total-pressure is low, which is when hatching is easiest for the insects and most likely to occur. When low barometric pressure acts to reduce total-pressure, higher humidity is typically present because higher humidity occurs incidentally with low barometric pressure systems. It occurs because a given volume of low pressure air contains fewer air molecules than an equal volume of high pressure air, and therefore contains more empty space that can be occupied by more molecules of water vapor. Thus, humidity is generally higher when barometric pressure is lower.

Low barometric pressure is also typically associated with rain, storminess, and slightly warmer air. The low pressure and high humidity always arrive before — often days before — any rain and storminess associated with a low barometric pressure system, and persist throughout the duration of the system. Higher pressure and the drier, colder air typically associated with it, settles in after the low barometric pressure passes through. It's a mini-sequence that never changes.

Aquatic insects have a hatching mechanism (ableness and the pressure rules) that takes advantage of this mini-sequence and, ideally, places the insects in a high humidity atmosphere immediately upon hatching. This scenario plays out often and well in rivers and most lakes, but there are major exceptions in the world's largest lakes, which are addressed in Chapter 10.

Aquatic insects need moist air to survive after hatching, and their temporary barometer-like characteristics greatly increase their chances for hatching into moister, warmer air. Those same characteristics also help them avoid the drier, colder air that can kill them. They play a key role in providing the insects with the highest chances for survival.

High humidity associated with low barometric pressure is not the only source of life-giving atmospheric moisture; there are others. Consider the following:

The approaching low barometric pressure — which precedes rain or storminess — brings favorable conditions that give insects the opportunity to hatch into a high humidity atmosphere without being crippled or killed by rain drops. When they hatch and fly off the water, they light on vegetation near the water so they can return for mating flights and laying eggs. The vegetation provides protective cover when the rain eventually arrives and recharges the earth with soaking moisture. The rain soon quits and fair weather returns, which means sunny skies, high pressure, cooler air, and lower humidity will likely prevail for a few days. Fortunately, the lower humidity will not be a factor near the vegetation where the insects have lit.

Characteristically, newly hatched insects stay on the ground or light on vegetation that grows from the moisture-laden earth near the water — on the grass, shrubs, or trees along the margins or lowlands near the water. While they linger there, the sun will bake the earth and create a certain amount of evaporation that raises the humidity in the vicinity of the margins and lowlands that satisfies some insects' need for moisture.

Things are a little more interesting for mayflies, however, because they show a preference for lighting on the *underside* of leaves of nearby vegetation. The leaves shield them from the cannonball effects of falling raindrops, afford lifesaving shade from the blistering sun, and give them another source of higher humidity. It's remarkable behavior because the leaves regulate the plant's moisture and temperature by a process called transpiration. The underside of leaves have tiny openings (stomata) that open and close to allow moisture to escape. The escaping moisture creates another little area with higher humidity near the leaf's surface that aids the insect's survival. Where vegetation is thick and plants are heavily foliated, transpiration from the leaves creates a small micro-climate with higher humidity. When the sun is high in the sky it causes higher evaporation of moisture from the plants, which then transpire moisture into the atmosphere at a higher rate, which in turn helps sustain higher humidity in the immediate vicinity.

It appears that natural selection that has favored emergence during low pressure conditions provides survival advantages to aquatic insects during every crucial step of their life cycle. Seems like it may have done the same for aquatic crustaceans; evidence supporting this notion is contained in old fishermen's proverbs, as discussed in Chapter 9.

Mutants

Despite evidence that supports postulations that I've proposed, it's important to remember that natural selection is always active and creating species mutants that behave differently than the masses of their brethren. Populations of these mutants are probably minimal, but they may appear at times that are completely contradictory to normal expectations. Their appearances would most likely not be significant events, but they may confuse unsuspecting observers, especially if they produce an unexpected and largely unpredictable bite. Such bites will probably remain rare for the foreseeable future.

Lastly, it's possible that social signals between the organisms may figure into the prompts for molting and hatching, but I'm not aware of any.

Chapter 8

Bite Notes

No matter how bleak the fishing outlook, if healthy fish are present, there is always a chance of coaxing them to bite. A natural or artificial bait probably exists that will catch almost any fish if it's used with the correct technique. There is always hope, although some days are certainly better than others. You can stack the odds in your favor, however, if you recognize the cause and characteristics of certain bites. With this in mind, this chapter contains insights into a variety of bites, some of which have never been reasonably explained.

Every fish species has evolved unique behaviors that keep it alive in its own special niche; and each behaves differently from all other species, even though the differences between some may be slight. Despite the behavioral differences, those same behaviors also have much in common. It's what they have in common that makes the bite easier to predict.

Behavior of healthy fish can be confusing at times, but as best as I can determine, it is always governed by at least one of three fundamental needs: (1) food, (2) safety and comfort, (3) reproduction. In other words, they must eat, they must protect themselves from environmental threats such as high temperatures, low oxygen and other adverse water conditions, and predators, and they must have a behavior pattern that results in successful spawning or, rarely, live birth (sharks). These needs cause fish to be in certain places at certain times, which are predictable if you have the right information. You'll see how they play out in examples that follow.

Leaf Drop Bites

Over the years, I've heard sensational stories about fishing in the fall. The tales were few and far between, but too tantalizing to ignore. They told about a few hardy fishermen enduring cold weather while making extraordinary catches of walleye, bass, and pike, but little word was getting out. It was as if a great secret was being protected. Sporting magazines also printed tales of unusually exciting fall fishing, but the articles didn't contain much that I thought could help me. I finally met a fishing guide who told me about a couple of his friends who were catching as many as 10 nice fish per outing with as few as 10 casts. They were throwing lures as they waded a lake shoreline in the mornings and evenings in very late fall. Several years later another friend told me about a fisherman he knew who was having comparable success while fishing from docks just before freeze up. He, too, was fishing mornings and evenings and throwing lures.

This sounded like my kind of fishing — catching lots of fish with little effort. Despite the promise of great fishing, it wasn't guaranteed. I needed to understand why the fishing was so good so I could get the timing right. The magazines frequently repeated the same tired mantra that the fish were intentionally feeding to fatten up for the long hard winter. Does a fish know it needs to fatten up for the winter? Who is the Dr. Doolittle that had a conversation with a fish that told him this? There had to be a better explanation, and there is.

Two common denominators were obvious in the stories: first, fish were biting during two periods of low light levels; second, the fish being caught were all predators, not prey fish. If they were all predators, it seemed logical that they had to be feeding on prey that was abundant and easy to catch, and inhabited the shallow water near shore. Something significant had to be occurring in the shallows to attract so many predators. At first, I strongly suspected that minnow species must be spawning in the thin water, but I was wrong.

I spent nearly a year researching more than 80 minnow species (true minnows, smelt, chubs, etc.), probably most if not all of the known minnow species in the Great Lakes region and Canada. Amazingly, I found that none of them spawn in the fall; they all spawn in spring and summer. It was a disappointing result, but much of the answer was still in the minnows, literally.

When minnow species spawn, they deposit approximately 250 to 6500 eggs, depending on the species, their size, and age. If 2000 minnows each lay 1000 eggs, it could result in two million new minnows. If several species spawn in the same lake, the number of new minnows can be staggering — many millions. They don't require much food when they first hatch, but how will the lake feed such a huge explosion of minnows when they grow up?

The eggs hatch in spring and summer when scores of other critters are also hatching and abundantly populating the food web. It's the time of year when food becomes plentiful. Enormous amounts of plankton, plus insect eggs and immatures become available as food for the masses of minnows (Sidebar #18: Plankton). The minnow eggs are also fed upon by many other organisms, including minnows. Most members of the food web that have not been eaten are thriving and growing. The populations of many other species are also exploding. As summer wears on, a large percentage of the new generation of minnows continue to thrive and grow on the abundance of food, even though their numbers are being steadily reduced by predators.

As fall approaches, the abundance of food is greatly diminished because it's been eaten. In addition, most of the great insect hatches, including smaller insects, are finished for the year; and many insect immatures have grown too large to be eaten by small minnows with tiny mouths. The seasonal temperature drop also reduces molting activity, so the immatures are not as available as food. Worse, older minnows have grown even larger, so more of them need still larger quantities of food, but food is becoming less plentiful. More and larger minnows are competing for a rapidly shrinking food supply.

By late fall, colder winds have eliminated the temperature stratification in most lakes so the water temperature is generally uniform from top to bottom (result of the fall "turnover" event). The turbulent winds of autumn also create plenty of wave action that oxygenates the water. Because of the improved water conditions, predator fish no longer confine their activities to isolated zones of low temperature and higher dissolved oxygen; they are more dispersed and roaming the entire lake for food.

Minnow species have also redistributed to their preferred habitats, such as open water, weed beds, drop-offs, etc. The multiplied hoards of little fish are easy prey for the roaming predators. It's a food bazaar for predators, but the minnows still face a dwindling food supply. How can Mother Nature feed so many tiny mouths when the food supply appears less adequate every day? The answer isn't exactly obvious, but if I'm right, the answer is simple: Leaf drop.

Near the same time as turnover, leaves on deciduous trees and plants that ring the lakeshore begin changing to the blazing colors of autumn. The trees and plants are going dormant for the season and soon drop their leaves. Literally tons of leaves drop into the water at the lake's edge, and wave action soon helps them settle to the bottom near shore.

The huge deposit of freshly fallen leaves is soon colonized by bacteria in the oxygen rich, wave-tossed water. The leaves are soon decom-

#18
Plankton

Plankton is the aggregate population of small and microscopic organisms that drift and float in great numbers in fresh and salt water, especially near the surface, although some are also associated with the bottom. There are two categories of plankton: (1) Plant (phytoplankton), (2) Animal (zooplankton). Both serve as food for fish and larger zooplankton species. Common characteristics of both are that they are generally limited to vertical movement, up or down, and they lack the ability for significant horizontal movement. Vertical movement of zooplankton is often related to light or the absence of it, therefore some are nocturnal and others are diurnal. Horizontal distribution is primarily caused by wind-driven movement of surface water. Many species manifest regular seasonal variations in abundance and will have peak populations at certain times of the year.

Common phytoplankton includes many species of algae and diatoms. Common zooplankton includes cladocera, copepods, mysidacea, and eggs of many organisms, although eggs are usually settled on the bottom and not drifting afloat.

posing from the bacterial attack, and the bacteria and its by-products are rapidly becoming a huge food source for tiny organisms like minuscule crustaceans that the large populations of minnows can eat. The decomposing leaves in the shallows form a large ring of food around the lake that, until ice forms, continues to attract insects, crustaceans, and the minnows that prey on them, and predator fish that prey on the minnows. The predators likely become conditioned to the presence of the abundant minnows and stay near them, which, in turn, makes the predators easy prey for hardy fishermen willing to brave chilly weather. In addition to leaf drop, weed beds in the shallows also begin dying and collapsing near this time, or shortly after, and provide additional plant material for bacterial decomposition.

From what I hear, it's a great bite that occurs every day, morning and evening, and lasts for weeks as predators enter the shallows looking for food. Barometric pressure or total-pressure is probably not an important factor in this bite.

When turnover occurs earlier in fall, just before leaf drop, deep circulating currents stir up bottom sediments that release nutrients that may sustain many plankton species in multiple niches throughout the lake. Depending on the species, they can be located in shallow or deep water and places in between, which would temporarily attract certain minnow and baitfish species to the specific niches populated with the various plankton species. The result would be disorganized, scattered bites occurring throughout the lake system (sound familiar?) as the plankton is moved around by wind and lake currents. The indefinite pattern would continue until submerged leaves or weed bed decomposition is in full swing later.

Eventually, ice will form over the shallows and kill the bite in most places. The bite stops because the ice stops all wave action that has been oxygenating the water. Bacteria are major oxygen consumers and they soon deplete the oxygen in the surrounding shallow water if it's not replenished by wave action or winter-hardy weeds that continue to photosynthesize and oxygenate the water. Snow cover on the ice sharply reduces any photosynthesis because it blocks light penetration. The shallow water under the ice near shore then soon becomes an oxygen depleted zone, which causes the minnows to abandon it, so the near-shore bite goes dead. Bacteria in the leaf litter will continue to decompose the leaves while the remaining oxygen lasts, but it will eventually suffer a major die-off from oxygen starvation and no longer provide adequate food for organisms the minnows are feeding upon. Interviews with many ice fishermen corroborate that the big predators are seldom caught in the near-shore shallows after ice-up. The minnows and predators drift farther offshore to weed beds that are still decomposing in deeper water with more oxygen. As spring approaches and days become longer with more sunlight, weeds begin growing and photosynthesizing again, infusing more oxygen into the shallow water, and the annual cycle begins again.

Leaf drop also creates good bites in river systems. Significant leaf drop can occur along the full length of some rivers. When leaf decomposition begins along the stream courses, the resulting material creates a continuous food supply that drifts to tiny prey organisms downstream. The mouths of rivers and creeks become collection areas for the tiny organisms and the minnows that feed on them, and the predator fish that feed on the minnows. It produces a hot bite. The same congregations of prey organisms should occur where streams widen into reservoirs behind dams.

The downstream areas can produce a good bite that lasts for an extended period. It's generally because of the gradual elevation drop along the stream, and the stream's length from north to south (south to north in the Southern Hemisphere), or a significant drop in altitude from its headwaters to its mouth.

Similar to the sequence of leaves changing color and dropping from north to south, and depending on a streams direction of drainage, leaves can change color and drop near the higher elevations of a stream's headwaters first. The color change and drop continues downhill along the stream all the way to the mouth, and it can take weeks along the longest rivers. Naturally, the leaves begin decomposing near the stream's headwaters at the highest elevation first. The decomposition then gradually progresses downstream as leaves drop in the lower elevations. Therefore, leaf drop and decomposition in a stream can begin earlier than they typically would in a lake located at a lower elevation. By occurring earlier and lasting longer, the bite would also begin earlier and last as long as adequate food produced by the decomposition is constantly drifting downstream. Organisms feeding on the decomposed material become available in increasing numbers as the season wears on. Streams oriented along east-west courses will experience decomposition along their full length over a shorter time span than the north-south streams.

Although ice-up doesn't generally occur in warmer latitudes, weed beds there still die and collapse late in the year, and bacteria break down the dead vegetation into food for organisms that attract bait fish or large crustaceans. The bait fish and crustaceans then attract predator fish, creating good bites.

Egg Hatch Bites

When fish species spawn, it's typical for a large segment of the population to spawn during the same short time period. Many thousands to millions of eggs are laid during that short period, and laid in approximately the same vicinity. Depending on the species, they are laid in a variety of places ranging from shallow sand and gravel bottoms to open water over silt. Some are deposited in prepared nests or redds, and others are simply extruded over a natural, undisturbed bottom. The eggs generally settle into the bottom where they remain until they hatch or are eaten by other organisms.

When eggs are first laid and resting undisturbed in the natural substrate, a significant percentage will remain unnoticed and therefore unmolested. As they mature and hatch, however, they become active as alevins (the nourishing egg yolk sac is still attached and not fully absorbed) and draw the attention of a wider range of predators. After the yolk sac is absorbed and the new hatchlings have gained some size and strength, known as fry at this stage, they must venture forth to find their own food. Because of their abundance and increased movement, they attract attention and are heavily preyed upon by small predator fish. Small predator fish then become numerous in the vicinity and, in turn, are fed upon by larger predator fish, and the bite is on.

Fortunately for the angler, good bites resulting from the development of eggs into alevin and fry can be predicted.

The eggs of each fish species require a unique amount of incubation time before they hatch. It's different for each species and is dependent on the water temperature, which means the eggs must absorb a certain amount of degree-day heat in order to hatch. In temperate latitudes, eggs fertilized in spring or early summer may hatch in a matter of days or weeks. Eggs fertilized in fall may incubate through the winter and hatch the following spring. When the eggs are finally hatching and causing a good bite, however, nearby terrestrial plants will also be developed to a certain stage. It's the botanical sequence thing again. Correlating the stage of plant development with the egg hatching will give you the necessary information for predicting egg hatch bites in following years.

Duck Bite

Sometimes a bite can be extremely localized.

Late one morning I witnessed six mallard ducks land in a river about 25 yards upstream of a steelhead fisherman who had hooked nothing yet for the day. Several fish were resting in a deep run within his casting distance, but showed no interest in his offerings. The ducks began tipping up and feeding in the bottom mud and vegetation. They were dislodging a noticeable amount of bottom material that drifted downstream through the fish and apparently excited them to bite. Within about five minutes the man's fly line was attached to a leaping steelhead as his reel screamed from the resistance of the drag. He landed the fish, and then caught another one immediately after the first one. Meanwhile, the ducks paddled far upstream, after which he hooked no more fish. Several other fishermen who were spaced 50 to 100 yards downstream caught nothing; probably because the drifting material was too widely dispersed to also stimulate the visible fish near them to bite.

Leeward Shoreline Bites

There are times when a bite continues to linger for a day or so after a cold front goes through, depending on time of year and location. A bite like that can be puzzling to explain. The first time I encountered one was on television.

I was watching a fishing program one morning when the host shocked me with news that he was having a great bite on the *first* day of a cold front positioned over his lake. His claim was completely counter-intuitive to everything I'd ever heard about cold front fishing; it wasn't supposed to be easy. I believe he was fishing on a day that followed pie hatches and pie molts, which should have made fishing slow and difficult. Fortunately, it had become my custom to observe and absorb as much as possible about the environmental conditions revealed by the TV camera on such shows.

The trees surrounding the lake were fully foliated, but the host did not reveal the date. As near as I could tell, he was catching smallmouth bass in 6 to 12 feet of water in a rather large lake. He did not mention any stomach contents sampled from the fish. By his own words I knew that the cold front had replaced a long spell of warmer weather. This probably meant that a thick layer of warm water covered the lake. The key element of his success appeared to be the wind. He was fishing the downwind (leeward) side of the lake. A slight breeze was blowing small waves (no whitecaps) into the shore line where he was fishing.

I surmised that the cold air behind the front was not significantly colder, so the thick layer of warm surface water was cooling very slowly. The wind was now moving the warmer water toward the shoreline where he was fishing. It seems reasonable that the water, which was still relatively warm, was probably carrying a great, drifting load of top-water zooplankton suspended in it. As the zooplankton was driven toward the leeward shoreline it became more abundant and concentrated, which probably caused baitfish to pounce on it, and the baitfish were soon preyed upon by the smallmouths.

Years have passed, but I believe my suppositions were essentially correct. Since watching that fishing program, I have personally experienced great bites on the leeward shoreline on windy days, and had good success when using indigenous minnows. I've also since met several fishermen who knew about the wind effect long before I figured it out.

Another thing that could have caused a good bite during the cold front weather is one (or more) of the indigenous minnow species was spawning or staging for spawning. Their concentrated numbers would certainly attract predators and create a good bite. It's a possibility that reinforces the need to keep good fishing logs. Spawning would repeat at the same location every year, whereas wind-blown plankton could be driven to any shoreline on the lake. It would be helpful to know that one or the other is causing the bite in future years.

When plankton is being blown from one side of a lake to another, it can cause baitfish to appear almost anywhere in the open expanse of the lake and create a good bite out there. Panic stricken minnows leaping out of the water often signal the existence of predatory fish below. When the baitfish and predators are not visible to the angler, kingfishers, ospreys, eagles, terns, and seagulls often betray their location.

I have noticed in small farm ponds that a majority of fish will migrate to the leeward side in high wind to feed on windblown food. A few fish remain on the windward side, but the majority followed the food during the times that I checked. I have not checked enough to know if this is consistent behavior, but I suspect it is in ponds and lakes that are small and where passages in lakes are narrow.

I also once watched a program featuring a well-known walleye fisherman who visited a large lake that had been producing very few walleyes for several weeks. He was with a local fishing guide who was stumped by the poor action. During their first outing on the lake, the wind was kicking up small waves that were breaking on the leeward side. The fisherman encouraged the guide to steer the boat to a boulder-strewn area where the leeward waves were breaking, whereupon he immediately began catching walleyes. He explained that turbulence from the waves was dislodging food from the bottom and minnows were feeding on the stirred up feast. The minnows were seeking refuge from the turbulence behind large rocks and boulders, and the walleyes were attacking them there; and that's where he was throwing his lure.

Fish Hunger

Fish are opportunistic feeders and critically dependent on the regular availability of food where they live. They feed when food is available, and generally inhabit a comfortable and safe location when it's not. They venture out of their comfortable and safe location to seek food if, like Pavlov's dog and based on their past experiences, they expect food to be available in certain places.

This phenomenon is acutely evident in walleye and trout that emerge from the depths each morning or evening to feed on insect hatches that have occurred at approximately the same time on previous days. They may forego the insects and feed instead on the minnows or other prey that are feeding on the insects. They also venture forth when their ultrasensitive lateral lines detect the vibrations that indicate adult insects or immatures, or other foods like crustaceans or bait fish, are vulnerable to predation. They'll also move from comfort and safety to prowl for food if they're simply hungry. Simple hunger, however, is a condition that's very difficult for a fisherman to predict.

Some will be hungry while other fish are not. Some will get food in serendipitous circumstances when others don't, so the ones that have fed won't be hungry when others are. The ones that have fed may have encountered and eaten a crayfish or two, or several minnows that came too close. After feeding, they may become lethargic while other fish remain hungry and on the prowl. Those that are sated are less likely to be responsive to food temptations (and imitations), and unfortunately may be the only fish encountered by a fisherman.

I witnessed a possible example of hunger that controlled a bite in the Boardman River near my home on March 12, 2005. Pressure had been low for several days and spiked lower and lowest on this date at 12:53a.m., and then began to slowly rise. Most unexpectedly, a friend hooked seven steelhead the next morning between 6:30a.m and 10:30a.m. He kept two hatchery raised ones (fin clipped) so I could check the stomach contents. The stomach of each fish was empty. Based on falling total-pressure, it seems as though pie molts should have occurred at certain times during the falling pressure period, and perhaps they did, but there was no evidence of it in the stomachs. Perhaps there were no molts.

I suspect that there were no molts, even for the previous day or two, and the fish were becoming acutely hungry and began feeding as soon as morning light began to break. The possible absence of a molt may be because of a catastrophic loss of the organism's previous year's generation, which should have been present this year but wasn't. Its loss and subsequent absence may be attributable to a heavy rain or heavy snowmelt runoff the year before.

Another possibility could be that an organism had molted and waited until daylight to become active, but was too difficult to catch. In other words, the molt triggered a bite because of the organism's availability several hours later, but the individuals were so elusive that none made it into the stomachs of the fish I checked. This scenario seems somewhat improbable because it appears to violate the principle of self-preservation — hatching in the dark, but becoming active a second time during daylight. It seems like a poor survival strategy. The organism is more vulnerable to predators in daylight, which appears to contradict the advantages it may have had if it molted in the dark.

It's puzzling that such a good bite occurred approximately six hours after the lowest instance of total-pressure and during the period when pressure was rising, which would suppress molts. Sheer hunger seems the most plausible explanation because it's simple and more logical than the others **(Sidebar #8: Ockham's Razor)**. The episode causes me to think that fish, especially steelhead, may feed unconditionally at my latitude after three days of a dearth of natural food.

Interestingly, not all fish will feed, even if they have empty stomachs, but a higher percentage will feed if ample food makes an appearance. Then again, some will even skip eating for the duration of the appearance. Perhaps they've been spooked, distracted, or have an ailment that affects their feeding behavior. It's difficult to know why they behave in such a contrary manner. Despite the contrary few, however, the best fishing approach is to time your efforts for when you expect the most fish to feed, which is almost always when abundant food makes a temporary appearance.

Your new understanding of barometric pressure and temperature influences will enable you to predict when their food will make that appearance in streams, reservoirs, and small lakes. Big lakes offer their own unique challenges, some of which are addressed in Chapter 10.

Bites During Hatches of Large Insects

Another interesting bite behavior occurs during hatches of large insects. When insects such as large mayflies, moths, or large stoneflies are abundant on the water, smaller fish become sated first and quit feeding earlier during a big hatch. As the hatch continues, generally, it seems that only the progressively larger fish continue to feed. It's a natural progression because smaller fish have smaller stomachs, which fill up much sooner than the larger stomachs of larger fish. It takes longer for larger fish to fill their larger stomachs, so they feed longer. The largest fish tend to feed the longest (unless they prey on vulnerable smaller fish and fill up sooner). This phenomenon often leads to a unique opportunity.

As a good hatch wanes and finally stops, the largest fish have often not filled their stomachs before the hatch ends. They are still hungry and in a state of elevated anticipation, so they lie in wait for more insects to enter their feeding lane or area, even though no more insects are appearing. They can still be in a strong feeding mode for a considerable amount of time after a hatch is done. Smaller fish have typically quit feeding, but the trophy fish are still prowling or waiting in ambush, and are now more vulnerable to a fisherman's offerings. I have caught many trophy fish during my four decades of flyfishing, particularly big brown trout in the hour *after* a major hatch has ended. It's also been my experience that, after about an hour or so after a hatch ends, the bite will lose its intensity and fade into a period of very difficult fishing. The reason can be partly because some of the fish are sated from a great feeding event and probably no longer hungry. It's also possible that they no longer expect more food to arrive because so much time has elapsed since the last insect drifted by. They become inactive because food is no longer available to keep them activated. Either way, the majority of the easy trophy bite is usually finished.

Trophy Fish Caught During Good Bites

Taxidermists and sporting good store owners have told me that nearly 100% of trophy fish, of all species, are caught when the angler is having a good day catching lots of fish. They say that very few trophy fish are caught as an only fish for the day. Big fish are almost always caught as one of a batch on a day when they are biting well. Therefore, if you're interested in catching trophy fish, the underlying message here is to go fishing on days when fishing will be good, which you are now better able to determine. If trophy fish are more catchable on these days, you may further improve your odds by using lures, flies, or bait that are larger and perhaps more appealing to larger fish.

Floodwater Bites

Floodwater usually wreaks havoc on hatches and associated bites, but it can also be responsible for bites that would not occur otherwise. This is especially true for anadromous fish like steelhead and salmon that migrate up rivers to spawn in the spring, summer, or fall.

These big fish generally arrive in the same streams during the same months every year, but their arrival is always erratic. They may show up during the same week as the previous year, or a week earlier or later. Predicting which week and day they will arrive is problematic, and every year is different. It has always been an issue given to chance, and fishermen annually waste large sums on expensive fishing trips that they hope will coincide with the appearance of fish in the stretch of river they will be fishing. More often than not, however, the fish are not there or not as abundant as expected. Fishing guides and lodge owners live with this disappointment every season. Guided clients commonly hear the guides and owners say, "You should have been here last week," or, "You're probably about a week early."

One of the biggest reasons for the fish's erratic appearance is unsuitable water temperature. While the fish are still in the sea or large lakes like the Great lakes, they begin to stage in offshore areas near the mouths of the rivers they will soon ascend. If the seawater or lake water surrounding the river mouths is too cold or too warm, it acts as a barrier that the fish are reluctant to cross.

Wind is the primary cause when warmer or cooler water surrounds the regions around river mouths. If wind is blowing toward the river mouth it is generally blowing warm water in that direction and replacing cooler water that was there previously. If it's blowing away from the river mouth it's moving warm water away from the mouth and allowing colder water to replace it. An exception would be when snowmelt fills the river with cold water which ultimately dumps into the waters surrounding the mouth. Wind would have little effect until the cold water drains out. For more on water temperature patterns caused by wind, see Chapters 10 and 12. (Sidebar #19: Hot Water Floats)

Eventually, spawning fish must enter the rivers, but most will delay entry until the water temperature near the mouth is more to their liking. A few fish almost always filter into the rivers when temperatures are less than ideal, but they can be so sparsely distributed that fishing is exasperating and relatively unproductive. Predicting when river temperatures will be suitable hinges greatly on wind direction at the mouth — or the occurrence of high water or floodwater that flows from the river.

Steelhead and salmon migrations really fire up when rain brings high water or floodwater that inundates a river system during their respective spawning season. Sudden high water brings a rush of new fish up the river, sometimes hundreds to thousands of fish. It almost guarantees a good bite. Experienced fishermen are familiar with this cause and effect, although I've only ever heard them attribute the high water migrations to increased "flow." Increased flow isn't the entire answer, and the salmon bite isn't quite the kind of bite you would normally expect. Increased total-pressure is not a factor.

Increased flow may have its most dramatic effect when it reaches the water surrounding the mouth of the river. The heavier flow has a greater flowing force that may punch through warmer water that has been maintaining a temperature barrier surrounding the mouth. Such temperature barriers can be very extensive, so a large, increased flow of river water would be required to break through such a barrier. Floodwater and high water can do that. The heavier, cooler flow of floodwater will punch through the warm water barrier, and fish will then migrate upstream within the volume of cooler floodwater/high water that's pouring through the barrier, all the way upstream to awaiting anglers. Charter captains have told me that a difference of only two-to-three degrees Fahrenheit can sometimes be enough to put fish on the move through the barrier; the difference needed would depend on the species of fish that want to swim through it. It's another case where good logs will provide answers for the years ahead.

19

Hot Water Floats

Think of a hot air balloon; it rises upward through the atmosphere. The hot air in the balloon is less dense than the colder air surrounding the balloon so the balloon rises, and continues rising toward the top of the colder air surrounding it. Hot smoke from a fire rises in the same manner for the same reasons.

Warm water generally behaves the same way; it rises toward the top of cold water. You can see a prime example of this in hot water heaters commonly used in most homes. The cold water pipe feeds water into the tank, then a flame or electric element heats the cold water until it's hot; the hot water then rises to the top of the tank and is available to use in your kitchen and bathroom. The water in the tank is now stratified. No matter how much hot water you use, cold water to replace it will regularly flow into the bottom of the tank and is heated, which causes it to rise naturally to the top of the tank. The warm water rises because it is less dense and lighter than the heavier, denser cold water at the bottom. The warm water floats on top of the denser cold water below.

Warm and cold water behave exactly the same way in lakes and the sea. Warm water is always positioned as the top layer, with few exceptions, or working its way upward to be the top layer.

Water is a strange substance, however, and exhibits two strange exceptions to the behavior described above:

1. When water freezes, at 32 degrees F, it expands and becomes solid ice. The expansion makes the ice less dense than liquid water, so the ice floats despite its colder temperature.

2. Freshwater is densest and heaviest when it reaches 39 degrees Fahrenheit (39 deg F). This means that water at 39 deg F will sink below water that is only 33, 34, 35, 36, 37, and 38 deg..

For the continued, entire text of this sidebar, see **Appendix E**

A large amount of rainwater also has another effect: It dilutes the concentration of minerals and chemical compounds that comprise the normal daily stew of the river. During periods without rain, the water level in a river drops a small amount each day. As the drop occurs, the concentration of minerals, and chemical compounds can become greater, giving the river a stronger and more distinct olfactory signature (odor). It's much like strong coffee at the bottom of a pot after too much moisture has evaporated out. The result is a strong, highly concentrated brew. Pouring fresh water into the pot with the old coffee will dilute and weaken its odor. The same principle applies to river water.

Fish are known to distinguish different odors that comprise only a few parts per billion of water volume. When floodwater or high water courses down a river into a lake or ocean, it greatly dilutes the concentrations of all elements in the river water, which changes and probably reduces its odor. Fish may sense this as a "freshening" of the water, and a signal that spawning conditions are immediately favorable. Floodwater may also have the effect of scouring more silt etc. from the streambed and suspending much of the increased amount in the flow, which may also give the river water a "freshened" odor. Either way, the fish come, in impressive numbers, although the entire annual spawning population normally will not migrate upstream as a result of one high water event. The one event will simply trigger a respectable quantity of fish to immediately move upstream, and more will come later as they become more "ripe' for the season. Interestingly, if the spawning season is just beginning, many of the fish may swim back downstream out of the river if high water drains out too quickly and causes the river to drop close to its former low level.

Rain that produces high water or floodwater during the normal spawning season will almost always produce an upstream migration of many fish. An exception is when rain produces heavy snowmelt. Cold snowmelt, especially if it flows over frozen ground before reaching the river, may lower the river temperature and cause further delay of any significant migration. This occasionally happens during spring thaw in temperate and higher latitudes and altitudes.

Every stream drainage or watershed warms or cools water in its own unique way and must be considered independently of all other drainages. Rivers unimpeded by dams have significantly different heating and cooling characteristics than rivers with dams and their reservoirs, and tailwaters. Because of these unique features, a stream thermometer is essential equipment for determining how your particular river responds to high water and runoff. A fresh influx of fish and the bite they bring are often heavily dependent on the temperature dynamics of the stream. Good logs of your readings and other observations will reveal valuable information that can improve your fishing in years to come.

The downside to salmon moving with floodwater is that they may move too far. I recall fishing the Pere Marquette River one year when torrential rains flooded the river over its banks in places. The water was very dirty and many large pods of fish migrated unseen over three-fourths the length of the river, over 30 miles. My friends and I were fishing the middle portion of the river and never saw a single fish, although thousands were passing through right in front of our noses. When the water receded there were still no fish in our section of river, but we learned that the upper reaches of the river, mostly private water, were now stuffed with fresh, chrome salmon. Anecdotal reports among fisherman along the river cause me to believe that most fish made the 40 mile trip in less than 48 hours.

In rivers impeded only by dams, floodwater can cause large populations of fish to collect in the tailwater immediately below the first dam and possibly upstream dams if fish ladders are part of the river system. The quality of the natural bite in these tailwater populations will vary wildly, but usually negatively because fish are commonly and constantly harassed by crowds of fishermen. Savvy fishermen know that the harassment often causes fish to shift to a higher or lower position in the water column, so they adjust their fishing technique to ply uncharacteristic depths, which often proves successful. The uncharacteristic depths are generally within just a foot or two of the level that the fish usually occupy. It's a situation wherein the location of the bite shifts, but not much.

Despite suppressing hatches and molts, floodwater can also cause unseen bites by washing terrestrial organisms like earthworms, ants, beetles, and other insects into the water. At such times, fish may be less selective due to a variety of organisms in the water, none of which may be overly abundant. Although a bite may occur, it's generally more difficult to locate due to increased flow and discoloration from silt load, which often cause fish to seek non-typical locations that they can tolerate better until conditions improve.

Latent Feeding Reaction in Salmon

When high water causes a new batch of fish to enter a river, they are the fish that seem to be most receptive to anglers' offerings. They are fresh and full of vitality. This is particularly significant in the case of salmon. Conventional wisdom holds that salmon no longer feed after beginning their upstream spawning migration. I've seen behavior that corroborates this suspicion, and also some that challenges it.

There is a considerable amount of film documentation that shows anglers catching spawning-run salmon on hardware such as metal spoons and plugs. Some of the fish will also take skein spawn into their mouths, and some will swallow it when it's on a hook suspended under a float; and they are often fair hooked on an assortment of flies. In most cases, however, the bait or lure is seldom swallowed because, depending on the species, many have lost their ability to swallow by this point in their life cycle. Many, but *not all* Chinook (King) salmon lose the ability to swallow even before they enter the rivers, but many Coho salmon (Silver Salmon) don't lose the ability to swallow until much later and farther upstream.

The fish may appear to be feeding, but this is generally a deceptive bite, especially after the fish have been in a river for more than a few days. It's been my experience with Chinooks that their bite is a latent feeding reaction. It can be characterized as somewhat of a "second thought."

Shortly before Chinooks enter a river, they are actively catching their food and feeding. Catching food is an instinctive activity that they've been doing for several years before making their spawning run. It's been their primary activity in life, and they are naturally conditioned to do it, probably like a habit. If instinct has driven them to do it every day for years, but they have suddenly lost their ability to swallow, it seems reasonable that some residue of their instinctive drive to eat may persist in the form of a latent feeding reaction. This means they may sometimes go through the motions of catching food simply by force of habit. It's a reaction that can be likened to the motions of someone who has recently quit smoking. During the first couple weeks after quitting, through sheer force of habit and without conscious control, the ex-smoker will unwittingly react to a stimulus and go through the motions of reaching for a cigarette. It's a latent reaction for cigarettes that eventually fades. A latent feeding reaction in salmon is just like it.

In my experience, the latent reaction is generally the same every time. If a fly or bait approaches close enough to a fish's face, and perhaps looks like food that the fish is familiar with, it will sometimes react by briefly snapping its mouth open and shut. It doesn't necessarily include flaring of the gills. I have seen this happen many times. I use small flies (size #6-#8) and try to bump the fish on the nose with them. When the fly gets close and the fish's mouth snaps open, the act of opening its mouth creates a void and low pressure zone in the mouth cavity, allowing water to rush in, carrying the fly into the mouth with it, as though it is vacuumed in. The fish are always facing upstream, so the current also helps push the fly very rapidly into the open-mouth space. It all happens in a split second. When the mouth closes and traps the fly, the line simply stops and draws tight with little or no indication of a bite telegraphed up the line. It's extremely subtle until gentle force is applied to the line to check if a fish is on the other end. If a fish is there, all subtlety soon vanishes.

The latent feeding reaction is also experienced by anglers using plugs and spoons. A popular tactic for non-feeding Chinooks in the Great Lakes region is to anchor a boat above a favorite river pool and let a wobbling lure dangle in the pool in a stationary position. An occasional fish moving through the pool will be overcome by its instincts and slam the wobbling lure that probably resembles an injured baitfish.

The sudden presence of a significant quantity of fresh salmon with a high tendency for latent feeding reactions is the usual result of rain that brings high water or floodwater during spawning season. The greatly increased quantity of fish promises the possibility of increased fishing success, even though the bite may not be clearly definable as natural instead of induced by the angler.

Baitfish Spawning Sequence

A spawning sequence that's commonly overlooked is that of the baitfish, such as small shad and minnows. Their spawning events will cause vigorous natural bites when larger predators key on hoards of the helpless little fish. A big advantage of knowing the baitfish spawning periods is that they may occur during the fishing season when it's legal to keep the predators. The bite may be nearly as good as when the predators spawn.

Fish Location in Turbid Water

When water in lakes and reservoirs rises from rain runoff, vegetation such as grass and brush along the shoreline and banks becomes flooded. Fish often migrate to these flooded edges, perhaps because they temporarily provide refuge for baitfish and good ambush cover for the predators.

151

While the water is turbid and off-color, the grass lines and brush lines also provide fish with navigational signposts they can follow while visibility is limited to very short distances, often only inches.

In larger water, turbidity also has the effect of driving suspended fish to the bottom for a similar reason. They can get their bearings for navigational purposes when in visual contact with the bottom.

During many years of fishing in rivers at night, I've seen numerous instances of fish navigating closer to the bank on the darkest nights, especially in dirty water. They betrayed their presence near the bank by occasional porpoising. The porpoising, too, may have been attempts to regain navigational bearings by taking a look around above the water.

Ice Fishing

Chapter 6 contained references to lousy fishing resulting from large hatches and molts that produced so much food that an angler's offerings were lost in the overwhelming mass of insects. This can happen at any time of year, even when ice fishing.

An expert river guide and ice fisherman who uses a variety of electronic gadgetry told me his best fishing day of the season (ice fishing season) occurred on a day when barometric pressure was the highest it had been all year. Assorted panfish ate everything he lowered through his hole in the ice. It was great fun because he could see the fish on his underwater camera as they approached and inhaled his bait. During the next day, however, barometric pressure plummeted and he had a far more difficult day of fishing. He caught a few fish, but was disappointed because he used all his considerable skills and equipment and only had mediocre results.

I quizzed him about what he observed with his underwater camera while fishing was poor during the low pressure day. He said the fish were active and appeared to be feeding, but they would only approach his bait slowly, and refuse to bite it. After refusing his bait the fish resumed their other activities that looked like feeding. I suggested that the fish were probably selectively feeding on something that was abundant and small. The low pressure probably caused a significant pie molt, perhaps of a tiny crustacean species, and the fish were keying on it to the exclusion of most other food. He agreed because of what he saw on his camera. He had not checked stomach contents, so we were both left guessing about the identity of the food, , but not why it was abundant. The high and low pressure rules appeared to be just as valid through the ice as in open water.

Water has peculiar properties, and one peculiarity is that it expands when it freezes and forms ice, which makes ice less dense than warm water, so it floats. Floating ice, such as a frozen lake surface, does not form a barrier to barometric pressure; it simply conveys the pressure to the water below. It has the same effect on ice-covered water as it has on open water.

An analogy would be to place a piece of plywood, two-feet square, in the middle of a patch of mud. The board would be pressing against the mud with the pressure of its own weight, resulting in the board making a slight impression in the mud. If you then walk on the plywood, thereby putting more pressure on it, the impression left in the mud would be deeper and more distinct than before. Clearly, the mud under the plywood experiences the change in pressure placed atop the plywood. Barometric pressure is felt the same way in the water under the hard ice of a frozen lake.

The effect is possible because large sheets of ice have some flexibility. This is manifested during spring when gusting winds and its changing pressure often cause ice on lakes to undulate up and down until it breaks up.

If a lake has an open inlet or outlet, barometric pressure is also readily transferred to the water under the ice via the pressure that it applies on those open waters. The same thing happens when you cut a hole in it. **(Sidebar #19: Hot Water Floats,** and **Sidebar #20: Pressure Transfer)**

In my neck of the woods, it seems that ice fishermen have considerably more success catching panfish in late morning through late afternoon. It also seems they have better success where the ice is bare and not covered with snow. This circumstance causes me to speculate that more solar energy penetrates through bare ice and is absorbed by food organisms, probably crustaceans that become activated by the sun's light. When the strong light causes them to become active, they attract the attention of predators and a good bite ensues in the bare ice area. It's also possible that some bare ice areas or snow covered areas may be located over better fishing habitat than others. Fish may also be sensitive to the movement of people or vehicles and their shadows cast through the ice in bare ice areas, which might compromise the bite. It's something to watch for.

Stomach Contents

Speaking of stomach contents, I almost always check the stomach contents of every fish I clean. Sometimes the decomposing food items or their parts are easily identified and sometimes not. Identification of any item is always valuable because it may be the reason for a bite during the same calendar period in following years. The benefits of identifying such stomach contents have been extolled for many years. Not so well known is what can be learned by inspecting the contents of a fish's intestine, which lies further down the system between the stomach and the vent.

Stomachs are most frequently empty, but the intestine commonly contains undigested remnants of insect legs, crustacean parts, and baitfish spinal columns that were incompletely dissolved by stomach acids. Each, if correctly identified, can be used to determine calendar period bites in future years. You'll know what the fish will be feeding on next year at roughly the same time, and have a better idea about what to offer them for best success.

Triggered Bites
Thus far, most of this book has dealt with identifying times when good, natural bites are likely to occur. Putting yourself in position when

---

#20

Pressure Transfer

Blaise Pascal, 1623 – 1662 A.D, elucidated his principle of transmission of pressure in what is now known as Pascal's Principle. It applies to all fluids, which includes gases and liquids that are completely enclosed and at rest. It states that the "pressure applied to an enclosed fluid is transferred equally in all directions without loss, and acts with equal force on equal surfaces."

A lake completely covered by a single pressure system, whether ice-covered or not, and has an open inlet or open outlet or not, can be considered to be completely enclosed by the system and primarily subject to Pascal's Principle. Flow pressure of an open inlet and relief of that pressure that's provided by an open outlet are commonly in equilibrium or close to it. This makes them insignificant factors in the net pressure change experienced by a lake when it is newly covered by a single barometric pressure system.

---

natural bites occur will help you catch far more fish. Natural bites, however, can have a down side; they may not last very long, they can occur at inconvenient times, and it's not always easy to identify what fish are eating during those bites.

For these reasons fishermen have developed methods and devices that artificially trigger fish to bite or strike, often referred to as a reaction bite or reaction strike, despite whether they are feeding naturally or not. An artificially triggered bite is a completely different phenomenon than a natural bite which is actually natural feeding.

Fish feeding naturally are past the threshold of being triggered to bite; they're already biting vigorously because nature has conveniently provided the trigger for you. You just need to convince them that your offering is the same or a similar menu item that they are already eating, and they will eat it too. Experienced fishermen know it's easier to catch a fish by offering it something that resembles what it's already eating, versus trying to trigger a bite when you have scant idea what the fish may want and the many steps of trial and error that accompany that approach.

Still, natural feeding events don't always occur when an angler can be on the water, which frequently makes the trial and error approach necessary. Such an approach requires the angler to methodically and somewhat randomly figure out what will trigger at least one fish to bite. If he's lucky, his offering may trigger a few more to bite and he will have a satisfactory fishing experience. Generally, however, fishing success is spotty and far more difficult when anglers must figure out the trigger instead of fishing when nature provides it.

Artificially triggered bites can occur for different reasons. They can be predatory reactions to eat what appears to be injured or vulnerable prey, even though the vulnerable prey doesn't necessarily need to resemble anything in the real world. Many times it only needs to be suggestive of something real and edible, and suggestively vulnerable or provocative. They can also have a completely different basis when fish are in their reproductive state. The bites can be expressions of aggression toward intruders perceived as threats to eggs, hatchlings, or nests.

I'm not going to wander very far into the subject of triggered bites. This work is primarily about natural bites, not artificially triggered ones. Small libraries have been written about how to artificially trigger bites from most species of fish of interest to fishermen. Contemporary fishing magazines and catalogs are chock-full of old and new techniques and tackle used to catch them. Many well-known fishermen also offer classes that can make all of us better at triggering artificial bites; but none of the books, magazines, and courses can put you on the water at the right time for more-productive natural bites as can your new understanding of sequences, degree-days, and total-pressure.

The enormous task of explaining the causes of *triggered* bites can be sensed in **Sidebar #21: Artificial Lure Features**. It's a moderately comprehensive list of features incorporated in just artificial lures that are used to trigger bites.

The extensive variety of lure features has evolved because fishermen are constantly exploring new ways to trigger fish to bite. The variety of offerings continues to grow because fishermen have learned that fish often become less reactive to lures that they see on a regular basis. At times, fish will only respond to something new that they haven't seen before. Some lures are consistent producers to a certain degree, but an unfamiliar lure will often produce a better result. This is frequently seen during tournaments and spawning activity. Fishermen break out their tried-and-true lures and flies that have been productive in the past. Unfortunately, many of the artificials resemble each other so closely that some fish become indifferent because they have been overexposed to their use. It seems they eventually recognize them as counterfeit. This phenomenon is even more pronounced when fish have been repeatedly caught and released.

There are fish, however, which are exceptions and never seem to learn. In year 2005, a friend of mine caught and released the same brown trout twice within a half hour on a Hendrikson fly pattern while fishing the Holy Waters of the AuSable River in Michigan's Lower Peninsula. It was about 15-16 inches long. Exactly a year later, he caught the same trout four times within an hour and a half on the same Hendrikson pattern in the same location. It had grown to 17-18 inches long. He knew it was the same fish because the right side of its mandible was severely deformed and its mouth could not close; it was very open on the right side. The deformity caused the fish to rise in an unusual and unmistakable manner: It would rise and flop to the right to feed. Sadly, another angler eventually caught it and kept it because of its odd appearance.

In addition to lure features, a few methods employed to present them to fish include spincasting, baitcasting, fly rodding, downrigging, Carolina rigging, Texas rigging, drop shot rigging, varied retrieves, various trolling methods (including long lining), jigging, and dead drifting.

21

Artificial Lure Features

Baitfish (injured)
Baitfish-like
Baitholder
Ball style
Battery operated
Beaded
Bladed
Bleeding
Brass
Bright
Bullet-like
Bullet shape
Buoyancy- neutral
Buzzbait
Cavitied
Chenilled
Chrome
Churning
Clawed
Collared
Compact
Concave front
Count-down
Cranked
Crawfish-like
Curly-tailed
Dancing
Darting
Deep diving
Double-lobed-lipped
Dragged
Dull

Exagerrated-motion
Extra large
Fat
Feathered
Fingerling-like
Flashing
Flashy
Flat
Flickering
Flipper tail
Flippered
Floaters
Floating
Floating diver
Flourescent
Fluttering
Football shape
Forked
Frog-like
Gapped
Glow color
Glowing
Grub-like
Gurgling
Hackled
Haired
Half-waved
Hammered- finish
Hard
Hollow
Holographic
Hooks (double)
Hooks (single)
Hooks (triple)

Hopped
Jerk bait
Jerky
Jittery
Jointed
Kinked
Large
Leech-like
Legged
Life-like
Lipless
Lipped (large, medium, small)
Lizard-like
Long
Long, short-slender, fat,
Medium length
Medium depth
Medium soft
Metal
Minnow-like
Multi-tone
Noisy
Nose-hooked
One-piece
Paddle-tailed
Painted
Panfish-like
Plastic
Popping
propellered
Pulsating
Rattles
Realistic
Ribbed

Rippled
Rocking
Rolling
Rotating
Round
Rubber
Scaled
Scent-seeping
Scooped
Scoop-like
Screen printed
Shad-like
Shallow diving
Shiny
Sinking
Skirted
Snagless
Soft
Spinnerbait
Spoonlike
Stickbait
Surface bait
Suspending
Swimbait
Trailers
Translucent
Tubed
Twist-tailed
Vibrating
Weedless
Weighted
Wiggling
Wobbling
Worm-like
Wounded
Yarned

Chumming

A technique that occupies the gray area between triggered bites and natural bites is the practice of ***chumming***. Chumming consists of scattering an abundant amount of a food item in the water for the purpose of triggering fish to eat it. Once the fish are triggered into feeding, they no longer require additional triggering and will feed the same as they would during a natural bite. It's a common saltwater technique that often uses ground up oily fish.

Chumming is also applied in freshwater in various forms. A heavily perforated container is commonly filled with a food item that will leach into the surrounding water and attract target fish like catfish.

The technique is also called ***hotshotting*** when fish eggs are used as chum and thrown by the handful into river currents to trigger bites by brown trout, steelhead, and salmon. It creates the type of active bite that occurs behind or downstream of egg-laying hens during active spawning, with which most fishermen are familiar. It's a technique that works despite changes in total-pressure.

Chumming is practiced in many forms and stirs poignant ethical debate in some angling circles.

Same Depth Fishing

A simple rule touted by expert bass fishermen states that you should continue fishing at the same depth at which you've just caught a fish. In other words, if you've caught a fish at 10 feet below the surface, continue fishing at 10 feet for your best chance of catching another. This is probably good advice immediately following a catch, but advice that should be heeded for only a short time, perhaps no more than an hour or two in some cases, longer in others. The rule needs a closer look.

The rule implies that something exists or is occurring at that depth that will cause the bite to continue. The cause is probably an insect or crustacean molt that may also be attracting baitfish and may only last for a limited time. When the molt or hatch is finished, the bite will probably evaporate. Bites of this nature often occur on one day but not the next. This typically happens because molts or hatches causing the bites are subject to the high pressure and low pressure rules. The bites will only occur again the next day in the same place at the same time if environmental conditions for the molts are still favorably aligned with the pressure rules.

A similar bite may occur in other areas of a lake where the bottom substrate and water depth is the same as where the original bite occurred. If conditions remain the same or become more favorable, additional molting and related bites should occur as long as some of the organisms still need to molt to the next instar or adult stage that their brethren have already achieved in the days prior.

Spawning Occurs on North Side First

When frozen lakes thaw in the spring in the Northern Hemisphere, the angle of light and heat from the sun strikes the shoreline and lake bottom at a more direct angle on the north side of the lake than on the south side. This causes the ice to melt and the water to warm up sooner on the north side of many lakes first. As the water continues to warm sooner on the north side, fish will begin spawning sooner on that side if suitable habitat is available. Generally, expect the spawning bite to occur there sooner than on the south side.

The effect is exactly the opposite in the Southern Hemisphere. Spawning will usually occur on the south side of the lakes because the angle of light and heat from the sun strikes the shoreline and lake bottom at a more direct angle on the south side than on the north side if suitable habitat is available. Generally, expect the spawning bite to occur there sooner than on the north side.

Fishing Transition Lines

Habitat edges like weed lines, brush lines, drop-off lines, the transition lines where silt beds meet sand, and others, are known to be high percentage fishing locations. Any boundary line where different habitats, or flow conditions, meet is a prime location. Different habitat on each side of the line is the key because it's likely that one set of organisms dwell on one side of the line and different organisms dwell on the other side. If a fish swims along the transition line separating the two habitats, its opportunities for finding food are appreciably enhanced. Edible organisms may be active on one side of the line when others are not active and available on the other side. At times they may be active on both sides. For fish, the transition lines are high percentage food lines. For anglers, these are especially good places to fish when conditions are favorable for pie hatches and pie molts, and after several days of stable weather. At such times the odds go way up for a good bite on either side of the line; and two habitats can be fished in a single pass.

Think like the Predator

Many predator fish can tolerate a broad temperature range, even though they may be found in a much narrower temperature range that's typical for their species. Fishermen often catch them when plying waters in the typical temperature range, but many times they do not. The reason for failure is often because fish are not located in their typical temperature range; they have left it to locate prey.

A helpful fishing strategy in this circumstance would be to learn the typical temperature range, habits, and habitat of the prey species commonly targeted by the predators. Your chances of finding the bite will be greatly improved if you have a better understanding and focused technique for finding the prey. Think like the predator.

Bites on a Freshened Wind or Hard Rain

It's commonly heard among bass and walleye fishermen that fishing is difficult on the calmest days, but the bite improves when the wind returns. They say, "We need wind." An energetic ripple on the water seems to make a significant difference.

When water is calm it's easier to see things through the surface because optical distortion (diffraction) is so minimal. Images of prey or predators can be seen more clearly from under or above the surface. Conversely, when ripples or waves traverse the surface, optical distortion (diffusion) is so great that images from the other side of the surface are shattered into so many pieces (facets) that the images can no longer be identified on the viewers' side. Predators are less able to identify fish under the surface, and fish are less able to identify predators overhead. Anglers have long known that fish seem quite comfortable under the broken surface water of riffles in streams, as if they are protected from above. Fish act as if they are safer, and are not as easily spooked under broken surfaces, even in shallow areas. Ripples caused by a freshening wind seem to have a similar effect.

It could be conjectured that fish become conditioned to the wind as a signal that food will soon be available, and they enter an elevated state of anticipation of food because of it. It may trigger them to become more active because threats from above are greatly diminished under the broken surface, allowing them to move about and forage with less jeopardy. Ripples and waves would also create a steady drone of noise vibrations that partly mask or attenuate the vibrations given off by the movement of predator fish through the water, making ambush easier for them. It may give them a stealth advantage.

Perhaps a significant proportion of other aquatic organisms are also less active when wind and surface water are calm. Calm conditions would make their movements much easier to detect. If they were easier to detect they would be easier to prey upon, and possibly become naturally selected out of the gene pool — extinct. If, however, they become less active during calm conditions, their odds of survival would improve. Once again, if they become active during the drone of ripples and wave action, the noise would partly mask their movements and vibrations and aid their survival.

It therefore follows that fish may correlate the drone with the appearance of food, which may raise the fish's inclination to feed; making them more responsive to anglers' offerings after the wind freshens.

Hard rain also creates a significant barrier of optical distortion and stealth conditions that may trigger a good bite. For example, a friend and his son were recently fishing for Atlantic salmon on the Bonaventure River in Quebec, Canada. The area is replete with avian predators — eagles, ospreys, kingfishers, cormorants, and mergansers — that regularly patrol the river; a factor seemingly not lost on the fish population. Wind was calm and the river's surface was like glass. Salmon were plentiful but refused all offerings until a light rain began to fall and soon became a torrential downpour. Surprisingly, a vigorous bite turned on during the peak of the downpour, and both fishermen were soon battling fish. Fish rose from the bottom of the Bonaventure to attack the same offerings they had adamantly refused under calm, clear conditions earlier.

The heavy rain would have created similar bite conditions as those arising from a freshening wind. Optical surface distortion would have been maximized during the downpour and completely obliterated any view through it, masking the fish's presence from predators above. Also, the loud thrum of raindrops, akin to a sustained blast of noise vibrations, would have given predatory fish a clear stealth advantage while rain was pounding the surface.

Rain appears to be a factor in this bite, but maybe it's not. Rain can occur coincidentally with a strong, underwater molting event unseen by fishermen. A strong molt could cause similar feeding activity, especially if the rain occurs during an insect's or crustacean's preferred time of day. If a good bite continues after the rain stops, and no insect hatches are apparent, an unseen underwater molt must be considered as a cause of the bite, despite the rain. Rain is a regular occurrence during low pressure conditions that are conducive to molting. Thus, knowledge of the local three-to-four day barometric pressure, and total-pressure history would be helpful in isolating the cause of good bites during rain events. This is just another reminder that the pressure rules are always in play.

Single Food Choice Limits Bite Response

During the coldest months, insect molting slows precipitously, but some species of aquatic crustaceans are more readily available. I've seen days when total-pressure had been dropping for many hours, but fishing success remained low.

There are days when fish may have only one choice of food to eat and the bite will be limited to only the one item, no matter what else is offered to the fish. I've seen what appeared to be this situation when a friend was jig-fishing for steelhead during a February day a few years ago.

Barometric pressure (total-pressure) had been falling for many hours, so the probability of molting was good, but he couldn't catch a fish. After several hours of bone-chilling fishing, and many jig pattern changes, he finally caught a nice fish and we checked the stomach contents. The fish had been feeding solely on tiny freshwater shrimp, locally known as scuds. The scuds were of different sizes and stages of development. Some appeared to be soft-shelled and others hard-shelled. All were olive-drab color, so they were probably the same species, but perhaps different generations. An insect seine collected only drifting scuds on this day and the following day, but no other food items. A high population of active scuds was also found under rocks in the stream.

The experience indicates that the fish was forced to feed on the only food choice available. Oddly, the single food choice seems to have put the fish in a selective feeding mode. It fed only on the scuds, even though it was offered many other choices of jig patterns. The successful jig pattern has proved effective during the same cold period in subsequent years.

Ice fishermen also report that swarms of freshwater shrimp have appeared in their holes near the end of winter, often near late morning to mid-afternoon. During this time of year when the bite is good, it's typically during this period of the day after the sun has radiated some energy to the organisms under the ice.

The appearances of the crustaceans during these colder months may indicate that their threshold temperatures for degree-day absorption are much lower for their development than that for most other indigenous organisms. If so, then they can be expected to be primary food species responsible for many good bites during the entire cold period.

Dog Days of August

Why is the bite so difficult to find in lakes during the "Dog Days" of August?

There are several reasons: 1. Water temperatures at the surface and upper part of the water column are very warm and the upper water levels contain low concentrations of dissolved oxygen, which compromises the level of activity that a fish can maintain in the upper column. Fish become easily stressed under such conditions so they spend less time there. In shallow lakes, if the water gets too warm from top to bottom, limiting dissolved oxygen, fish become so stressed that they become less active simply to survive. 2. Deeper lakes become temperature stratified, so fish spend more time in deeper water in their preferred temperature range, which is cooler and contains more dissolved oxygen. Fish are then more difficult to locate. Also, larger areas of such lakes will hold fewer fish because of the stratification, so there is a substantially reduced area of productive water. 3. Food is readily abundant, making long foraging trips less necessary, and probably needed less frequently, which means fish are probably less hungry so they travel less to feed. 4. Weed and algae growth is at its maximum, creating large areas of protective cover that are difficult to fish.

The best fishing may occur in the first hour or so after first daylight in the morning, especially if a breeze has blown through the night. The breeze will oxygenate the surface water, and cool it, causing it to sink through the water column and oxygenate the water below. As daylight occurs, photosynthesis further oxygenates the cooler water. Cooler water with more oxygen is favorable for activating fish and a good bite.

Dawn and Dusk Bites

With respect to many of the larger predator fish, it's common for natural bites to occur when dawn is breaking and dusk is deepening. These are times when they commonly emerge to prowl for food. Depending on their hunger, some may be predisposed to bite, whether or not food is readily available. It's not unusual for the morning bite to be concluded by the time the sun climbs to the horizon, but the evening bite may last several hours into the night. This behavior seems consistent in all waters, from streams to the largest lakes.

Conversely, some prey fish become less active at these times and assume behavior that makes them less vulnerable to predators through the night. The bite of these species may slow or stop, although as dawn breaks they resume their characteristic activity cycle again, including feeding more actively. Light is a major influencing factor for some of these species. For example, they can be induced to bite at night if an artificial light is positioned over water in a manner that attracts small aquatic organisms and nocturnal insects to the light. When the organisms congregate near the light the prey fish, e.g., crappie and smelt, pounce on them in a vigorous bite. Naturally, when prey fish actively feed in such a nocturnal congregation, larger predator fish soon take notice. The result can be a multiple species bite.

Surface Bite Diminishes at Night

During warm summer months, bites occurring at night near the surface can be compromised due to the shutdown of photosynthesis as darkness falls, which slowly causes a deficit of dissolved oxygen in the warm upper water levels. As the darkness of night wears on, dissolved oxygen diminishes further in the upper levels and they become still less hospitable for roaming fish. Deep into the night, the oxygen deficit can cause the surface bite to approach zero, causing fish to abandon the upper levels. As daylight breaks, however, photosynthesis again infuses oxygen into the upper levels, making them hospitable once more for roaming fish and a morning bite.

A Television Bite

Don't always believe what you see and hear. I've included this little story just to reinforce your power of observation.

I was watching a popular fishing show on TV wherein the professional fishing host and guest were steadily catching smallmouth bass on a large lake in New York State. One was using a crankbait and the other was using a tube jig. A scented gel had been applied to both. The fishermen were extolling the merits of the gel and assuring viewers that it made their lures smell good to fish and caused them to bite. They were giving the gel a lot of credit for their success and recommending that viewers buy some The entire presentation appeared valid and legitimate, and I was duly im-

164

pressed — until the camera zoomed out and panned the surroundings.

The camera briefly showed a storm line with tall, billowing cumulus clouds approaching in the distance. I instantly knew the area was undergoing a pressure change that had been occurring for hours, and a strong molting event was probably occurring while the host and guest were fishing and filming their presentation. They were fishing in a protected bay area that probably had a silt bottom harboring an abundance of food organisms that had become very active. The wind was also blowing from the lake into the protected bay, delivering a load of suspended plankton to their location. It was a classic hot bite situation, despite the scent on the lures.

I truly believe the host and guest were convinced the scent deserved high credit for their success, and they were not trying to deceive anyone. However, they just didn't understand the circumstances and conditions in which they were fishing. It's likely that fishing in the same spot the next day would have been radically less successful, scent or no scent. The storm would have moved through and probably replaced the low pressure conditions with a cold air mass and high pressure.

The Challenges

Knowing why a bite has occurred can frequently be determined by checking the contents of a fish's stomach and intestines. Conversely, there is no comparable method for checking why a bite has not occurred. How can a wild fish's state of appetite response be determined if it has not been caught and examined? How can it be predicted? Those are the challenges.

More bites will be addressed at **www.PredictingTheBite.com.**

Chapter 9

Fishing Winds
and Old Proverbs

Over the ages, fishermen have developed a few proverbs or old sayings that are generally regarded as reflecting patterns of fish behavior in relation to certain environmental conditions. All are related to wind, storms, high water, or quality of fishing, and all seem to be about the bite. Seven of them are discused here. The narrative is generally limited to the Northern Hemisphere, although the discussion is applicable in both hemispheres. Illustrations for the Southern Hemisphere are located at the end of the chapter in Figure 9-3.

The understanding developed in earlier chapters about total pressure, hatches, and molts, facilitates a better examination of these old sayings. Some of them are true at times, but false at others. A couple are almost always true, but none offer very clear insight. Some have been repeated often enough that they have acquired status as truth, although most contain only partial truth.

Truthful or not, they have certainly flavored traditional fishing lore. They are pronouncements repeated by generations of hard-bitten fishermen who found that the proverbs occasionally and exactly described their experiences on the water. Their history is difficult to ignore, and they probably ring true for a fisherman somewhere every day.

Proverbs

A. "Wind from the east, fishing is least. "

B. "Wind from the west, fishing is best."

C. "Wind from the south puts the bait in the fish's mouth."

D. "Wind from the north, fishermen do not venture forth."

E. "Fishing is best just before a storm."

F. "Fishing goes dead for three to four days after a cold front goes through."

G. "Fishing improves after three to four days of stable weather."

Despite their shortcomings, they collectively harbor valuable clues that helped solve some of the challenges discussed in previous chapters.

For example, proverb **F**, "Fishing goes dead for three to four days after a cold front goes through," is true so frequently that it helped lead me to the realization of the state of ableness and its three to four day effect on fishing in temperate latitudes. The proverb is an old messenger bearing a clue that it finally surrendered. The state of ableness is also supported by proverb **G**, which states, "Fishing improves after three to four days of stable weather." The lesson of this proverb was conveyed in the charts of Chapter 6 when hatches and molts began to recur again after 3-4 days of high barometric pressure, which is the usual trademark of stable weather. In similar manner, every proverb, has its own unique and somewhat cryptic message.

In the material that follows, the explanation for proverb **A** is far more detailed than explanations for the other proverbs. A deeper understanding of the factors affecting proverb **A** allows quicker and deeper insight into several other proverbs without the need for as much explanation.

East Wind

Proverb **A**, *"Wind from the east, fishing is least,"* is one of the most common, but least informative and least valuable of all the proverbs. To understand it better, only rudimentary knowledge about wind *direction* is needed. You don't need to become a meteorologist to understand a few facts about wind direction. They're simple to learn, enjoyable to know, and they eliminate many of the mysteries from fishing.

Figure 9-1 depicts the classic comma-shape of low barometric pressure systems that are common in the Northern Hemisphere. Notice the arrows around the perimeter that indicate the *counterclockwise* wind directions that occur within the system. The winds always rotate counterclockwise in these systems. The systems are often seen in local weather forecast radar images and infrared satellite images. Wind, rain, and lower barometric pressure are its common characteristics.

Low Barometric Pressure System in the Northern Hemisphere

Counterclockwise Rotation of Ascending Warm air

Figure 9-1

As the arrows indicate, wind directions associated with this low barometric pressure system can come from any direction of the compass. The wind direction you experience depends upon your location in relation to the system. For example, if you are located at **A**, the wind is from the

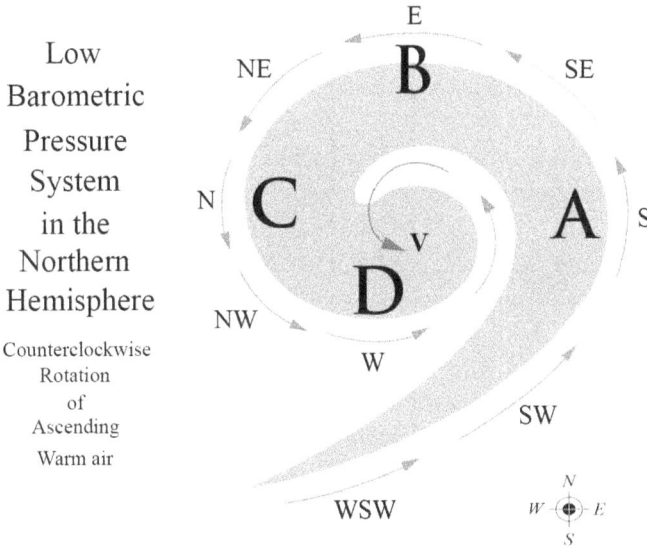

south; if you are at **B**, the wind is from the east; if at **C** it's north, and west if at **D**. If you are at the center of the spiral near **v**, the winds will tend to be from nearly all directions and are simply referred to as *variable*. I've seen comma-shape systems that were as small as three to four hundred miles long from north to south, to a few large enough to cover most of Canada and the United States combined.

The bottom portion of Figure 9-2 again shows the same low pressure system that's in Figure 9-1. The upper portion of Figure 9-2, however, depicts an idealized high barometric pressure system with the same comma shape, but it's upside down. The upside down comma is a normal shape and orientation for high pressure systems in the Northern Hemisphere. Notice the arrows around the perimeter that indicate the *clockwise* wind directions that occur within the system. The arrows also indicate that wind directions associated with the high pressure system can come from any direction of the compass, just like they do within a low pressure system. Both systems can contain winds from all directions. Once again, the wind direction you experience from a high pressure system is dependent upon your location in relation to the system. For example, if you are located at **A**, the wind is from the south; if you are at **B**, the wind is from the east; if at **C** it's north, and west if at **D**; and again, variable winds are located near the **v** in the center of the spiral.

Generally, upside down commas of high barometric pressure systems are seldom seen on weather forecasts because they contain so few clouds. High pressure air contains little moisture, so skies remain relatively clear and little or nothing shows on radar. A few high level clouds may be visible on infrared satellite images, but they, too, seldom reveal much but open space in a high barometric pressure system.

An exception is when clouds form and accumulate at the leading edges of cold fronts — the cold fronts being the edges of high pressure systems or areas. The clouds form as the edges of cold air masses encroach into higher humidity in lower pressure areas.

High pressure systems are also constantly breaking down because air from high pressure systems moves to low pressure regions. The moving air is the wind, which is nature's symptom indicating that the different pressures of the two systems are trying to become equal. The same phenomenon occurs when you remove the valve stem from a fully inflated car tire. There is high pressure air in the tire, but when the valve stem is removed, the high pressure air flows outward through the open stem until

High
Barometric
Pressure
System
in the
Northern
Hemisphere

Clockwise
Rotation
of
Descending
Cold Air

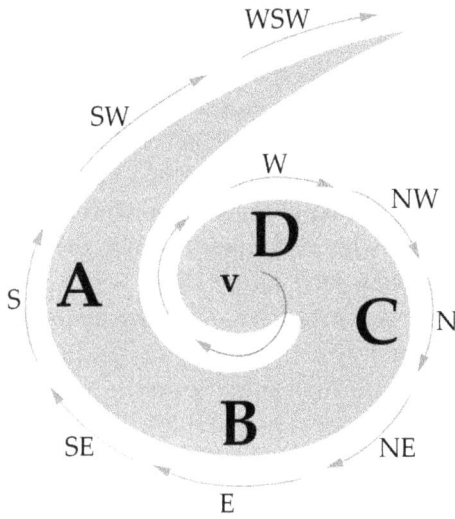

WSW

SW

W

NW

D

A

S

v

C

N

B

SE

NE

E

N
W ⊕ E
S

X

Low
Barometric
Pressure
System
in the
Northern
Hemisphere

Counterclockwise
Rotation
of
Ascending
Warm air

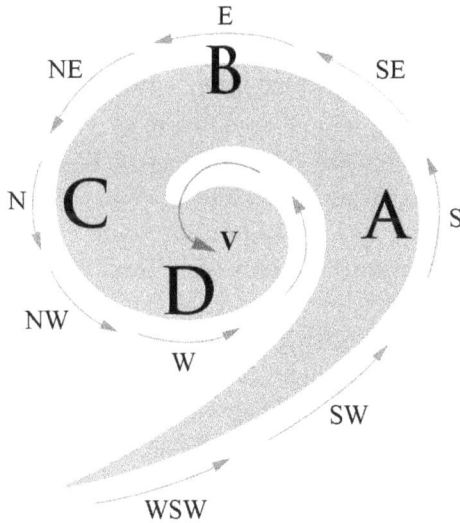

E

NE

B

SE

N

C

A

S

v

D

NW

W

SW

WSW

Figure 9-2

all the pressurized air is gone from inside the tire. The air pressure inside the tire is then equal to the air pressure outside. When the high pressure air flows out of the tire, it creates a noticeable wind, but when the pressure inside the tire and the pressure outside become equal, the wind stops. Low pressure air from the outside never flows into the high pressure air inside the tire. High pressure always flows toward regions of low pressure.

High barometric pressure systems and low barometric pressure systems interact with each other in much the same way. It's this interaction between systems that causes changes in the shape of the systems. A high pressure system may have a comma shape, but when it starts leaking air into a nearby low pressure system, its shape can change and become unrecognizable as a high pressure system. High pressure areas are more often the shape of the areas between low pressure areas, and they're constantly changing shape. Both high and low pressure systems can become segmented and disorganized by their interactions, causing only a segment to arrive in a region and move through as a front. Variations are endless.

At times it may seem easier to predict air movement and wind direction, but it's still a difficult task. It seems that you will always need more data and information than you have. I learned long ago to rely on local weather forecasts and wind maps available on the internet. They get it right far more often than I do.

Focusing closer on proverb **A**, if you were standing on the bold **X** positioned between both systems in Figure 9-2, you would experience an east wind from both systems. You would be on the north end of the low pressure system, and on the south end of the high pressure system, and in the path of an east wind from each. Now imagine yourself on a lake somewhere and wind is blowing from the east. Would you know if it's coming from a high pressure system or low pressure system without the aid of a barometer? In most instances you would not. I have tried to make this guess and similar ones for years, but know of no reliable way to be accurate except by using a barometer. For a little fun, however, there may be a method you could explore: I have seen peeled balsam branches from Maine, that will droop during periods of low barometric pressure and higher humidity, but then they assume a more upward and erect posture during high barometric pressure and lower humidity. I had one for several years, which was simply called a "weather stick," and it always correctly indicated the current weather.

Knowing that an east wind can be produced by either low barometric pressure or high barometric pressure provides a clue to the actual meaning of proverb **A**. Low pressure systems cause pie hatching and pie molting and good bites, so an east wind would seem like a good thing, especially for river fishermen. The bite would be occurring in both rivers and lakes, but access to the bite can be difficult on lakes. On lakes the winds can be too high and cause large dangerous waves that keep anglers off the water. Hurricane forecasters know that the east winds of a hurricane are the most powerful, and all hurricanes are low pressure systems. So east winds from low barometric pressure systems would create larger waves than most other winds from the same system. Lightning associated with low pressure systems may also keep anglers off lakes and rivers, even though a great bite may be in progress.

It's well known among seasoned freshwater fishermen that, on average, overcast days and rainy days produce decidedly better fishing. An east wind is often an integral part of the weather conditions on those gray days, and can be a harbinger of great fishing opportunities. Despite the possibility of great fishing, the turbulent water can be difficult and perhaps impossible to access on those days. Naturally, fishing would then be least.

High barometric pressure also produces east winds, but the fishing circumstances are considerably different simply because of the higher pressure. The *high pressure rule* (Chapter 5) comes into play, which means a good bite may not occur for up to several days because of the state of ableness issues explained in the charts of Chapter 6. The reduced bite could endure for a day or two or more and be directly attributed to the high barometric pressure. If high barometric pressure remains stable for several days, however, then the bite should resume at an elevated, normal pace. This would be the case no matter which direction the wind is blowing, although the wind direction can cause the location of the bite to shift with it.

A shift in the bite location can occur when the wind blows plankton away from one shore and toward another, which is then followed by baitfish and other organisms, which are followed by predator fish. Many fishermen, however, usually avoid shorelines experiencing breaking waves, instead preferring sheltered, calmer waters, which often causes them to miss some better bites. Ironically, they most often seek the calmer waters of the windward shore, which has had a substantial portion of the plankton blown away from it. They opt for comfort and safety over the chances of finding a better bite, although many are unaware of their mistake. They go where the probability for fishing success is reduced, and perhaps is least.

East winds also create the illusion of lousy fishing. Prevailing winds over land are generally from a westerly direction in both the Northern and Southern Hemispheres. Prevailing winds create environments in lakes that are enhanced every time the prevailing wind blows. Plankton, detritus, and all else that can be moved by the prevailing wind and waves, settles in certain areas on a regular basis. It settles there and is churned up and resettles repeatedly. The locations where this occurs become regular haunts for fish because of the richness and abundance of food that is so readily available. Fishermen also visit them repeatedly because they know these locations harbor fish on a regular basis. Fishermen also have a general habit of fishing mostly during fair weather, which most often means during prevailing westerly winds. This causes them to usually have about the same kind of success in the same places, because they usually fish the same places during similar conditions, and at the same time of year. To their dismay, when the wind switches to the opposite direction and becomes easterly, suspended and drifting plankton is blown away from these locations and is soon followed by baitfish and predators. Voilà! The old reliable fishing hole has been rendered disappointingly unproductive by the easterly wind. Fishing should still be good, however, but probably somewhere to the west. They just need to recognize the illusion. This is addressed at length in Chapter 12.

If a high barometric pressure system replaces a low barometric pressure system, then it's likely that pie hatches and pie molts occurred just prior to the high barometric pressure moving in. If a fisherman was kept off the water by a strong east wind from the low pressure system, but he returns when winds are calm because high barometric pressure moved in, and fishing is poor in the first few days during high pressure, then it would naturally look like poor fishing could be attributable to the powerful east wind that kept him off the water earlier. In actuality, the wind and its direction have little to do with poor fishing success at this point. The earlier low barometric pressure that caused the pie hatches and pie molts is the true culprit, along with the high barometric pressure that replaced it and curbed hatches and molts for a short while thereafter.

So, *"Wind from the east, fishing is least"* is a misleading proverb. It can cause fishermen to think that fishing is lousy, or, more correctly, that the bite is lousy when an east wind blows. Obviously, that is not true.

Fishing is least because bad weather accompanying strong east winds can keep fishermen off the water until the weather settles down. Some of the best times for fishing success in freshwater occur when the wind blows from the east or any other direction if it is part of a low barometric pressure system; and, after a short recovery period, fishing success can be just as productive in an east wind that is part of a high barometric pressure system. Because of the advanced fishing knowledge we possess today, proverb **A** should be interpreted as mostly a cryptic insinuation against fishing in unsafe conditions, not a reflection on the bite. "Fishing" and the "bite" are two completely different subjects, and the proverb contains no mention of a bite. The term "fishing" in the proverb may imply "bite," but the meaning is unclear. The old saw probably deserves to be treated more as a trite platitude than a time-proven proverb.

West Wind

Proverb **B**, *"Wind from the west, fishing is best,"* has some fishing value in it because it's probably true more often than not. Part of the explanation for proverb **A** also applies here and is repeated in abridged form.

Long-term prevailing winds over land generally have a westerly component: they are northwesterly, westerly, or southwesterly. In one way or another they prevail from the west. They are also characteristically associated with high barometric pressure, which is normally more prevalent than low pressure.

The winds create enriched environments in lakes that are reinforced every time the prevailing wind blows. Plankton, and all else that can be moved by the prevailing westerly wind and waves, regularly settles in certain areas. It settles there and is churned up and resettles repeatedly. These locations become regular haunts for fish because food is so readily available.

Fishermen also visit them repeatedly because they know these locations harbor fish on a regular basis. Fishermen also have a habit of fishing mostly during fair weather, which means during prevailing westerly winds. This causes them to usually have about the same kind of success in the same places because they usually fish them during similar conditions, and at the same time of year. This pattern of fishing would give rise to a statement like proverb **B**, that fishing is best when wind is from the west. When the wind direction changes, however, success in these locations usually changes for the worse. It's because, in these locations, bottom plankton (benthic plankton) is not being stirred up by wave action, and suspended plankton is blown to a new location and therefore followed by the baitfish and predators. Food availability and fishing success is completely changed by a different wind.

The following example gives you a feel for how to predict a different wind.

Low barometric pressure systems will cause drastic changes in wind direction. As a low barometric pressure system approaches, the high pressure prevailing winds can change direction because they are being drawn to the area of low barometric pressure that is approaching. How much the winds change will depend on where the low barometric pressure system moves through the local area. For example, if the system remains east of your lake, the prevailing winds over your lake will still be blowing to the east as usual because they are drawn to the low pressure in that direction. Conversely, if the low pressure system remains to the west of your lake, the prevailing winds over your lake could reverse and blow to the west because they are being drawn to the low pressure in that direction. If the entire low pressure system moves in a path directly over your lake, then it will experience most of the changing and variable wind directions contained in the low barometric pressure system. The plankton and all that moves with it can be blown in several different directions in a matter of a day or two, but there is a silver lining.

The silver lining is that your lake is now under the influence of the low barometric pressure system. The low pressure is causing hatches and molts to occur, which are triggering good bites. Even better, the old familiar haunts that provide good fishing during prevailing westerlies are probably where much of the hatching and molting is occurring. Those haunts are the environmental niches providing life support for a great variety and quantity of aquatic insects and crustaceans that comprise the lower levels of the aquatic food web. Fish will certainly know where to find them. Total pressure will be changing around the rim of the lakeshore as the winds change direction, so duration of the direction becomes a factor.

Even though a lake may continually experience prevailing westerlies and its effects on the leeward eastern side, the windward side should not be ignored. This is true no matter which direction the wind is coming from. The windward side may still harbor a good bite if it's protected from the wind by vegetation and high terrain along the shore that negate the wind's effects.

South Wind

Proverb **C**, *"Wind from the south puts the bait in the fish's mouth"* is a weak metaphor that has no clear meaning, but it provides an excuse to examine the effects of south winds, which can be beneficial for most fishermen.

It's probably safe to presume, in the Northern Hemisphere, that "Wind from the south" implies that the wind is warm. Warm winds begin to blow after the cold winds of winter; they make the water in lakes and streams warm. When the water begins warming, it triggers the entire sequence of spawning of various fish species throughout the spring and early summer; and every spawning species is vulnerable to an angling technique of one kind or another. It's far easier to put bait in their mouth when you know where they have congregated for spawning activities.

When cold weather settles in during late fall, winter, and early spring, relatively few fishermen are on most lakes and streams. Many find it too cold and uncomfortable for fishing and would rather wait for warmer weather to better enjoy their time on the water. Cold temperatures also slow fish's metabolism which often makes fishing more difficult and less productive than fishing in warm weather. Cold water, dissolved oxygen, and sparse food also cause fish to move to places unfamiliar to fishermen who only fish during warm weather. They are often unable to find fish so they can trigger them to bite. Cold weather fishing, and particularly ice fishing, is far more challenging and less productive for the average fisherman than fishing during warm weather in warmer water. Certainly most fishermen would agree that it's easier to get bait into a fish's mouth during warm weather than cold.

Beneficial circumstances are also created when south winds blow across very large, deep lakes. Many of these lakes harbor both warm water fish species and cold water fish species. They include lake trout, salmon, whitefish, smallmouth bass, largemouth bass, catfish, brown trout, rainbow trout, bluegills, walleyes, yellow perch and many others. When the top layer of water warms in spring and a south wind blows the large volume of warm water to the leeward north end, fishermen there will see an influx of warm-water species entering shallower water in their end of the lake. Conversely, fishermen at the southern end of the lake will see their waters chill down as the warm water is blown to the north. As the warm water is blown northward, cooler, deeper water wells up and replaces it, and species that prefer the cooler temperatures will enter the shallower areas at the south end. The effect is illustrated further in Chapter 10.

North Wind
Proverb **D**: "*Wind from the north, fishermen do not venture forth.*"

Once again, the proverb is cryptic and bears no clear meaning. There are numerous variations of this old saying, but they all convey about the same incomplete message. Some early versions don't even include the word "fishermen." It may actually be a phrase born of superstition about the sea. It may also be a respectful tribute to the character and power of north wind, or a slander against it. Whatever its origin, the proverb whispers a connotation that something negative can occur when the north wind blows, but the message has been lost in time. Nonetheless, it's worth examining how north winds affect some fishing circumstances today.

When strong winds blow across lakes, whether from the north or any other direction, the waves hitting the leeward shore can be large and turbulent. This is particularly true if a drop-off is near the leeward shore because the drop- off causes the waves to build very fast, and very large over a short distance. If strong winds are from the north, the south shore would experience pounding waves. It's no place to launch a fishing boat. When wind and waves are high, wading fishermen can also encounter life-threatening rip currents on bigger waters. On the plus side, pounding surf carries, and churns up, large quantities of plankton which is followed by baitfish and predators, particularly fish like walleyes. In saltwater surf, many fishermen have seen this result in wave crests loaded with terrorized baitfish being savaged by bluefish during feeding frenzies. It's a spectacle no fisherman ever forgets.

"North wind" often means a cold wind, which means, if it's colder than recent winds, it's probably associated with high barometric pressure. Recall that colder, heavier air is the cause and essence of high barometric pressure. Therefore, in lieu of a barometer, a new, cold north wind would be an indicator that hatches and molts, and some good bites have ceased for a short while.

One benefit of a north wind is similar to that for a south wind as explained in the details for proverb **C**. The benefit occurs when a north wind blows across very large, deep lakes that contain warm water fish species and cold water species (See proverb **C** for a short list of species). When the top layer of water warms in spring and a north wind blows the large volume of warm water to the leeward south end, fishermen there will see an influx of species – species that prefer the warmer water -- entering shallower water in their end of the lake. Conversely, fishermen at the north end will see their waters chill down as the warm water is blown to the south. As the warm water is blown southward, cooler, deeper water wells up and replaces it, and species that prefer cooler temperatures will enter the shallower areas at the north end.

In early spring, the temperature of the warm top layer may only be two to five degrees warmer than the underlying water, but it can cause significant fish movement. If the warmer water is blown into the region of river and creek mouths, it can break down cold water barriers that keep some fish from entering the streams to spawn. This is true of winds from all directions, and the benefit is seen in streams on the leeward side of big waters.

Not all north winds are cold. As illustrated in Figure 9-2, low barometric pressure systems contain north winds on the west side and near the center of the spiral. These are warm north winds compared to north winds associated with high barometric pressure systems. The north wind on the west side of the low barometric pressure system can have a long fetch, which can cause it to persist for a significant amount of time. While it persists, it can blow plankton to the opposite side of a pond, lake, or reservoir. When the plankton gets to the opposite side, it may stay there for a prolonged period because there are no other winds from the low barometric pressure system that will blow it to a new location. The system not only moves the plankton around, but it also causes hatches and molts in places where it creates favorable total-pressure. The location and concentration of plankton can create a fishing opportunity that competes with locations producing hatches and molts. It can also just reinforce the bite if the plankton is blown into locations where the hatches and molts occur. This situation demonstrates the value of good fishing logs and weather records that can be used to develop a useful fishing strategy.

The duration of north winds near the center of the spiral of a low barometric pressure system are typically brief, but still last long enough to blow plankton in a single direction that can provide a brief but good bite. If the system stalls, the prevailing wind over your water may persist in one direction and create a predictable fishing opportunity.   Variable winds near the center of the spiral probably create the most unpredictable plankton bite because the wind can redistribute it in multiple directions.

Storms

Proverb **E**, *"Fishing is best just before a storm,"* is often true, but it depends on the character of the storm. The proverb, unfortunately, provides no clues that help define a storm. It also only refers to the time just before a storm, but offers no good meaning for "just before." Could it mean ten minutes, six hours, or a day or two? It also only implies a meaning for "fishing," which probably means catching fish, and I'll assume it does.

For most fishermen, the term "storm" means a rainstorm, thunderstorm, or snowstorm, but probably not just a windstorm without precipitation. Defining a storm is problematic because it's a lot like art; you know it when you see it, but what is it?

How much rain must fall before it's called a rain storm? Are a few drops of rain in the dust and one thunderclap a storm? Is a half hour of snow flurries a storm? Is a five minute downpour from a big cloud a storm; and will it cause fish to bite better? Is a gentle, daylong shower with no thunder or lightning a storm?

If a big thunderstorm misses your lake or stream by fifteen miles, does it affect fishing in your lake or not? If rain pours amid thunder and lightning for twenty minutes before arriving at your lake or stream, will that make your fishing better? An endless litany of these storm scenarios and their many variables can be cited without bringing you closer to understanding their effects on your fishing success or failure. Fortunately, fishermen don't need to know very much about the science of storms. A little knowledge goes a long way, and several short paragraphs should be perfectly adequate to explain most of this away.

Storms of every stripe are created by moist warm air that rises, which is then cooled in the upper atmosphere and condenses the moisture in it, and then the condensed moisture precipitates back to earth in wet or frozen form. Lifting mechanisms, air currents, moving air masses of different temperatures, dew points and many other factors are all part of the mix that create storms of every intensity level, from mild to severe. The staggering array of possibilities can be bewildering, but two simple properties are common to all of them; wind and barometric pressure.

Wind has already been addressed. Most of the remaining mysteries are peeled away with the help of barometric pressure. The question, "which storms affect your fishing" is answered by how much each storm affects total-pressure.

All rainstorms and thunderstorms contain a column of air being lifted upwards (updraft) from underneath the storm, which causes low barometric pressure under the storm. This causes air near the ground in the surrounding area to also move toward the storm, and it replaces the air that's being lifted upward. In a nutshell, the updraft in the storm sucks air toward the storm from the surrounding area. It's acting like your household vacuum cleaner. As the air from the surrounding area is sucked toward the storm, the area where the air is coming from also begins to have a drop in barometric pressure. The pressure is dropping because air is being sucked away. This effect of air moving toward the storm and creating low barometric pressure, sometimes deep low pressure in the area where it came from, can extend outward hundreds of miles from a big storm. Conversely, the distance and pressure drop can be almost negligible when storms are small and isolated.

Big storms usually mean big barometric pressure drops, although the pressure drop becomes smaller as the distance from the storm becomes greater. Small storms usually mean small barometric pressure drops or no meaningful drop at all.

Meteorologists give storms numerous names and classifications, but barometric pressure, as it affects total-pressure, is the great equalizer. No matter what kind of storm is approaching, it only needs to be considered in terms of its winds and barometric pressure, and how its barometric pressure will affect total-pressure, and how the total-pressure affects hatches and molts when you are out there fishing.

An abundance of anecdotal evidence supports the notion that fishing can be fabulous just before a storm, but also that fishing can be terrible just before a storm. The evidence is inconsistent. Obviously, a major reason for the inconsistency is the fact that not all storms are created equal. You can sort out "which is which" by watching the affects of the winds and total pressure. It's that simple. A better bite will occur just before a storm if total-pressure drops enough to cause a hatch or molt, which would most likely be, or include, pie hatches and pie molts that will normally occur at that time of day. If you are present when that occurs, and employ good fishing techniques, your efforts may be rewarded in good measure; and your success will raise the count of celebratory tales in anecdotal evidence.

I won't name all the various kinds of storms, but most fishermen encounter one form of thunderstorm on a regular basis if they do much fishing during the summer. It's the brief, but sometimes violent thunderstorm that pops up on a summer afternoon. They are known by several names, including single cell, pulse, local, and popcorn storms. They are a product of local heating of the land, and they form quite rapidly and impact a relatively small area.. Their duration is usually brief, generally affecting an area for twenty minutes or less, but they can be deadly and deserve respect. They are an example of a small storm that typically has little or no significant barometric pressure drop associated with it, and therefore no meaningful affect on total pressure. The only way this type of storm will affect your fishing is to drive you off the water until it passes.

Fishing during the days or hours that precede the arrival of big storms — when barometric pressure is plunging and causing total-pressure to plunge before stormy weather occurs — can produce fishing at its best. Pie hatches and/or pie molts can be the result, producing a very active bite. It can also produce temptation to stay too long.

A proper fishing barometer that records pressure during the days and nights when such storms are nearby would be an invaluable asset.

Cold Fronts
Proverb **F**, "*Fishing goes dead for three to four days after a cold front goes through,*" is frequently true. It also contains a generous dose of ambiguity.

The definition of fishing, once again, is left to the imagination, but I will assume that it means catching fish and the efforts required to catch more.

The definition of a cold front is also left to the imagination, so it can only be addressed by speculating about its meaning. I will assume that it means a strong cold front, which is usually associated with a three to four day disruption of good fishing near the 45th parallel.

Another ambiguity is the phrase "goes through." Does this mean that a cold front has completely passed through the area, along with the cold air mass that came with it? Is the front the only important feature, or is all or part of the cold air mass behind it important too? Which part influences the fishing?

The answer is simple and once again demystified with a barometer Cold fronts have long been associated with fishing that suddenly becomes unproductive and remains lousy, sometimes for days. It's a valid correlation when fronts are strong, but when fronts are weak they only have a

182

weak affect that can go unnoticed.

Strong cold fronts bring big increases in barometric pressure, increases on the order of 40-125 points or more. A big increase in barometric pressure usually occurs after a very low barometric pressure event. After these low pressure events occur, pressure must rise a large amount just to return to a normal level, which is basically what happens when a strong cold front arrives. When a big increase in barometric pressure follows deep low barometric pressure, hatches and molts are soon reduced to such a low level that organisms and baitfish that feed on the emergers have little to feed upon, and they become markedly less active. The predator fish also then become markedly inactive, perhaps because resting, inactive baitfish become difficult to find. The bite is extremely diminished, and will probably remain so until hatches and molts recover, which can take up to several days depending on pressure and temperature in most instances.

The big increase in pressure brings the *high pressure rule* into effect, which roughly states: High barometric pressure hinders hatches and molts and causes them to slow down and occur later during the state of ableness. It's this phenomenon that causes fishing to grind to a near halt. Recall that this scenario is explained in detail in Chapter 6 for Figure 6-3, Days 7, 8, 9, and 10.

With respect to barometric pressure, strong and weak cold fronts are basically the same phenomenon; they are varying degrees of the same thing. Being the same thing means they both cause the same effects on fishing, but one has a proportionately greater effect than the other.
The strong front causes a longer lasting effect than the weak front. It causes a significantly diminished bite that lasts longer than a weak front can cause. Higher pressure of the strong front prevents hatches and molts for a longer period of time than is prevented by the lower high barometric pressure of a weak front. The barometric pressure of a weak front will prevent hatches and molts for a shorter time, so the bite will recover a day or two sooner.

In a few words, the high barometric pressure that accompanies strong fronts causes *longer* spells of poor fishing, which usually improve after three to four days. The lower high barometric pressure accompanying weak fronts causes *short* spells of poor fishing, which usually recover after only a day or two. This is the typical pattern in temperate latitudes. Shorter delays are probably more typical in subtropical latitudes because of the greater availability of degree-day heat.

Fishermen have long associated cold fronts with diminished fishing, and rightly so, but the unseen, unfelt, high barometric pressure that moves in with a cold air mass is the fundamental cause of the decline in good fishing. The boundary line of the cold air mass (the front) and the fact that the air is cold, and that more cold air is moving with and behind the boundary line have very little immediate effect on fishing. The real cause is the elevated *weight* of the cold, denser air; it's the greater force that the weight of the colder air exerts in the form of higher barometric pressure. Of course, higher barometric pressure has a detrimental effect only if it increases total-pressure.

Gradually, however, cold air temperatures ushered in by fronts do contribute to a diminished bite. The cold air cools the top layer of water on a lake or stream, and then the cooled, heavier water sinks through the warmer water just below it. This process of cooling and sinking continues throughout the duration of the presence of the cold air mass above.

The cooler water may have a dramatically suppressing effect on the availability of plankton that occupy and drift in the upper levels. Evidence supporting this idea dwells in the fact that the natural bite is so diminished. If larger crustaceans and baitfish were feeding on the plankton in the cooler water, the bite would be active instead of painfully slow. This suggests that at least some plankton, which is likely comprised of tiny crustaceans and other tiny invertebrates, is not readily available at that time. If fish are not activated to feed on it, it may mean the plankton is significantly scarce. Perhaps the temperature drop deactivates the plankton and causes it to precipitate downward. The cooled water may also have a negative effect on algae and bacteria that some plankton feed upon, causing a large percentage of plankton to vacate the upper levels. It's also possible that, somehow, the higher barometric pressure has interfered with the life processes and normal activity of some of the microscopic organisms in the upper levels. These examples strongly suggest that crustaceans react to the natural conditions in a manner extremely similar to that of the aquatic insects. Both are arthropods, so there may be reasonable probability to expect it.

If the natural bite has gone dead because hatches, molts, and plankton are mostly unavailable, wind may still offer a fishing strategy. If wind is brisk enough to drive waves against a shoreline, there may be enough churning of the bottom detritus and micro-life to activate a natural bite in that area. The wind may also re-concentrate a diminished and well dispersed plankton population into the area where waves are lapping the lee-ward shoreline.

Stable Weather

Proverb **G**, "*Fishing improves after three to four days of stable weather,*" is handy for predicting the return of good fishing.

As defined in proverb **F**, the meaning of "Fishing" in this proverb remains the same — catching fish and the efforts required to catch more. However, "Fishing improves," and "stable weather" beg a closer look.

"Fishing improves" implies that fishing could be better, and perhaps has a ring of disappointment about recent fishing, but the remainder of the proverb indicates that weather can provide a remedy.

Stable weather implies that the weather is not changing, or at least not changing very much. When weather is not changing, it's an indication that barometric pressure is also not changing much and is relatively stable. So the proverb can be paraphrased as "Fishing improves if barometric pressure is stable for three to four days."

Barometric pressure can be stable over a broad range, either high or low. When it's low, however, weather is not usually very stable. It brings intermittent wind, rain, and generally unsettled conditions. When low barometric pressure systems are very large, they can provide steady, stable weather only when the *edge* of the system exerts its influence on your area. This is not a likely scenario that will persist for three to four days. If it does occur, it's also likely that the low barometric pressure has caused fishing to improve long before three to four days have passed because pie hatches and pie molts will already have been induced. It seems highly unlikely that the proverb is alluding to stable weather associated with low barometric pressure.

Conversely, stable weather associated with high barometric pressure occurs much more frequently, and is generally longer lasting in most geographic locations. If the stable weather is more frequent and longer lasting, then it will improve fishing more often, and the bite will remain improved for longer periods. This pattern correlates perfectly with fishing expectations that are based on the state of ableness. There is little doubt that the proverb is alluding to stable weather associated with high barometric pressure.

If unsettled conditions and a cold front have put a damper on fishing, three to four sunny days with zephyr breezes will bring back the hatches, molts, and plankton that create good bites.

An alternative explanation for fishing that improves after three to four days may simply be that fish have reached such an acute level of hunger that it drives them to hunt and prowl again. It's probably safe to assume that hunger also plays a part in the explanation above.

Figure 9-3 illustrates typical barometric pressure system wind directions in the Southern Hemisphere.Their directions are exactly opposite of the directions in the Northern Hemisphere.

Low Barometric Pressure System in the Southern Hemisphere

Clockwise Rotation of Ascending Warm Air

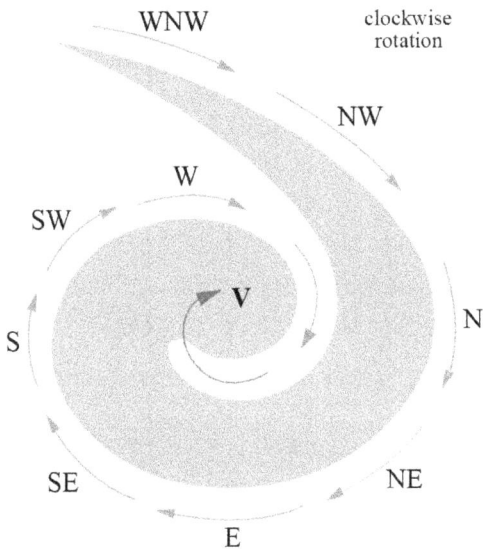

High Barometric Pressure System in the Southern Hemisphere

Counterclockwise Rotation of Descending Cold Air

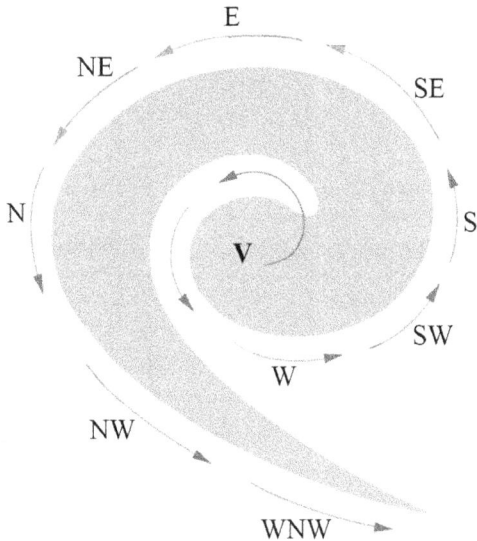

Figure 9-3

187

Chapter 10

Lakes: Big and Small

Charter captains and recreational anglers who consistently catch fish in the world's largest lakes deserve a tip of the hat. They've worked hard to learn to catch numerous species of fish throughout the entire season. They know approximately when certain species will arrive, which temperatures they prefer, how long they will be in the area, and the best tackle for catching them. Eventually, most of these seasoned fishermen know what other fishermen know, but some will have a secret bag of tricks that gives them a competitive edge. The secret bag of tricks, in most instances, is simply better knowledge. This chapter should add to that bag of tricks.

One secret not yet in any of their bags is how barometric pressure influences fish behavior in big water. Most captains believe there is a correlation, but it's still a mystery to them. Interestingly, the influence of barometric pressure is generally different in big water than it is in small water.

The ways that weather systems affect fish behavior in lakes, especially the largest lakes, is extremely complex. Wind, barometric pressure, and temperature cause all sorts of mysterious things to happen in large lakes. The thermocline can undulate in wave fashion, the earth's spin causes water to deviate off course from wind direction, and water near shore can move in unexpected ways. There are many more. They are phenomena that most fishermen would never notice, nor have efficient means for detecting and evaluating during an average day of fishing. Some of the complexity, however, can be simplified for the average fisherman's advantage.

The intent here is to improve every fisherman's odds by discussing a few of the phenomena that occur regularly. Being aware of them and having a rudimentary understanding will make you far more effective in predicting where your target fish will be located, and where a good bite could occur and where it may not.

I've included a few simplified illustrations that convey the concepts and develop your instincts for them, although they are not meant to describe every variation in nature. The first few illustrations address the affects of barometric pressure on big water and where the bite has a higher probability of occurring. The final illustrations address wind-driven water movement (currents) and temperature and how to use the information for higher percentage fishing. Both will give you a powerful new ability to predict when and where to go for successful fishing, before you leave home.

Everything presented in previous chapters applies to all streams and small lakes across the globe, but additional factors must be considered when fishing the planet's largest lakes.

Lake Sizes Defined

For the sake of expediency, the difference between a small lake and the largest lakes shall be defined somewhat arbitrarily by how they are affected by wind and barometric weather systems:

If the unobstructed fetch of the wind is no longer than two miles across a lake, the lake shall be considered a small lake. If the unobstructed fetch is longer than two miles, but less than 75 miles, the lake shall be considered a large lake. If the lake is longer than 75 miles it shall be considered one of the world's largest lakes. The largest lakes differ from large lakes because the largest can have more than one weather system (barometric pressure system) hovering over them. Remember that these are arbitrary sizes and the material that follows can often apply to more than one lake size category. Also, I will frequently refer to large and largest lakes collectively as ***big water***.

The world's largest lakes are scattered across several continents. They include the Great Lakes in the United States and Canada, Lake Ladoga and Baikal in Russia, Lake Victoria — which is bordered by Kenya, Tanzania, and Uganda, and a few more. Canada has the most, which include Great Bear Lake, Lake Winnipeg, Great Slave Lake, and Lake Athabasca. Some are much larger in surface area than others, ranging from 31,000 sq. mi. for Lake Superior, to only 3,000 sq. mi. for Lake Athabasca.

These large bodies of water, like smaller lakes, are also replete with aquatic insects and crustaceans that contribute to the base of their food web. Total-pressure affects these organisms in the same way that it affects organisms in small lakes, which makes their activity and good bites more predictable. The way in which total-pressure is created, however, is often not what you would expect. It's greatly affected by the length and/or width of the lake. Also, weather systems traveling over the largest lakes normally require several hours to days to traverse the full length or width of the lake due to their variable speed. They can approach from every point on the compass.

Selecting Useful Water Behavior Factors

I live one and a half miles from the eastern shore of Lake Michigan (East Grand Traverse Bay) which is over 300 miles long. For 25 years I've watched countless shoreline episodes of lake water receding from the shallows and exposing large gravel flats, only to see the flats completely re-submerged a few hours or a day later. Most fluctuations ranged from three to eight inches. The wits in local tackle shops speculated that the fluctuations were due to wind direction, which wasn't much of an explanation on windless days. Naturally, the fluctuations caused changes in total-pressure, so they required a closer look.

Few fishing tasks are as daunting as trying to determine how water behaves in lakes that are actually inland seas. Watching the water height as it changes on a measuring stick hammered into the bottom near shore does not provide much information about a lake. There are many factors that contribute to the behavior of water in its basin, and they all influence how fish behave in it as well. Many of them, however, are extremely complicated and require far too much technology and manpower to be of any practical use for fishermen.

I have tried to identify the most useful and simple ones that I'm confident most fishermen will find beneficial and practical. I used two guidelines in my selection process: (1) A fisherman must be able to use it to catch more fish when all he knows is the local weather report and the weather history for the past couple days, and, (2) The information is not common knowledge among a high percentage of recreational fishermen.

A better understanding of these factors will help you find the bite in big water and certainly increase your odds for successful fishing. They're based on some easy-to-understand affects of wind, temperature, and total-pressure.

Drinking Straw in a Beverage Effect

When a low barometric pressure system begins crossing one of the world's largest lakes, only a portion of the lake is first covered by the system. While that low pressure system is advancing onto the lake, a higher barometric pressure system is usually at the other end or side of the lake. In this situation, each end or side is experiencing a significantly different barometric pressure. This is a common occurrence on the largest lakes. Small lakes are generally too small to be significantly affected by more than one system. (Sidebar #22: Small Lake Pressure)

#22

Small Lake Pressure

When new barometric pressure systems begin overspreading smaller lakes, the systems create a slightly different barometric pressure at one end of the lake than that which exists at the other. The difference, at most, may only be a point or two over most small lakes, and maybe a few more points over the largest small lakes. If a significant difference does occur, its duration will likely be brief and inconsequential in most instances because of the speed of the system. The pressure difference is so insignificant that it causes very little change in total-pressure and water displacement, and no practical impact on hatches and molts.

The pressure systems are so large in relation to the size of smaller lakes and reservoirs, and the pressure gradient is so small over such short distances, that the difference in pressure from one end of a small lake to the other would seldom, if ever, have any measurable effect on fishing.

Figure 10-1 illustrates the effect that two different pressure systems can have on a very large lake. Note that the illustration is for lakes that are 75 to 400 miles long. It shows how water can be displaced by barometric pressure, and how total-pressure can be affected, up or down.

A low barometric pressure system is located at one end of the lake while high barometric pressure is located at the other. This scenario is

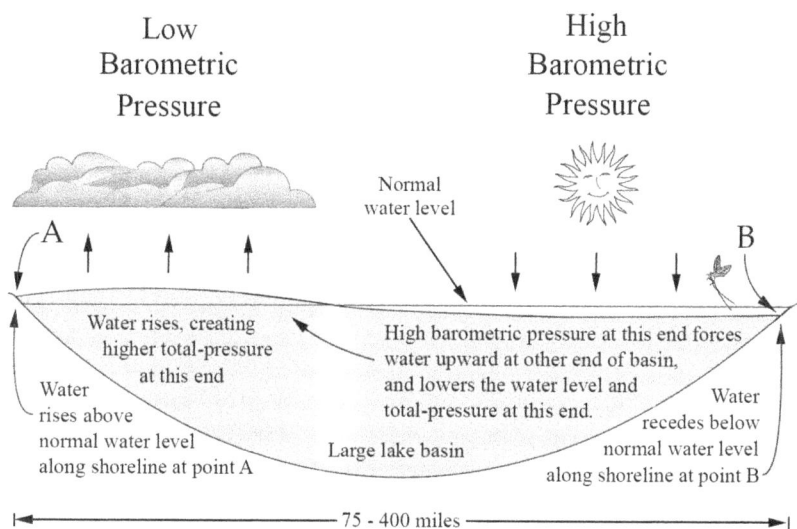

Low
Barometric
Pressure

High
Barometric
Pressure

Normal
water level

A

B

Water rises, creating
higher total-pressure
at this end

High barometric pressure at this end forces
water upward at other end of basin,
and lowers the water level and
total-pressure at this end.

Water
rises above
normal water level
along shoreline at point A

Large lake basin

Water
recedes below
normal water level
along shoreline at point B

75 - 400 miles

Figure 10-1

Imagine ordering a soft drink in a glass with a straw. To drink the beverage, you suck on the straw to draw the liquid up to your mouth. The liquid comes up through the straw as soon as you suck on it and reduce the pressure in the straw. You have created low pressure in the straw at the same time that the atmospheric pressure is pushing down on the top of the beverage in the glass. The pressure pushing down on the beverage is a higher pressure than the lower pressure you created in the straw. As a result, the beverage is pushed up through the straw by the higher pressure of the atmosphere that is pushing on the top of the exposed beverage in the glass. The higher atmospheric pressure pushes the liquid up the straw toward the lower pressure you created at the other end of it. The liquid is pushed up a path of least resistance.

The scenario in Figure 10-1 is the same, but on a bigger scale. The water in the lake basin behaves like the beverage in the glass. The low barometric pressure system acts like your mouth and the straw. It creates the same type of suction, and a path of least resistance where the water can be pushed upward. The higher atmospheric pressure at the other end of the lake is the force that can push water into it. The greater the difference between the low pressure and high pressure at opposite ends of the lake, the higher the water can be pushed upward under the low pressure system. As the water swells upward under the low barometric pressure system, to-tal-pressure is increased under the swell because the water is now deeper, which hinders hatches and molts in that part of the lake. In turn, the water depth is lowered directly under the high pressure system that is forcing water upward at the other end of the lake. The effect of the pressure dif-ference on water level is noticeable along the shoreline as depicted at **A** and **B**.

In the region where the water depth has been lowered under the area of high barometric pressure, the result is that total-pressure has also been lowered. The lower total-pressure that now exists under the high pressure system is conducive to causing pie hatches and pie molts. The hatches and molts will occur directly under the *high pressure system,* and the bite un-der it may be a good one. This is a bite that will occur because a low baro-metric pressure system has overspread *part* of the lake, but the bite will occur in the part of the lake where there is high barometric pressure, not *where the low barometric pressure is located.* It's possible that a fisher-man hundreds of miles away will experience a great bite under clear skies because of it. This is completely opposite of what occurs in small lakes, where pie hatches and pie molts occur only under low barometric pressure systems. The greatest affect on hatches and molts is near shorelines and bays where the water is shallow and harbors more insect life.

If the fisherman in the example above keeps logs, he would prob-ably note a great day of fishing under high barometric pressure conditions, and dutifully record one barometer reading. This is typical of almost every log entry I've ever seen, and it's basically meaningless. As you now know, one reading reveals little or nothing about how fish behavior is influenced by barometric pressure, and never reveals a consistent behavior pattern.

Barometric Pressure and Wind Effects On Bites

Figure 10-2 depicts the same conditions as those in Figure 10-1 but wind is added, which creates an ambiguous or uncertain situation near area **A**.

Wind is pushing the bulging water ahead of the low barometric pressure system. As the wind pushes the water ahead, the water level recedes near the shoreline at area **A**. It's questionable whether or not wind can lower the bulging water level enough to create a low total-pressure condition in this area, directly under the low barometric pressure system. As wind blows the bulging water away, the low barometric pressure keeps sucking more water upward. It's difficult to predict how the water level will vary because every storm is different. Each converges on a lake at a different location from a different direction with a different pressure and wind speed. If the barometric pressure isn't very low, then the swell won't be very high, but wind speeds will also not be very high, so the wind may not be able to blow enough water away from the shoreline to create a low total-pressure condition. If barometric pressure is quite low, then the swell will be higher, and wind speeds will also be higher, but again the wind may not be strong enough to blow enough water away from the shoreline to create low total-pressure. If the wind is strong enough to drop the water level low enough, weather and wave conditions may then be too dangerous to be on the water.

I mention this situation because I have not seen how it plays out in

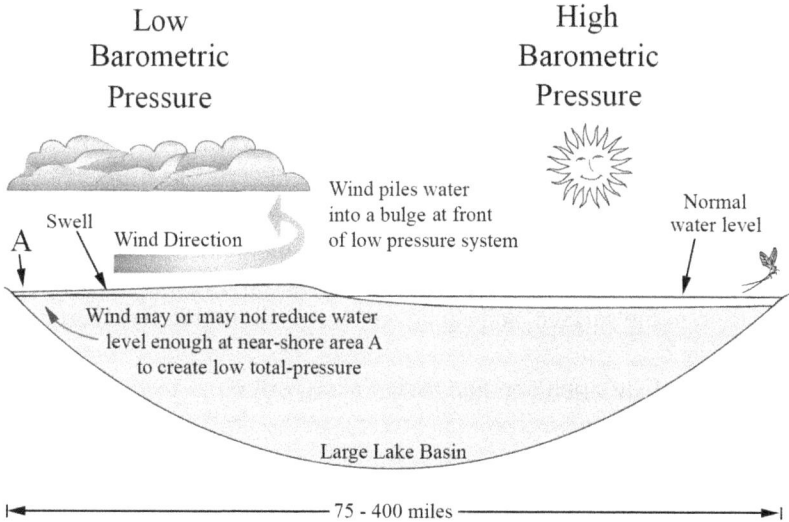

Figure 10-2

reality, but it's a block of knowledge that needs to be obtained. It would be useful because the wind blowing from shore and out over the water will generally yield calmer water near shore, which is usually safe for boaters. Whether or not a bite can be predicted in that safe calm water is dependent on whether total-pressure becomes high or low. This information takes time to collect and interpret, and it's only possible by keeping good logs of the water level, environmental conditions, and fishing success over a number of years.

The logs will eventually become still more valuable as they shed light on the conditions that influence the behavior of organisms occupying unique niches in the calm water areas near **A**. The ultimate result will be the capability to regularly, and accurately, predict the bite in the area near **A**.

Logs of this type can be constructed and kept at local tackle shops. Shop owners could develop the logs rapidly with cooperation from their many customers. Fishermen love to chat and speculate about reasons for good or bad fishing, so it would be an entertaining, educational, magnetic activity that's perhaps viral in nature. It would be a community effort that benefits everyone. The logs would be an invaluable aid for near-shore fishing. Shop owners who develop and share such logs can expect to attract many loyal patrons.

Charter captains want to please their paying clients by catching limits of fish as soon as possible after leaving the dock. They prefer not to travel far for good fishing if they can avoid it. Recreational fishermen also prefer familiar and productive fishing grounds that can be reached within reasonable travel time. Therefore, most fishing on the largest lakes is usually conducted within a few miles of shore. The best big-water fishermen also know that near-shore waters are where the best fishing conditions occur most frequently. They know that wind forces layers of water at different temperatures toward shore or away from it, or upward or downward in relation to the surface, and each condition is favorable for a certain species of fish.

Better fishermen conduct their fishing efforts according to the water temperatures preferred by the target species, and on the wind patterns that produce those temperatures in the fishing grounds. They study wind and water temperature and rely on this knowledge to locate target species because enormous volumes of water are devoid of fish in the largest lakes. They also know what the fish eat at different times of the year, and a little about the behavior of the organisms being eaten, which helps refine their ability to locate the desired species. The remainder of their arsenal usually consists of fishing methods and preferred tackle. Their success improves as they include more of this type of information in their logs.

One thing freshwater fishermen don't worry about much, though, is tide. Tide is probably almost never a factor that affects fishing on the largest lakes because it's usually so small and brief. For example, the highest annual tide for Lake Michigan is reported to be approximately only 1.75 - 2.4 inches (equal to about 13 to 17 points of barometric pressure) over a three hundred mile fetch, in January when almost no one is fishing in open water; and the peak lasts only a couple hours. Such a tide could be easily offset by a gentle wind blowing in a conflicting direction. The tide is much lower during the remainder of the year, and basically unnoticeable to the average person standing on the shore.

Pressure Gradient Effects on the Bite

Figure 10-3 scrutinizes low barometric pressure in a way that can be easily overlooked, and will help you recognize locations where good bites could soon occur. It shows a large lake completely overspread by a low barometric pressure system. It's an idealistic example for instructional purposes only.

Low pressure systems usually contain a region that has the lowest pressure within the system, and such a region is located above **C** in Figure 10-3. As the distance increases away from **C**, the barometric pressure increases at those farther distances, which is depicted on the gradient bar at the base of the clouds. This can result in significant pressure differences between the lowest pressure region at **C** and the distant locations. It's a *pressure gradient* that exists within the system that might not ordinarily be recognized by the casual fisherman.

In this example, the higher barometric pressure of the distant locations surrounds the lowest pressure region at the core of the system. The higher pressure locations, such as those above **A** and **B**, act to push water toward the lowest pressure region at the center of the system, and create a water swell under it (**C**). It's the straw in the glass again. Even though the entire system is a low barometric pressure system, the pressure gradient within the system creates pressure at **A** and **B** that is higher than the lowest pressure at the center of the system. The higher pressure near shorelines at **A** and **B** causes the water level to recede at **A** and **B**, resulting

197

Entire lake is covered by low barometric pressure system

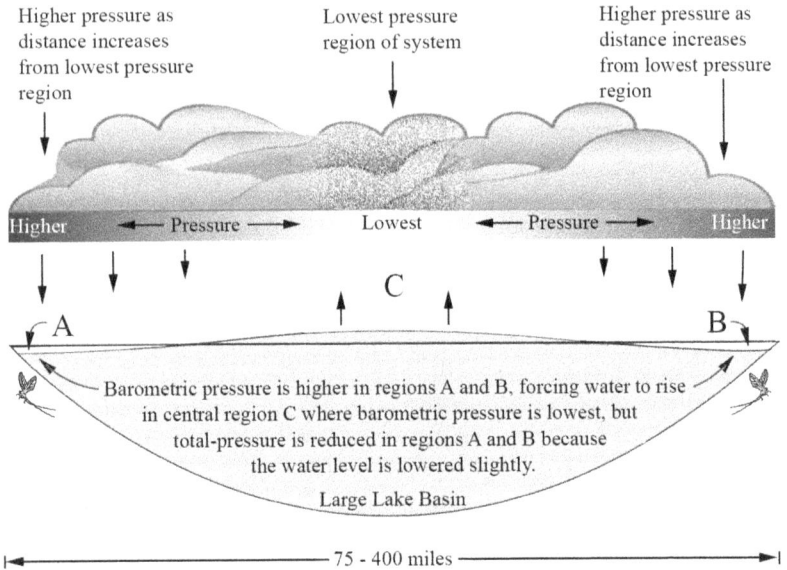

Higher pressure as distance increases from lowest pressure region

Lowest pressure region of system

Higher pressure as distance increases from lowest pressure region

Higher ← Pressure → Lowest ← Pressure → Higher

C

A

B

Barometric pressure is higher in regions A and B, forcing water to rise in central region C where barometric pressure is lowest, but total-pressure is reduced in regions A and B because the water level is lowered slightly.

Large Lake Basin

75 - 400 miles

Figure 10-3

in lower total-pressure near those shorelines. If low total-pressure lingers long enough near **A** and **B**, it may then produce additional pie hatches and pie molts and very active bites in those regions. Conditions are favorable for it.

Although barometric pressure may be favorable for hatches and molts, wind direction may be unfavorable for either **A** or **B** because it may push too much water into one of them, but the other may still produce a good bite. It's unlikely that a typical low barometric pressure system will produce multiple regions like **A** and **B**, but it's entirely feasible that at least one low total-pressure region like them will occur near a shoreline somewhere on the lake. Knowing how these systems work allows you to predict where low total-pressure will occur, and therefore where a surprising bite could occur.

If you can't get to a location like **A** or **B** when conditions are right, you can still gather information from boaters who fished those waters when you couldn't. Chatting with other fishermen at launches and marinas, or on marine radios can give you very valuable information for future reference. You only need to ask if they caught anything, which species they caught, and what time they caught it.

These few details will give you far more information than is obvious to the other fishermen. If you know the species, you will know or can easily learn the water temperature it was probably caught in; and you'll probably be able to learn its preferred forage for that time of year, so the catch is a tip-off that certain forage might be available on that date. You'll know that either the fish or the forage could have been feeding on insects or crustaceans that were available on that date at a certain time of day. Recall that hatches and, quite possibly, molts occur at a preferred time of day, so the pressure conditions that are conducive to them must coincide with those preferred times.

The answers you get to the three simple questions may validate your suspicions that a good bite occurred for good reasons, exactly where you thought it might. When you enter the information in your logs, your secret bag of tricks will be a little fuller.

Effects of Larger Pressure Systems on the Bite

Figure 10-4 illustrates a very large low barometric pressure system that has overspread an entire large lake and the region surrounding it. It's similar to the previous examples, but the system is much larger and provides practical insight for those times when big systems overspread your water.

The region of lowest barometric pressure within the system is converging onto shoreline **B**. The bulging water level under it, partly supported by wind, has created high total-pressure near **B**, which hinders hatches and molts in that region, probably for miles offshore in the largest lakes. It's another example that jibes with the high pressure rule.

Before the lowest barometric pressure region reached shoreline **B**, however, it drew water away from shoreline **B**, which would have caused a low total-pressure condition there. This could have caused pie hatches and molts, and a good bite a few hours earlier near that shoreline. As the lowest pressure region approached **B**, however, with its swell that increased total-pressure, hatches, molting, and the bite would have been suppressed. The swell would cause a lull in the action (high pressure rule again).

As the system continues to move in the direction of shoreline **B**, the lowest pressure region will also continue to move in that direction and eventually move off the lake, and the lake will no longer be affected by

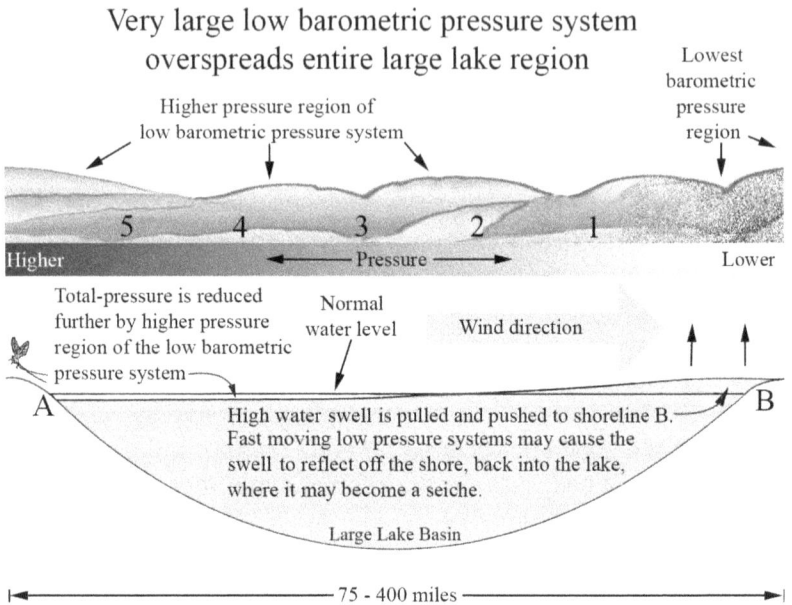

Very large low barometric pressure system overspreads entire large lake region

Lowest barometric pressure region

Higher pressure region of low barometric pressure system

5   4   3   2   1

Higher ———— Pressure ————> Lower

Total-pressure is reduced further by higher pressure region of the low barometric pressure system

Normal water level

Wind direction

A

High water swell is pulled and pushed to shoreline B. Fast moving low pressure systems may cause the swell to reflect off the shore, back into the lake, where it may become a seiche.

B

Large Lake Basin

|———————— 75 - 400 miles ————————|

Figure 10-4

it. The remainder of the system trailing behind it, however, and still positioned over the lake, still has barometric pressure that ranges from low to higher, with the lowest remaining barometric pressure region now located at position **1**. Immediately following position **1** is position **2**, which has slightly higher pressure than position **1**; position **2** is then followed by position **3** which has slightly higher pressure still, and so forth through all the positions, each one with slightly higher pressure than the one that preceded it. Even though each position has slightly higher pressure, they are still relatively low barometric pressure values as evidenced by the fact that they are part of the total low barometric pressure system. Positions **1** through **5** simply represent a pressure gradient within the system.

As position **1** converges onto shoreline **B**, it, too, will bring the swell to the shoreline with it, although the swell will be smaller because the pressure at position **1** is higher than the pressure in the original lowest pressure region moving ahead of it (higher pressure won't cause the water to rise as far). After position **1** moves onshore, position **2** is then the lowest pressure region over the lake and will keep the swell at the shoreline, although the swell is now getting smaller because the pressure at **2** isn't

200

as low. As each successive position — **1** through **5** — moves onshore, the difference in barometric pressure over the lake at shoreline **B** becomes less and less, causing the swell to continuously lose height. The swell will disappear when there is no longer an area of low pressure over the lake at that location, and there is no driving wind to create and maintain a swell at the shoreline. As the barometric pressure diminishes, the swell will also diminish and recede back into the lake and travel as a long wave to the opposite shore. That type of wave is called a seiche (pronounced "say-sh"). It will continue to travel back and forth between the shores until it dies out. It's like a wave of water that sloshes back and forth in your bathtub and finally subsides.

Seiches, Swells, and Death Trap Hatches

In big water there is no practical way for fishermen to predict when most seiches will occur, or how high they will be, or how long they will affect a certain location. Generally, if they are a rather high wave (2-3 ft. or more) they may only last a couple hours or less and not affect fish behavior very much; if they are long, low waves (2-12 inches) they may last longer, and maybe long enough to keep total-pressure high enough to hinder hatches, molts, and bites. On the largest lakes, small seiches are probably sloshing back and forth very subtly every day. They can be caused by a steady wind, an almost imperceptible tide, and uneven barometric pressure. Their occurrence and affect is probably at a minimum, if not zero, after a prolonged period (two to three days?) of stable high pressure over the entire lake region. Stable high pressure often creates prolonged calm conditions and therefore few seiches. Without interference from a long-lasting seiche of sufficient magnitude (about two inches or more), the odds of correctly predicting the location of a bite would increase.

An interesting example of the swells produced by low pressure systems is seen in the Hawaiian Islands. Surfers eagerly await the formation of strong, fast-moving low pressure systems in the northwestern Pacific Ocean because they create large swells that deliver gigantic waves to the islands' shorelines. Another example is the high storm surges produced by hurricanes, which are systems with extremely low barometric pressure.

While the water was piling up on shoreline **B** in Figure 10-4, the higher barometric pressure at the other end of the large system was causing lower total-pressure along shoreline **A**. Wind has blown a substantial amount of water away from the shore near **A**, and the low barometric pressure on the other side of the lake has drawn even more water away from shoreline **A**. Because the entire system is very large, its effects have been prolonged over the lake. This means that the region near shoreline **A** has had low total-pressure for an extended period. Once again, this is a favorable condition for hatches and molts and a good bite near **A**.

As you can see by the previous examples, low *total-pressure* can frequently occur under high barometric pressure regions on big water, which is a surprising and counterintuitive development. It's also seriously problematic because those conditions will induce insects to hatch under low total-pressure conditions (as usual), but they must face the death trap of a strong surface film. They are at risk of hatching out of the state of ableness too soon to penetrate the formidable film. Recall from Chapter 4 that high barometric pressure creates a strong and formidable surface film. In this case, it seems that the strong surface film would naturally select against small insect species.

My first impression of this development was that it could only mean that the biggest and strongest insects could hatch and successfully struggle through the strong film. As I investigated further, my suspicions appeared corroborated because I found no other fishermen who could recall ever seeing small mayflies, stoneflies, or caddisflies hatching from the big water of Lake Michigan. Only flies larger than those imitated on size 14 hooks and larger were mentioned by the most expert fishermen.

In my region of the lake there were no smaller insects known to local fishermen other than one major exception: midges — millions of them. I can offer no known explanation for their presence, just speculation. My best guess is that, because they develop through a pupa stage, via natural selection they are among the first species whereby the pupa have evolved a method, perhaps involving capillary forces, for creating a hole through the surface film through which they can emerge. If this is indeed an exception, I suspect there are more in other large lakes around the globe.

I also suspect that a higher number and variety of crustaceans have evolved to occupy big water because they have no need to scramble through a surface film. Perhaps they now occupy the underwater niches that have not been occupied by small aquatic insects. This could be understandable because, if the Great Lakes were formed by the last ice age about 10,000 years ago, natural selection has not had much time to produce small insects with extraordinary abilities to conquer strong surface films in this water.

Currents in Big Water

Figures 10-5 through Figure 10-7 depict how wind creates a variety of currents in big water, and how it influences water temperature near shore. Knowledge of the near-shore water temperatures and currents is the mother's milk of successful fishing on big water. The illustrated effects are completely dependent on the wind's speed, its duration and direction. Bear in mind that there is always a lag time between the onset of wind and the useful effects it produces. Some effects may develop within a few hours; others may develop only after several days of steady wind. A few unfamiliar terms are introduced, but it's not imperative that you remember them.

The depictions are grossly simplified versions of the complex behavior of wind and water in large basins, but they are efficiently instructional. Their purpose is to give you a quick, practical sense of how wind influences water so you can use the information to catch fish immediately, or know when to stay home and save your gas money. You will learn about several different currents, but there are more that have been omitted. Fortunately they all lead to one simple fishing technique that you may find enlightening.

Nearly every captain I've explained this stuff to has had a minor eureka moment upon hearing it.

Stratification, and Thermocline Effects on Bite Location

Figure 10-5 illustrates a phenomenon produced by wind in the largest lakes after they stratify into different temperature layers. Stratification commonly forms and persists from sometime during spring through sometime in fall, depending on latitude and altitude. In the Northern Hemisphere, lakes warm and stratify in their southern regions first; in the Southern Hemisphere they warm and stratify in their northern regions first. Shallower water warms sooner in spring in both, and also cools sooner in the fall. The pattern of warming and stratification is part of the natural sequence of life re-emerging in the spring at an average approximate rate of 70 miles toward the poles every 10 days (45th parallel). (Recall from Chapter 8, small lakes warm in the opposite direction because of the combined effects of their small size and the angle of the sun.)

Early in the season before stratification is complete, the thermocline will be at the surface of the lake but often many miles from shore. This situation is famous for *scum line* fishing which will not be addressed here because the situation, cause, and bite are already well explained in other literature.

Notice that the wind is blowing toward shoreline **B**, blowing all the warm water from shoreline **A** in that direction, and causing the water level to rise on the leeward side of the lake at **B**. My guess is that the rise would probably be only a matter of inches and would vary, depending on the wind strength, direction, and duration. As the amount of warm water increases near **B**, so does the increasing burden of its weight, which pushes downward on the cooler water below it. The cooler water below then sinks a little deeper. The sinking is known as ***downwelling***. This process continues as long as the wind blows toward **B**, causing the colder water below to downwell still deeper.

This works neatly because of the properties of water at different temperatures. Cold water is denser and heavier than warm water, which causes water at different temperatures to separate or stratify into layers that have the same density and temperature. It's somewhat like cards in a deck that can slip around on each other. Common knowledge about these layers is that the warmest, less dense layers occupy the upper region of the water column, and the cooler, denser layers occupy the lower region of the water column. This is commonly true, and swimmers experience this type of layering when their toes feel cold water a few feet below the warmer surface layer. The wind, however, almost constantly separates warm layers from the cold layers in big water in a manner that frequently leaves warm water near the surface at one shoreline, and cold water near the surface at the opposite shoreline. Wind constantly shifts the less dense warmer layers to and fro around the lake basin. (Sidebar #23: Water Density)

The warmer water continues to separate into layers of slightly dif-

---

#23
Water Density

A good example of water density differences occurs in home hot water heaters. The less dense hot water rests on top of the denser cold water below. Cold water enters the bottom of the tank and is then heated, which reduces its density. Its reduced density causes it to float to the top of the tank as useful hot water. More cold water then flows in under the hot water and the process is repeated.

ferent temperature as depicted by the light and dark diagonal banding near **B**. The banding represents subtle temperature and density layers from the surface to the thermocline. When diagonal banding meets the diagonal slope of the shoreline it sets up a condition known as ***wedging***. There are other versions of wedging not included here, but the principle is similar in each case. Wedging traps a small thermally driven current (***wedge current***) between the warm water layers. Wedge current exists where wind direction parallels the shoreline. It flows counterclockwise near the shoreline in the Northern Hemisphere, but clockwise in the Southern Hemisphere. It's typically a slow current, on the order of less than a half-mile per hour and is represented by the graphic swirl near **B**.

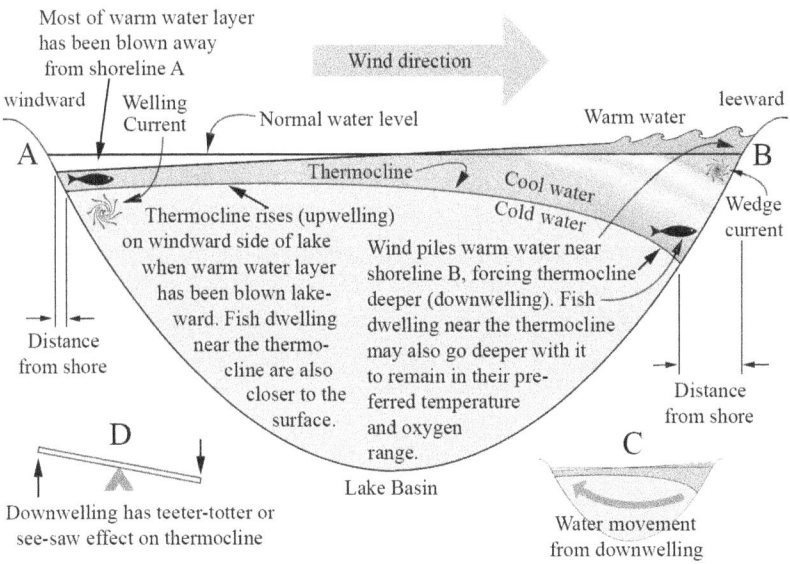

Most of warm water layer has been blown away from shoreline A

Wind direction

windward | Welling Current | Normal water level | Warm water | leeward

A

B

Thermocline

Cool water

Cold water

Wedge current

Thermocline rises (upwelling) on windward side of lake when warm water layer has been blown lakeward. Fish dwelling near the thermocline are also closer to the surface.

Wind piles warm water near shoreline B, forcing thermocline deeper (downwelling). Fish dwelling near the thermocline may also go deeper with it to remain in their preferred temperature and oxygen range.

Distance from shore

Distance from shore

D

C

Lake Basin

Downwelling has teeter-totter or see-saw effect on thermocline

Water movement from downwelling

Figure 10-5

The warmer surface water of the lake is separated from the colder water below by a thin region between them called the ***thermocline***. Temperatures change abruptly across the thermocline, going from warm to cold within just a few feet or yards in many instances, which is reflective of the swimmers' experiences mentioned above. Typical temperature range of the thermocline is roughly 39-46 degrees F (4-8 deg C). When surface water pushes the thermocline deeper, it also pushes it farther from shore when there is a sloping shoreline as shown near **B**. Depending on the lake's size and the slope of its bottom, the thermocline can be a considerable distance from shore, sometimes miles. This is characteristic of the leeward side after wind has blown from one direction for several days; warm surface water is always forced toward the leeward shoreline, and to the right of the leeward shore as explained later. As the thermocline goes deeper and farther offshore, many fish species will also migrate deeper and farther from shore as they try to remain in their preferred temperature and oxygen range. You must move with them to stay with any possible bite. Understanding wind influences on the water will help you do that.

The situation is different on the windward side near shoreline **A**. The warm surface water has been blown away from **A**, so there is no layering or wedging located above the thermocline. There is also no burden of extra water blowing into shoreline **A** to cause downwelling of the thermocline. In fact, the opposite has occurred. With a reduced weight burden on the thermocline near **A**, the thermocline has been forced upward by the downwelling on the opposite side of the basin and is now near the surface. The coldest water is now near the surface at **A**. This is known as *upwelling*, the opposite of downwelling. Upwelling also causes fish species dwelling near the upwelled thermocline to reposition closer to the surface and shoreline. They move closer so they can remain in their preferred temperature and oxygen range. **(Sidebar #24: Upwelling and Downwelling)**

When the wind is moving water to the leeward side of the lake and causing downwelling on that side and upwelling on the other side, it also creates a current in the cold water under the thermocline as shown at **C**. This occurs because downwelling puts pressure on the water below and puts it in motion toward the opposite shore. In large basins the volume of water being moved can be enormous, perhaps many cubic miles of water, which will cause swift currents in certain places. Good logs allow good predictions of where those swift currents will be, and reveal which winds cause them.

Coriolis Effect and Ekman Drift

When water under the thermocline is put in motion by downwelling, the moving water shows a marked tendency to constantly drift clockwise a few degrees to the right. The clockwise drift, called *Ekman drift*, is caused by the earth's spin and how it affects stacked layers of water that

24

Upwelling and Downwelling

Upwelling is caused by two primary factors: The absence of the weight of warm water on the windward side of a lake, and the constant wind-delivery of more water and its additional weight to the leeward side of a lake, which causes downwelling on the leeward side.

When the downwelling — sinking of the thermocline — is occurring, the downwelling hydraulically forces the denser water below the thermocline to push upward on the thermocline from its bottom side throughout the lake system. The warm water load on the leeward side keeps the thermocline from rising on that side, but the downwelling hydraulically forces the thermocline to rise in all other regions where less warm water burden is pressing down on it. With no warm water weight burden on the thermocline near the windward shore, the thermocline is hydraulically pushed much closer to the surface in that region. It upwells. Given the nature of fluid dynamics, the hydraulic effects are rapid, even over hundreds of underwater miles. The hydraulics are dramatically aided by the different densities of the water layers at different temperatures, the restraining boundaries of the lake basin, and atmospheric pressure against the water's surface.

have different temperatures and therefore different densities. The layers can slip past each other, with a little friction, like books in a stack. It's the same force that causes water to spiral clockwise down a drain in the Northern Hemisphere, or counterclockwise in the Southern Hemisphere.

The clockwise current under the thermocline, which I've termed a welling current, is represented by the graphic swirl under the fish near **A**. Structures in the lake basin and the shape of the basin may cause turbulence in the across-basin water movement that can cause welling currents to flow in a variety of directions for short distances, depending on where the downwelling occurs. Every lake will have its own unique characteristics. Turbulent currents under the thermocline are probably only a factor if you seek fish species that dwell in the coldest water, perhaps in water less than 50 degrees Fahrenheit (10 deg C) when the lake is stratified.

The result of downwelling of the thermocline near one shore is that it usually causes upwelling of the thermocline somewhere on an opposite shore. The action-reaction resembles a teeter-totter or see-saw action as shown in **D** of Figure 10-5; when one side goes down, the other side goes up. The mid-section of the device, however, does not move up and down very far, and the mid-lake section of the thermocline commonly behaves in the same manner; its vertical movement is usually far less than at the shorelines. Conversely there are situations when the thermocline is at the surface in mid-lake during stratification, but it's frequently very far from shore where few fishermen venture. As a general rule, downwelling occurs on the leeward side of the lake, and upwelling occurs on the windward side of the lake.

Figure 10-6 shows the affects of a south wind blowing over an elliptically shaped lake. The most important feature in the illustration is the flock of small curved arrows that each veer to the right. The arrows indicate the actual direction that the surface water is moving.

When wind blows over water, it causes the surface water to start moving. It starts moving in the same direction as the wind is blowing, however, in stratified water the earth's spin causes it to begin veering or drifting clockwise to the right. This clockwise drift is another example of Ekman drift as mentioned for Figure 10-5. It's a critical behavior of water movement that every big water fisherman should remember. Ekman drift must be factored into almost every wind-related prediction that big water fishermen make.

Dark shaded area **B** represents the approximate area where warm surface water will accumulate when a south wind blows it northward and it drifts to the right because of the earth's spin. Note that the warm water of area **B** has accumulated along most of the length of the eastern shore because of Ekman drift. This depiction is not representative of exactly what will occur in all lakes, but it does represent the trend that will occur in all lakes when wind blows over stratified water in the Northern Hemisphere. The blown water will generally move in the direction of the wind, but the entire moving body of blown water will veer to the right. There will always be a right-veering component in stratified water. This is important because the warm water in **B** is causing downwelling in **B**, and upwelling in light-shaded area **A**. Therefore the south wind, because of Ekman drift

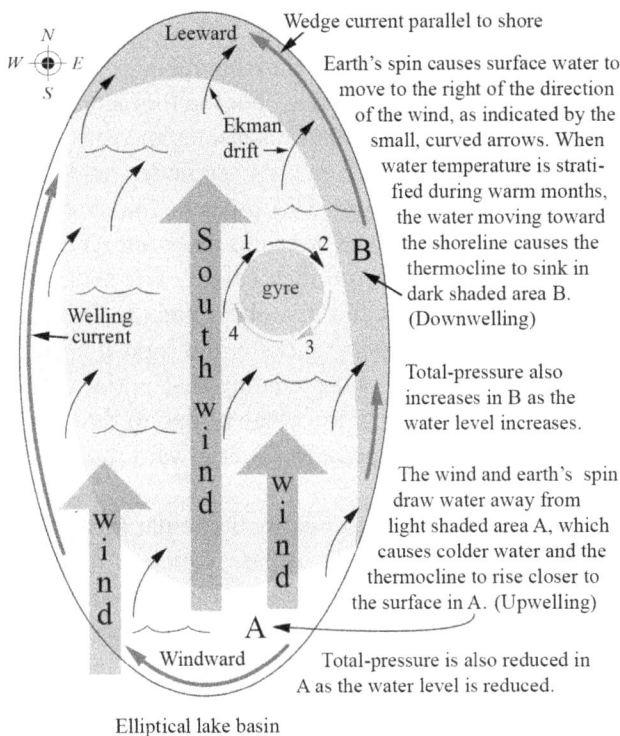

Figure 10-6

and the downwelling it caused in B, has forced the colder water near the thermocline to rise closer to the surface in **A**.

The shape of **A**, like that of **B**, is hypothetical and only represents a trend that might occur on any given lake. More specifically, the trend depicted is probably more likely with winds of short duration of perhaps less than a day or two.

Winds of long duration will cause surface water to accumulate in a pattern more like that depicted in Figure 10-10 as addressed later. Nonetheless, the explanations above result in a simple rule: *Wind-driven surface water moves in a downwind direction, but its movement trends to the right of the wind direction (in the Northern Hemisphere).* It trends to the left in the Southern Hemisphere.

The movement to the right, (left in Southern Hemisphere) caused by the earth's spin, is known as the ***Coriolis effect***. It is most pronounced and influential near the poles, but basically non-existent at the equator. Lakes near the equator will experience very little drift, so their wind-blown water movements will closely parallel the wind direction.

The *gyre* (Pronounced like "tire," but the first letter has a 'J' sound — think gyroscope.) in the illustration is also created by the wind. It is a large, slowly rotating mass of water. It's my understanding that it's not unusual for gyres to be as large as 15-25 miles in diameter, or more. They generally form far offshore when the wind has been blowing for a short time, perhaps only 6-10 hours and then ceases. The short wind duration acts like a pulse that puts the water in motion, and the Ekman drift causes the moving water to continuously move to the right until it forms a full circular motion. It's also my understanding that initial current speed at the perimeter of a gyre can be in the range of two to three miles per hour in the temperate latitudes, but perhaps faster toward the poles and slower toward the equator.

Gyres are included here because their circular movement has a current moving in all directions of the compass, which is indicated by arrows 1,2,3,4 positioned around the gyre. As gyres drift closer to shore, fishing captains may encounter them and notice a current moving in an unexpected direction.

The steady south wind in Figure 10-6 causes simple and predictable results, but wind and current conditions are often not that simple. Variable and short-duration winds will often create surface temperature patterns that are decidedly chaotic, disorderly, and confusing, but the general trends will be as already explained. The shoreline and basin shape of every lake is different, so each lake will respond to wind in its own unique manner, but their behavior trends will all be similar. Interestingly, their shape and long-axis orientation will make each lake more responsive to wind from one particular direction and less responsive to all others.

Mysterious Currents are Fish Producers

Figure 10-7 illustrates how gyre currents can become still more mysterious. Notice the arrows within the gyre that indicate two currents counter-rotating next to each other. This actually symbolizes a double-gyre that, in terms of size, can nearly match the dimensions of the lake in some instances.

Another unexpected current, the waltzing current is shown at C. A waltzing current is the beginning stage of a gyre, except the wind keeps blowing and prevents the current from forming into a full circular move-ment. The waltzing current has only half the circular movement of a gyre. It gets its name because it moves in continuous half circles as if dancing a waltz. Arrows 1 and 2 around the gyre represent how a waltzing current begins. At **C**, waltzing arrows X,Y,Z depict a waltzing current's typical motion, although its direction can vary.

The large arrow pointing from northeast to southwest indicates movement of the enormous volume of water that is displaced across the basin by downwelling. No doubt there are places within any basin where this large movement is felt more than others.

A cacophony of wind-driven currents that occur in stratified wa-ter is included in Figure 10-7, and they become more pronounced as wind speed increases. It's only a sampling, however, of the spec-trum of currents that arise in big water. Other important currents include those from river inlets and outlets, and from wave motions, e.g., seiches and rip currents.

Currents and temperature patterns in large bays of big waters, depending on the bay's shape, will generally behave somewhat inde-pendently of the larger lake. They also respond to wind much quicker because there is less water to move around. In the case of Lake Michi-gan, this semi-independent behav-ior is seen in Green Bay and both Grand Traverse bays. Water that surrounds peninsulas and points that jut into the lake will also exhibit independent behavior with certain winds, but not inconsistently with the principles presented here.

Research has shown that wind-driven currents in fully mixed, un-stratified water show a much closer relation to wind direction and will

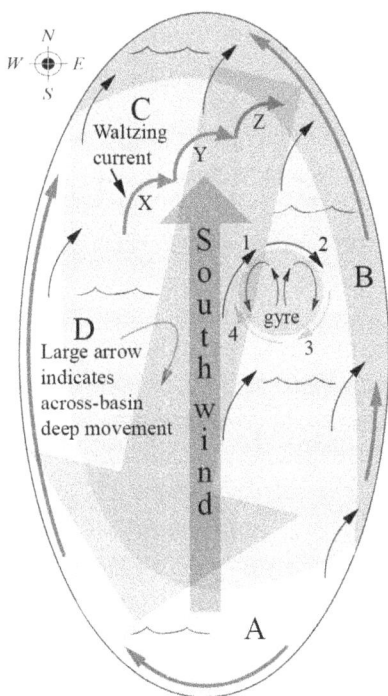

Cacophony of currents in
an elliptical lake basin

Figure 10-7

closely parallel wind direction in many cases. The Coriolis force is far less influential in fully mixed water, so there is much less Ekman drift. (Clifford H. Mortimer, 2004, Lake Michigan in Motion, Madison, Wisconsin, University of Wisconsin Press,)

Despite the wide variety of currents in big water and their mysterious causes, I submit that they give big-water fishermen a distinct fishing advantage. The advantage lies in the fact that fish almost always face into a current; their normal behavior is to face upstream. Currents are like streams in big water, so it's probably reasonable to assume that fish are normally facing upstream in them. The currents would bring them food and oxygen with the least amount of work. Baitfish would also be facing into the current, which would make them easier to ambush from behind because they are all facing one direction — upstream.

Savvy charter captains who troll (or drift fish) have long known that they will catch more fish by trolling in one direction than in the opposite direction through a certain section of water. The reason, however, has remained a mystery.

It's common to hear fishing reports, especially on marine radios, about lousy fishing near a local port, yet some captains will catch their limit when fishing the same water at the same time as others. Often it's because they were trolling in a different direction than the parade of local boat traffic. Quite likely the successful fishermen were trolling in the same direction that a current was moving; they were trolling downstream with the current. Trolling with the current allows fish to see the bait coming; it puts it in their face in the natural flow of the current. It's the way they are accustomed to seeing food approach. The bait isn't coming from behind and startling them. It takes advantage of the natural way that they feed, i.e., it exploits the natural bite.

In this age of electronic fish finders and global positioning systems (GPS), it's relatively easy to locate fish, determine their depth, and mark their position. Assuming they are facing upstream into some kind of current, the next step is to determine which way the current is flowing. This can be done by lowering a line with a weight to the level that the fish are at. The line should drift away from the boat in the direction of the current flow. This can get tricky if the wind is blowing the boat in one direction but the deeper current is moving in another. In this case it may be prudent to troll the bait in at least two or three directions through the fish. When trolling downstream with the current, it would be necessary to troll artificial lures faster than the speed of the current in order to create the action designed into the lure.

Generally, most currents in big water extend for miles. They are currents on a grand scale and can be trolled for substantial distances. Even some of the shortest currents, which I suspect are probably near river mouths, offer reasonable opportunity for trolling or drift fishing in a single direction for a reasonable period before a direction change must be made.

For fishing in currents, big water fishermen can take a lesson from experienced stream fishermen. The stream folks know they will seldom catch a fish by retrieving their lure, fly, or bait upstream. Almost all stream fish are caught when the enticement is retrieved or moving in a downstream direction or perhaps exhibiting motion while holding in a stationary position in the current. Fish are also caught when the enticement is presented across-current, but still moving downstream. There is almost always a downstream vector in its travel. It's probably not too unreasonable to assume that the downstream vector is also important in big water currents as well, because it's the natural way that food is moved by water.

In summary, it's not very important to understand the cause or name of a current. It's more important to realize that when fish are located, it's highly probable they are swimming in a current and facing upstream in it as well. To catch them, your odds improve if you present your enticement in a way that they are accustomed to encountering their natural food. It should be moving downstream (with the current) toward them at a speed yielding best results, or exhibiting motion while holding a stationary position in the current where they can see it.

River fishermen use a boating technique called drop-back trolling that may be effective in some big water currents. The boat is maintained in an upstream position while lures are allowed to hang in the current downstream from the boat. The boat is then allowed to drift downstream, but it drifts a little slower than the current is moving. Holding the boat to a slower drift also holds the lures to a slower drift. The slower drift causes the lures to exhibit their proper motion. The technique presents lures to fish before the boat travels over them. In big water, if the lures are dropped back far enough from the boat, it would help minimize the problem of scattering fish with engine noise, prop noise, sonar noise (fishfinders), and line singing. It has far more chance of improving the bite instead of compromising it.

Water Temperature Patterns Caused by Wind

Figure 10-8 is a quick reference that depicts how wind direction influences the water temperature in different areas of a stratified lake (Northern Hemisphere). A perfectly round lake (and basin) is used in all four examples. Using a round lake and basin means that the results, theoretically, will always be symmetrical for each wind direction. Only one wind direction and its Ekman drift are depicted in each example, along with just the areas where cold water (**A**) and warm water (**B**) will result from that particular wind.

The depictions in all four examples are hypothetical and only meant to imply the trend that might be expected on any given lake under ideal circumstances. For example, if a wind from the north blows over *your* lake, as shown over the round lake, you can expect warm water to accumulate in your lake in a region that roughly corresponds to region **B** (southerly and westerly) in the corresponding illustration for a north wind in Figure 10-8. You can expect cold water to ascend toward the surface in your lake in a region that roughly corresponds to region **A** (northerly and easterly). If the wind is from the south over your lake, region **A** would be southerly and westerly, and **B** would be northerly and easterly; and so on and so forth for the other examples. Figure 10-9 is the same type of reference for the Southern Hemisphere.

When winds are calm, variable, or slow, surface water temperatures may not vary by more than several degrees across the entire lake for days. If this occurs, the latest surface temperature readings may not reveal enough information about the proximity of the thermocline to the surface. Daily surface temperature archives (satellite readings) that are available through university or government programs on the internet could then reveal where downwelling and upwelling occurred before the onset of the calm period. If surface temperature archives are inconclusive, wind archives may help you deduce how the water temperature pattern developed prior to the calm period.

A Personal Prediction Example

I've included the two depictions in Figure 10-10 as an example of how I would try to make a prediction of water temperature patterns in an elliptical lake basin. Figure 10-10 (**1**) depicts a hypothetical water temperature pattern that has developed after several days of stiff wind from the north. The prolonged north wind has driven all the warm water to

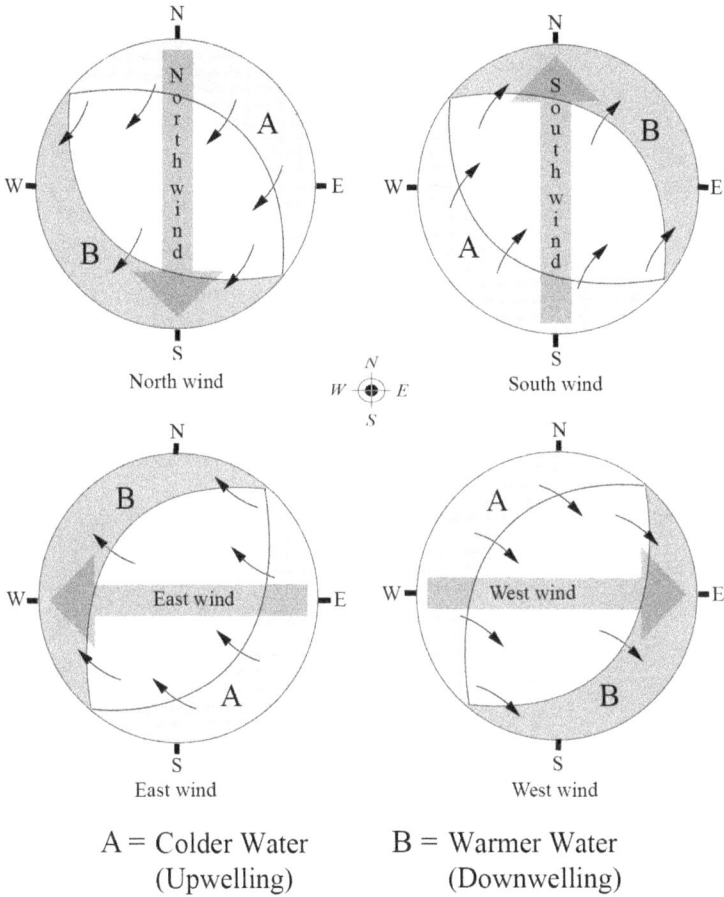

A = Colder Water   B = Warmer Water
    (Upwelling)   (Downwelling)

Wind influence on water temperature patterns in
a perfectly round lake in the Northern Hemisphere
(Stratified water)

Figure 10-8

the south end of the basin at **B**. In doing so, the warm water has created
downwelling of the thermocline at the south end, which in turn has caused
upwelling at the north end. Very cold water is now at the surface at the
north end in **D**. Ekman drift has also moved warm water away from the

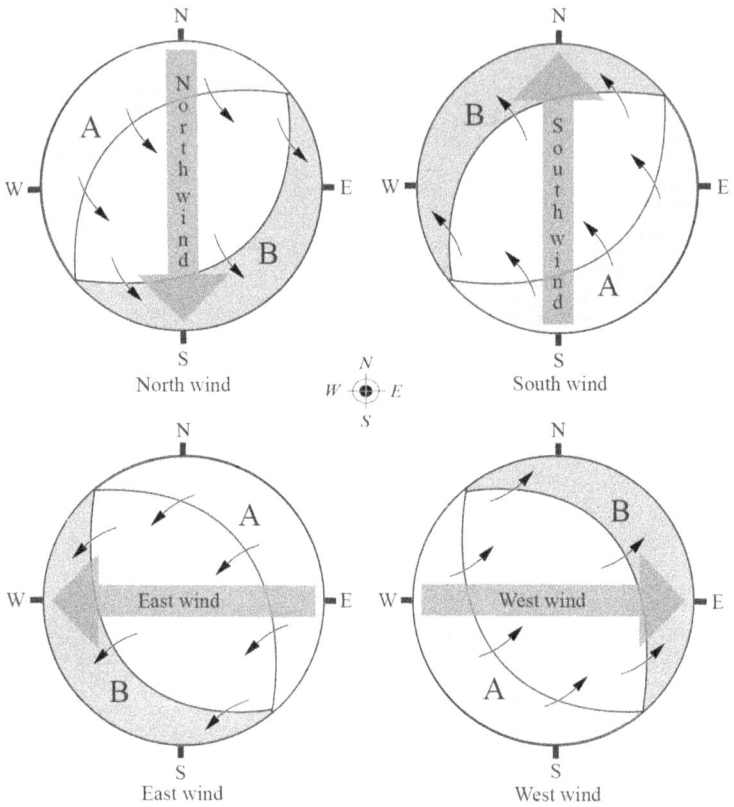

A = Colder Water   B = Warmer Water
(Upwelling)   (Downwelling)

Wind influence on water temperature patterns in
a perfectly round lake in the Southern Hemisphere
(Stratified water)

Figure 10-9

eastern shore, so downwelling at the south end also causes upwelling of the very cold water near the eastern shore. Area **A** is the region of cooler water remaining behind after the wind stripped off the warm water.

Figure 10-10 (**2**) is the type of sketch I might make when trying to determine if I should go fishing or not.

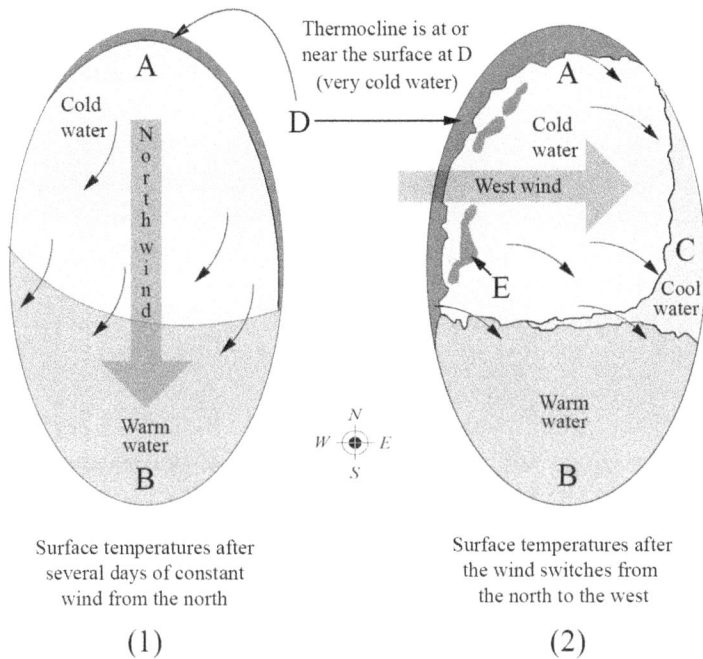

Thermocline is at or near the surface at D (very cold water)

Surface temperatures after several days of constant wind from the north

(1)

Surface temperatures after the wind switches from the north to the west

(2)

Figure 10-10

The wind has switched from north to west. The temperature pattern is one that might be expected after a day or two of steady west wind of moderate speed. The irregular temperature boundaries are more typical of actual conditions.

The surface of the cold water in **A** has had a day or two to warm up slightly and is being blown toward the eastern shore. It's not particularly warm or cold, but somewhere in between, so it's simply noted as cool water in **C**. It replaces a large portion of the very cold water of **D** that was near the eastern shore. After the cool water on top of **A** has blown easterly, the remaining water in most of **A** is still cold. As the wind continues to blow the cool water easterly to **C**, it causes more downwelling on the east side under **C**, and upwelling on the north and west side (**D**). **E** represents patches of very cold water **D** that upwell in unexpected places in the windward portion of the lake, and are common occurrences in big water because of variable and intermittent winds.

The warm water in **B** hasn't moved much because it's trapped by Ekman drift caused by the west wind. **B** needs a southerly or easterly wind

217

in order to spread to another region of the lake.

The underlying lesson in Figure 10-10 (**2**) is the importance of knowing which direction the wind has blown during the prior few days. Wind direction always has an effect on water temperature patterns, and each direction will have its own unique effects; and each effect will depend on how the water temperature patterns have developed during the previous several days. Brisker winds speed up the effects. Knowing how various winds affect your water is a key to finding and predicting a good bite, or a better bite.

As similarly noted in Chapter 9, an effect of winds and currents in big water is that they create special environments in various parts of the basin. Plankton, detritus, and all else that can be moved by wind and current will often settle in certain areas on a regular basis. It settles there and is churned up and resettles repeatedly. The locations where this occurs become regular haunts for fish because of the richness and regularity of the food that is so readily available. Finding these places will, again, plump your secret bag of tricks.

Predictable Ocean Water Levels

Barometric pressure and wind exert approximately the same affect on oceans as they do on the largest lakes. Oceans, however, are all interconnected and form a single, extremely large body of water, essentially the world's largest lake. Because of this singleness, all oceans are always under the influence of all low barometric pressure systems, all high barometric pressure systems, and all winds affecting all the other oceans. The presence of so many pressure systems scattered over the enormous expanse of the interconnected oceans permits a phenomenon within all the oceans that is very consistent: Wherever barometric pressure is high over ocean water, the water level is lower than normal; and vice versa — wherever barometric pressure is low over ocean water, the water level is higher than normal.

These are dependable occurrences because single barometric pressure systems are never large enough to overspread the entire oceanic expanse around the globe; the oceans are never under the exclusive influence of a single barometric pressure system. This situation allows each barometric pressure system to exert a predictable influence wherever it's located over uncontrolled oceanic water (no locks or man-made barriers) and that influence is essentially the same as put forth in the illustration:

in this chapter. The influences will be reflected further in the discussion about tides in Chapter 11.

Blocking Effect on Great Lakes

The above example of interconnected oceans may cause you to think that the interconnected Great Lakes also form a large, single body of water, which is somewhat true. However, some of the Great Lakes are isolated from the others by shipping locks which negate the influence of barometric pressure systems and winds that could influence the other lakes. Locks block most weather influences occurring on one lake so they are not communicated to an adjacent lake. This blocking effect must be factored into your predictions.

Small Lakes and Reservoirs

Predictions for small lakes and reservoirs are discussed in further detail in Chapter 12.

Summary of Strange Effects

In summary, big water behaves in challenging ways: Barometric pressure has an effect far different on big basin water, including oceans, than it has on small basin water. Water movements are strangely changed by wind, the earth's spin, and invisible density differences. Fortunately, effects of these forces and phenomena are no longer so mysterious. They can be used to determine and predict locations that are favorable for good bites throughout lake basins of every size. A brief weather history, current weather conditions, and a local forecast can regularly provide the information needed for accurate predictions.

Chapter 11

The Moon:
Salt and Fresh

This chapter is about the Moon's influence on fishing, and builds on the common knowledge about the Moon that average fishermen already have. Examples of how wind and barometric pressure help or hinder the Moon's influence are included.

Fishermen usually know that the Moon, with the Earth and Sun, causes high tides and low tides, and that they occur roughly twice every day about 12.5 hours apart in most locations around the world. Tide schedules and heights are generally available through local sources, software, or the internet. Some locations only have a single daily tide, or none. They also know there is a full moon about once per month, and other moon phases occur before and after the full moon. Many also know that a new moon, which occurs about two weeks before and after a full moon, means that the Moon is not visible for one night because it has risen and set during the day. Full moons and new moons bring the highest tides, and also the lowest tides within the same 25 hours.

Some of these moon behaviors exert a major influence on the bite, although the Moon is sometimes given more credit than it deserves. Its influence on saltwater fishing is most apparent because of the tides. Its effects on freshwater fishing may not be what we've been led to believe.

The influence on salt water is examined first, primarily in the inter-tidal zone. The influence on freshwater fishing is addressed last.

Saltwater

When the tide comes in, the water level rises along the coast to a maximum height called the *high water limit* (*high tide*), and then stops rising and pauses for a short period of time. The pause is known as *slack tide*, or more correctly, *high slack tide* and can last from a few minutes up to an hour or so. It's a period during which water stops moving toward the coast, and will soon begin receding back toward the sea. When the water recedes from the coast, meaning when the tides goes out, the water level soon drops to a much lower level called the *low water limit* (*low tide*). When reaching the low water limit, the water level stops dropping and again pauses for a short period of time. This pause is also known as slack tide, but more correctly as *low slack tide*.

In most locations the tide rises and falls at about the following rates: one-fourth within the first two hours, one-half within three hours, three-fourths within four hours, and complete by the end of six hours and 15 minutes.

Intertidal Zone

The high and low water limits are depicted in Figure 11-1. The height of both the high water limit and low water limit varies with every tide; some days they're higher and some days they're lower, depending on how the Sun, Moon, and Earth are aligned with each other, which changes constantly. The changes, however, are well understood and reflected in daily tide charts. It's another natural sequence that enables predictable fishing.

The coastal landscape between the high water limit and low water limit is known as the *intertidal zone*. The intertidal zone is covered with water at high tide, but fully exposed to air at low tide.

Fish follow the rising tide toward shore to feed on the abundant crustaceans and other food organisms in the intertidal zone. When fish come in with the tide, their behavior varies according to the shape of the land, so to speak.

The shape and characteristics of intertidal zones are varied and di-verse. Figure 11-1 depicts the typical ramp shape of most of them. The

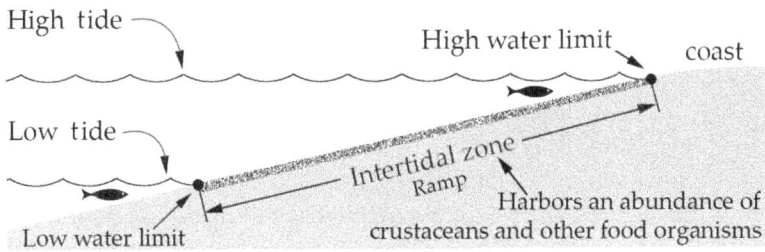

Figure 11-1

ramp is simply a bottom that slopes from the sea to dry land. Its slope can range from steep to gradual. If it's steep the intertidal zone will be narrow; if it's gradual the zone may be miles wide. It can be comprised of beach areas, expansive grassy flats, rocky flats, mud flats, boulder fields, sandbars, brackish bayous and estuaries, bays, rivers, alluvial fans and deltas, cliff sides, rocky outcrops, gravel and pebble fields, ditches, channels, cuts, canals, marshes, tidal pools, drop-offs, mangrove stands, fjords, jetties, breakwaters, combinations of these features, and more. The point being that the characteristics of intertidal zones normally change from one location to the next.

As the lay of the land changes along a coast, fishermen must deal with unique fishing circumstances created by tides in each location because most locations are different from all others. Regional ocean bottom and depths, and the shape and proximity of surrounding shores control the maximum and minimum height of tides that will occur locally. They can cause tides that vary from mere inches in height to dozens of feet.

Tide Bites

Fishing is subject to how the incoming and outgoing tides interact with the shape and physical features of the intertidal zone in any particular place. Tides repeatedly create significant currents in some locations and not others. Currents are commonly the key factor for locating fish at certain times during the tide cycle. For example, in the Gulf of Mexico near Louisiana, the tide moves inland for miles in some places. Shrimp and baitfish follow the rising water inland to feed on abundant organisms in tide pools, flooded marshlands, and shallow brackish lakes. The zone is interlaced with cuts and channels that the tides, shrimp, and baitfish follow.

223

Predator fish such as redfish follow them inland, but the bite is marginal until the tide goes slack.

During high slack tide, just before the tide recedes back to the sea, the predators become exceedingly active and the bite is on. Slack tide, however, is brief and soon gives way to the receding tide. As the tide recedes, shrimp and baitfish enter swift current lanes and attempt to return to the Gulf through the cuts, channels and ditches. Predators take up feeding positions in or next to the current lanes, and feast on the passing shrimp and baitfish as the current carries them into range. Savvy fishermen target the predators in the current lanes as the tide recedes. As the water level drops, predators also drop back accordingly. Note that the predators face upstream into the current, and fishing techniques must take this into account. The bite that occurs during slack tide in this fishery does not occur universally in other regions of the seas. Slack tide is regularly *not* a productive fishing period in many other regions.

In the preceding example, a good bite didn't occur on the rising tide, but occurred only on the high slack tide and falling tide. It's a bite that can continue so long as a receding current continues to carry food back toward the sea. In addition, when the tide drops to the point of low slack tide, all the food washed back is concentrated in the area just below the low water limit. During the low water slack, the washed back food will often cause good bites to continue just below the low water limit.

The bite is slow on the fast rising tide in this region because the tide penetrates miles inland, which requires fish to swim long distances to the ambush points where they customarily feed as the tide falls. Seemingly resident fish are slavish to the routine.

A unique but similar series of feeding events occurs along most stretches of intertidal coastline of every ocean every day. Predator fish are attracted to the thousands of crustacean species, e.g., shrimp, crabs, and baitfish that inhabit, roam, or drift into the unique coastal habitats throughout the great saltwater system covering the globe. They're attracted because of the potential for food and reproduction, two of the same elements that control organisms in freshwater.

Tides, ocean currents, and weather systems generally provide an abundance of plankton species for crustaceans and baitfish to thrive upon in the intertidal zone, which keeps predators in the vicinity. The abundance and availability of such food, however, may fluctuate with the seasons causing better fishing opportunities at different times of the year. When the organisms do become abundant, predator fish make their first appearances and descend on them, often in hoards, creating great bites.

Fourteen Day Limit

The date of their first appearances will vary from year to year, but will normally occur within **14 days** *before or after* a certain date. It could be within as little as one day or as many as 14, but it's usually five days or less. This is an important parameter, but I'm not sure what regulates it. My best guess (you may have a better one) is that there is a relationship with the time required for the Moon to orbit the Earth, which is approximately 27.3 days. Half that time is about 14 days, during which a full moon or new moon, or both will occur. Perhaps organisms are synchronizing with one of these moon events.

A preponderance of data that I've encountered in my lifetime seems to support the fact that natural sequence events recur every year within 14 days of certain dates. For example, if a fish spawns on May 1st one year, then May 1st is within 14 days of the average date that this particular fish will always spawn. The same rule applies to wildflowers blossoming, stages of tree foliation and defoliation, bird migrations, insect hatches, and all other natural events used as periodic indicators (For exceptions, see Chapter 2, How Sequences Unfold). Numerous years of data collection are usually necessary to discover the pivotal average date (expected date) on which each fish species spawn.

Recall that these events unfold in a reliably predictable manner because the orbit of the Earth around the Sun follows the same approximate and predictable path every day of every year. It's the steady orbit that exposes the Earth to approximately the same annual degree-day absorption that causes the same conditions to recur year after year, on or near the same date.

An example of the 14 day limit and annual timing attributed to the Moon occurs every spring in Raritan Bay off the coast of New Jersey and Staten Island, New York. Striped bass and bluefish fishermen there are familiar with the annual sequence of fish appearances that occur along the Jersey shore from south to north.

In the spring, as waters warm to 50-55 degrees F from south to north, baitfish such as alewives, blue back herring, and mackerel appear along the coast of southern New Jersey. As the warm water temperature advances northward, the baitfish also work their way north. Alewives and herring are there to spawn, but the mackerel are just advancing north-ward in pursuit of cooler water, and the bluefish are following them. When the 50-55 degree F water temperature reaches Raritan Bay, it's usually very near Mother's Day in early May, for which the locals have an adage: "Bluefish are in Raritan Bay by Mother's Day."

Not only are bluefish chasing bait in the bay, but resident striped bass are right on their heels, as are weakfish, and a vigorous seasonal bite ensues for weeks beyond Mother's Day. The predator fish hang around the shallow intertidal zone because the spawning alewives and herring move into rivers, bays, and lakes fed by freshwater. Herring are generally regarded to stage at sea and move onto the spawning grounds, en masse, near the time of the new moon or full moon nearest Mother's Day. Food for the predators is then extremely abundant, and fishing action can be fast every day. Because it's a bite that lasts for weeks, another adage could apply: "The height of the bite occurs before the full moon of June." Locally, it's felt that this fishing situation is clearly defined and well understood.

Remarkably, the herring spawning time is correlated to the timing of three different events — the new moon, the full moon, and Mother's Day.

Mother's Day in the USA always occurs on the second Sunday of May, so its calendar date can only vary by 3½ days, earlier or later. It will always occur on or between the 8th and 14th of May. The dates of the new moon and full moon wander around on the calendar by as much as two weeks (1/2 of the 27.3 day orbit), but either the new moon or full moon will always occur within a week of Mother's Day. It appears that Mother's Day is always the pivotal date and serious spawning will normally com-mence near the highest tide on either side of Mother's Day. It could be as much as a week before or a week after, but usually less in most years. The timing of the bite appears to be predictable, almost to the day every year. If local predictions based on the Moon are correct, you might be able to plan a fishing trip, years ahead, and hit a good bite.

I am suspicious, however, of claims of herring spawning near the new moon. The dark, new moon period may actually reduce herring spawning activity instead of facilitate it. I could be wrong, but my suspi-cions are based on the effects of melatonin on spawning as discussed near the end of this chapter.

Wind and Barometric Pressure Effects on Tides and Bites

The Moon is not the only influence on tides; wind and barometric pressure are also significant influences. Your fishing trips will be far more efficient and productive if you know how wind and barometric pressure affect the tides. You'll have a far better grasp of where to position yourself in the intertidal zone, and know the better times to be there.

Recall from Chapter 10 in the discussion of the world's largest lakes: When low barometric pressure systems and high barometric pressure systems exist over the same body of water, each will have a different effect on the water level. Low barometric pressure will cause a swell of water under it — the water level rises. High barometric pressure has the opposite effect; it pushes the water level lower. The exact same effects occur in the oceans and experienced sailors are familiar with them. They know that water rises and is deeper in shallow passages when barometric pressure is low. It facilitates safer sailing through the shallows. They also know to avoid certain routes during high pressure which creates shallow water, lest their keels will run aground.

Accordingly, high and low barometric pressure can each have dramatic affects on the level of the tides, and where you should anticipate the bite on the intertidal zone. The differences in tide levels due to high or low barometric pressure, and wind, are illustrated in Figure 11-2 through Figure 11-6. Fish symbols represent where to anticipate the bite. (Reminder: Standard barometric pressure at sea level is 29.92 in.Hg (inches of mercury) when the air temperature at sea level is 59 degrees F. Pressures below 29.92 are deemed low pressure; pressures above 29.92 are deemed high pressure.)

When the tide comes in and reaches high slack tide, the water will normally stop rising at that level. If barometric pressure is low and overspreads the region, a swell will form under it and the height of the swell will be added to the level of the high tide. The high tide will then consist of the normal high tide plus the height of the swell from the low barometric pressure as depicted in Figure 11-2. The added height of the swell will depend on how low the barometric pressure is — the lower the pressure, the higher the swell.

Consequences of the higher tide that includes the swell would be deeper flooding that flows farther inland, and faster current when the tide comes in and goes out. This would affect where a fisherman would best position himself to take advantage of the higher water. The bite on the high slack tide or receding tide may shift further inland, but he can anticipate it and be ready for it. This is an important advantage where the intertidal zone is miles wide because high slack tide doesn't last long, only a matter of minutes. **Warning: *Positioning yourself in front of, or in, a moving tide should be done with extreme caution and only after sufficient preparations are in place for your safety.***

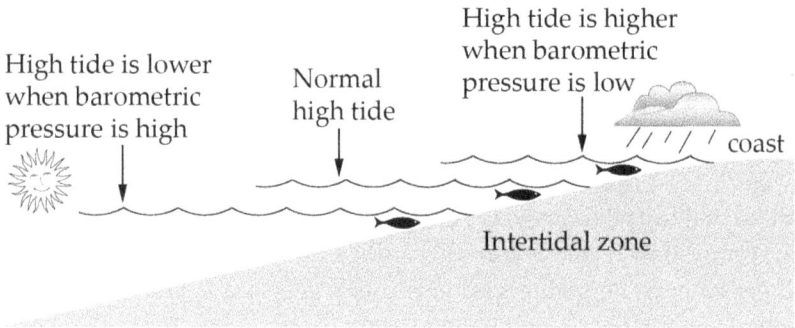

High tide is lower when barometric pressure is high

Normal high tide

High tide is higher when barometric pressure is low

coast

Intertidal zone

Figure 11-2

High barometric pressure has the opposite effect; it causes the water level to drop. The result: High tide is forced to a lower level.

The constant multitude of weather systems over the oceans guarantees a unique situation with respect to barometric pressure: High pressure lowers the water level, and low pressure raises it. They're always interacting and causing a seesaw effect on the water level in all locations. Fortunately for fishermen, behavior of the water under each system is predictable.

Knowing how barometric pressure affects tide levels is important for every fisherman who's trying to understand his fishing circumstances. It's also important to understand the effects of wind on tide levels. In big saltwater, barometric pressure and wind are inseparable bedfellows.

Figure 11-3 illustrates how wind can affect the level of high tide, which also has the same effect on low tide.

When wind is not blowing, the tide will come in at its normally expected level, as shown at **A**. If there is a wind, however, and it's blowing toward shore as shown at **B**, it will force more water from the open ocean toward shore and pile it up higher against the shore on top of the regular tide. The effect will look and behave like a higher-than-expected tide, but

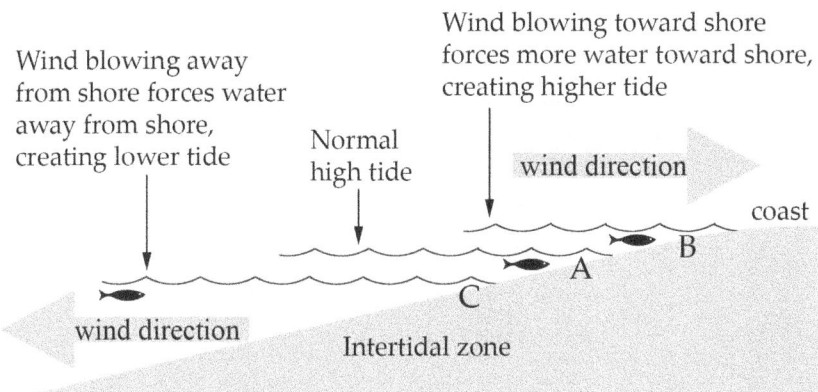

Wind blowing away from shore forces water away from shore, creating lower tide

Normal high tide

Wind blowing toward shore forces more water toward shore, creating higher tide

wind direction

coast

B

A

C

wind direction

Intertidal zone

Figure 11-3

it's simply a combination of normal tide and water forced toward shore by the wind. A preponderance of plankton would also be blown toward shore, normally causing a good bite near shore.

The opposite effect occurs when the wind is blowing offshore toward the ocean as shown at **C**.

The high tide will ordinarily come in as shown at **A**. When the wind is blowing offshore toward the ocean as shown at **C**, it will blow part of the incoming tide back toward the sea. The result is what appears to be a lower tide. In reality, it's a normal tide that has had some of its volume stripped away by an offshore wind. Depending on location and wind velocity, it's possible that an entire tide can be driven back to the sea. Steady high winds can drive the tide and even more of the sea further from land.

Notice that the fish symbol at **C** is far from the intertidal zone. Wind blowing away from land blows a preponderance of plankton away from the intertidal zone, often causing a very slow bite near shore because baitfish follow the plankton offshore. There is a bite, but it's farther out to sea, perhaps miles at times.

In summary, the tide will be higher if the barometric pressure is low and wind is blowing toward shore, but lower if the wind is blowing toward the ocean, blowing the plankton out to sea or closer to shore — and the bite follows the windblown plankton. Keeping logs of the wind speeds and directions will eventually reveal how much higher or lower the tide level will be during specific wind conditions.

Figure 11-4 depicts a more realistic scenario that includes tide, wind,

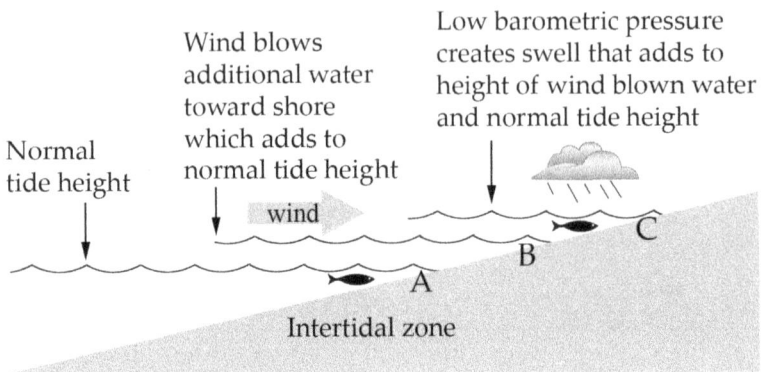

Figure 11-4

barometric pressure, and how they interact to create elevated tide levels.

Normal tide height is shown at **A**. Wind blowing toward shore forces more water toward shore and piles it on top of the normal tide as shown at **B**. Low barometric pressure then causes the tide and wind driven water to swell under it, which raises the water level still higher, as shown at **C**. In this circumstance, wind and low barometric pressure each added more height to the tide. The bite is then at **C**.

This becomes a quite different circumstance if the wind is blowing toward the ocean (not shown). The wind would strip water off the normal tide height and blow it back toward the ocean, so the normal tide height would be lower than expected. However, low barometric pressure would cause the lower than expected normal tide to swell, and the swell could raise the tide so it's near the normal level again. To an unwitting observer, it would appear that the normal expected tide level is normal, and is unaffected by the wind or low barometric pressure, which is not the case.

Predictions of realistic tide height should always include the expected tide height, and the effects of wind, and barometric pressure. Only good logs can provide the necessary information; there is no substitute.

Afternoon Heating Effects on Bite Location

A situation that occurs frequently during summer afternoons is illustrated in Figure 11-5.

Imagine a clear, warm sunny day at the coast with a cool breeze coming at you from the ocean. It's a "bluebird" day, typically produced by

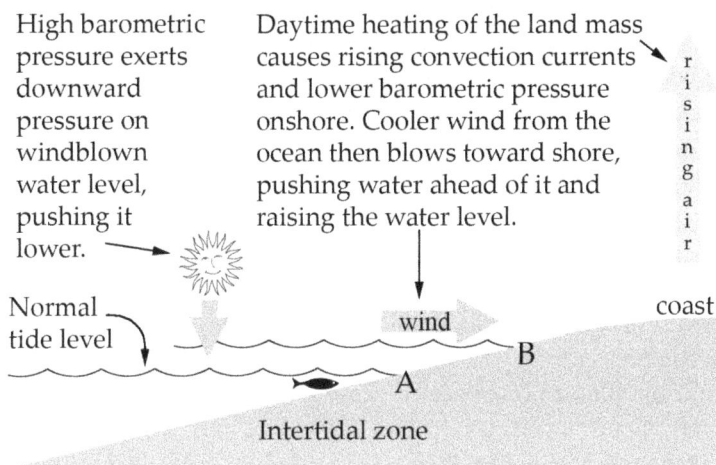

High barometric pressure exerts downward pressure on windblown water level, pushing it lower.

Daytime heating of the land mass causes rising convection currents and lower barometric pressure onshore. Cooler wind from the ocean then blows toward shore, pushing water ahead of it and raising the water level.

rising air

Normal tide level

wind

B

coast

A

Intertidal zone

Figure 11-5

high barometric pressure.

The summer sun heats the land which then heats the air over the land, causing the overland air to rise. The rising air is known as convection current. As the warm air over the land rises, other air moves in to take its place near the ground. The other air is cool air that migrates from the surface of the ocean. The cooler air is heavier so it stays near the ground until it, too, is heated and rises in the continuing cycle. The cooler air is felt onshore near the surface as a cool ocean breeze. The breeze will continue to blow as long as the warm convection current continues to rise, which is frequently most of the day. The continuous breeze pushes water toward shore, raising the water level accordingly.

If an incoming tide occurs during the daytime heating period, as shown at **A**, its level would be raised by the breeze as shown at **B**. The higher water level, however, may never actually occur or be observable because of the existing high barometric pressure. Even though the breeze acts to raise the water level, the high barometric pressure pushes downward on the water and may completely counteract the effects of the wind on the water level. The high pressure may offset any rise caused by the wind. The normal tide level may remain unchanged or close to it because of the interaction of the breeze and high barometric pressure. The level may even be lower than normal, depending on the velocity of the breeze or the level of the high barometric pressure. Once again, only good logs can ultimately foretell how high or low the tide level will be in the presence of certain winds and barometric pressures, and where the bite will be localized because of where the water stops rising, and plankton drift.

This set of conditions occurs near coastlines across the globe nearly every day, and often produces thunderstorms. The storms are frequently the type referenced in Chapter 9 as single cell, pulse, local, or popcorn storms. "Popcorn" is an apropos description because, at the time the storms are occurring or just preceding them, the sky is liberally populated with clouds resembling individual, popped kernels of corn. The associated barometric pressure drop is only a few points of short duration, and very local, having almost no impact on water level or a bite.

Plankton Moves the Bite

Figure 11-6 is the identical situation depicted in Figure 11-5, except the wind is blowing toward the ocean instead of toward land. The normal tide height is shown at **A**, but wind blows some of the tide back to sea and lowers the water level as shown at **B**. High barometric pressure lowers the water level still further as shown at **C**. Depending on location, the distance from **A** to **C** can be minimal to perhaps miles.

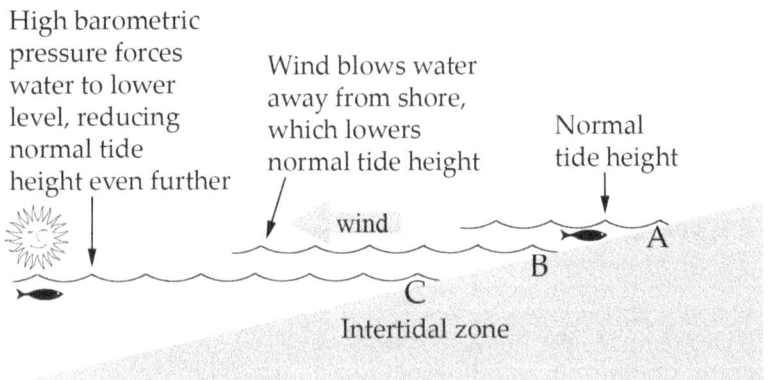

High barometric
pressure forces
water to lower   Wind blows water
level, reducing   away from shore,
normal tide   which lowers   Normal
height even further   normal tide height   tide height

wind

A

B

C

Intertidal zone

Figure 11-6

Notice that the fish symbol at **C** is once again far out to sea. Wind blowing away from land has blown plankton away from the intertidal zone, causing a slow bite near shore because baitfish followed the plankton. A better bite is farther offshore.

The bite may also suffer when wind blows parallel to the intertidal zone. It may blow the plankton farther down the shoreline from your location. You may need to relocate to the farthest downwind location possible, to where the shoreline becomes more perpendicular to the wind and traps the windblown plankton.

Recognizing Spring or Neap Tide

Figure 11-7 depicts the two high tides, called spring tide and neap tide that occur every day in most places. They occur about 50 minutes later on each successive day. I've included them because they are seldom at the same level. Spring tide is always as high or higher than neap tide even though both are high tides that always occur on the same day (approx. 25 hour period). In practical terms, if you fish a high tide in the morning, don't expect the high tide in the evening to rise to the same level; it will be higher or lower, depending on whether the morning tide was a spring or neap.

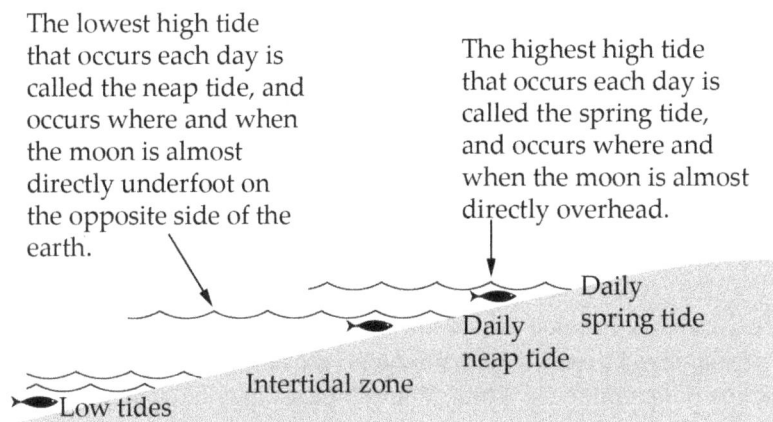

The lowest high tide that occurs each day is called the neap tide, and occurs where and when the moon is almost directly underfoot on the opposite side of the earth.

The highest high tide that occurs each day is called the spring tide, and occurs where and when the moon is almost directly overhead.

Daily spring tide

Daily neap tide

Intertidal zone

Low tides

Figure 11-7

Both are easy to identify while on the water. Spring tides, the highest high tides, occur when the Moon is in the sky on your side of the planet. In other words, if you can see the Moon, you'll experience a spring tide. The Moon's gravitational tug is greater because it's closer to you, so it pulls the tide higher. If you can't see the Moon because it's on the other side of the planet, you'll experience a neap tide, the lower high tide. The low tides will also recede to different levels. Position yourself accordingly in the intertidal zone for the ensuing bite.

Where to Take Water Temperature

Predicting the spring bite in Raritan Bay looks like it could also be accomplished by simply checking the water temperature during the appropriate time of year, but that's not a simple proposition. The trick lies in when and where the temperature is taken.

During daylight when the tide comes in, it's bringing cold sea water into the intertidal zone over a period of about six hours. During the six hours, the cold water floods into many different areas which are relatively shallow, and begins to warm up from solar radiation. This is especially true where the bottom is dark, which absorbs heat at a faster rate, and therefore heats the water faster. The result is that the outgoing tidewater is warmer than the water that came in, and warmer than the deeper water in the intertidal zone. There can be a significant temperature difference in different locations in the zone. Temperature samples would also be different, usually lower, if taken at night. Which temperature, at which location, at which time, is the one you want?

Water temperature could also be affected by rain or runoff into streams draining into the bay. The entire bay may not be affected, but some areas of it might be.

Wind is another factor affecting temperature. Cold breezes and overcast skies can keep shallow tidewater cooler than expected, especially at night if conditions persist through the entire tide cycle. When the cooler falling tide recedes back to the low water limit, the water below the low water limit may become even cooler when it mixes with the receding water. It may then be so chilled that it repels the baitfish sought by predators, which is unfavorable for a bite. Warm breezes may have the opposite effect, creating conditions that attract fish to the intertidal zone. It makes most of the aquatic food web more metabolically active, which normally results in a better bite.

In spring, areas within the intertidal zone with dark, muddy bottoms are often the first areas during the season to attract fish because the sun warms them first. Dark bottoms absorb heat faster. They also attract fish longer in the fall because they continue to absorb more heat as the surrounding areas begin to cool. Muddy bottoms also host far more food organisms than sandy areas.

Also, there are select areas in intertidal zones in which certain fish species prefer to spawn or patrol, each according to its needs. The areas are not all created equal. It's in the select areas that the species will be found from day to day, or year to year. When you become familiar with the select areas, the next step is to obtain the water temperature when the target fish or their baitfish have finally arrived. Obtaining temperatures, however, can be very difficult, but it's not the only option.

The temperature should be sampled where fish are swimming in the slack water near the high water limit, and in the nearest slack water below the low water limit, which may be too difficult in many locations. Ideally, the two temperature samples should be obtained within the same tide cycle, and repeated every day at the same location and time, and logged for the duration of the presence of the target fish. Sampling every two or three days would probably suffice. Alternative sampling patterns may be more effective in some areas.

The samples will yield an accurate and invaluable temperature pattern for predicting the appearances of the target species in years to come. One season of samples may be all that's necessary for a lifetime of fairly accurate predictions. Your immediate benefit will be far less time and money wasted on unproductive fishing excursions for the remainder of your lifetime. You'll know when to go fishing and when to stay home — but the catch is that someone must still obtain the temperatures.

Alternative to Temperature Sampling

If obtaining temperature samples is too difficult, an alternative is to rely on a local botanical indicator, which is something you should do anyway. Find a plant in the nearby area that's in a certain stage of budding, bloom, leaf growth, or seed development when the fish are in. Roadside wildflowers (weeds) and deciduous trees and shrubs near your home, even if located several miles from the seashore, are very good for this purpose. Select plants that will be in the same place every year, and those that go through the same annual stages. Recall from Chapter 2 that fishermen on Long Island, New York, know the local weakfish bite occurs when their French lilacs are in bloom. Botanicals are most reliable if located within ten miles north or south of where you're going to fish, and grow in the same place every year (recall the dormancy and re-emergence rates from Chapter 2). In subsequent years, it's advisable to identify botanicals that precede and follow your primary indicator. They will alert you to the upcoming event or inform you that you've missed it because your life became too busy.

If botanical indicators are unavailable, fish behavior can be correlated with any other natural sequence events that occur either onshore, in the water, celestially, or in any combination of the three. Examples might include bird nesting or migration, insect hatches, frogs singing, turtles nesting, or constellation positions in the night sky, to mention a few. There is always something that can be used. Saltwater fish, much like freshwater fish, predictably eat and spawn at certain times in known locations throughout the year. Sequential indicators can flag when those events occur.

Full Moon for a Full Catch of Flounder

As insinuated previously, the Moon appears to act as a timing marker that helps to facilitate spawning in salt water. An example of this timing occurs every fall in the Gulf of Mexico along the Louisiana coast.

When the moon is full in Late November or early December, great numbers of large, female southern flounders migrate from the inshore estuaries and rivers to offshore waters to spawn. They're locally known as doormat flounders because they're about the size of household doormats. The considerably smaller male flounders, which behave much like a separately distinct species, reside in the offshore water year-round. Neighborhood fishermen prefer to catch the doormat females. They've learned they will catch prodigious amounts of doormats on the day before, the day of and the day after the full moon. They anticipate those three days every year because the doormats are consistently caught on those days. The full moon tells them exactly when to be there. The correlation is well known in that vicinity.

Tide Destroys Ableness as a Prediction Tool

Tides have an obvious rhythm associated with the Moon, but they also create a rhythm that's easily overlooked: The constantly changing tide creates a constantly changing rhythm of total-pressure. When tide is low, total-pressure is low; when tide is high, total-pressure is high. This changing rhythm of total-pressure is perfectly synchronized with the flow of the tide. It changes from maximum to minimum every 12.5 hours over most of the intertidal zone. It's the saltwater version of the freshwater training phenomenon explained in Chapter 7. Crustaceans in the intertidal zone are certainly affected by it, and the high and low pressure rules still apply, but determining it's affect on fishing success is daunting and impractical. (Sidebar #25: No Insects)

The next three paragraphs describe the complicated conditions created by tide that eliminate the state of ableness as a bite prediction tool in the intertidal zone.

As tide rhythmically ebbs and flows twice over the intertidal zone in a 25 hour period (approx. one day), two things happen: (1) Water covers the lowest part of the zone for a longer period than it covers the uppermost part. The lowest part is covered with deeper water for approximately 22 hours per day, whereas the uppermost part is covered with shallower water for approximately just 2 hours per day. (2) Because of the water depths, the lowest part of the zone experiences much higher total-pressure for about 22 hours per day, but the uppermost part experiences only slightly higher total-pressure for approximately 2 hours per day. This pattern of disparity of total-pressure occurs at every point on the slope of the intertidal zone. While the tide is moving, total-pressure is changing constantly. The moving water creates a constantly fluctuating total-pressure gradient that is different at different times for all points on the intertidal zone. It's a nightmare for anyone trying to measure it.

Total-pressure is the essential factor here. It oscillates up and down, much like the training effect discussed in Chapter 7. Each point on the

---

#25

No Insects

The saltwater discussion in this chapter is directed more toward crustaceans than insects because only a rare few insects occupy the oceans. A rare few also occupy brackish water and saltwater marshes. I'm not aware that any are well understood sources of fish food that could be used to predict a bite. The dearth of insects is reflected in the absence of insect patterns used by fly fishermen in saltwater. Saltwater fly patterns for baitfish, worms, and crustaceans are common, but I'm not aware of any patterns that imitate saltwater insects.

slope of the zone experiences a different daily amount of total-pressure, and each point experiences it for a different amount of time. Therefore, crustaceans dwelling at different points on the zone will experience different amounts of total-pressure for different amounts of time. These differences will then have different influences on the state of ableness in each crustacean at all points up and down the zone. Tides and total-pressure are also different during every cycle, which complicates the matter. Wind speed and direction are also factors because they control how much additional water gets piled up or how low the water level becomes when driven offshore.

Under such circumstances, it's basically impossible for anglers to predict when molting will occur and cause crustaceans to become more active and available as fish food. There is just too much total-pressure variability that occurs too frequently at too many points over the distance of the zone's slope. Thus, even though the state of ableness is still in play, it's not a practical paradigm for predicting daily bites in the intertidal zone.

Despite the loss of the state of ableness as a predictive tool, barometric pressure patterns may still be useful. Extended periods of steady barometric pressure, either high or low, and steady winds which yield steady total-pressure, may result in periods of steady molting that induce more vigorous feeding by predators in the zone. The weather pattern for a better bite may simply be an extended period (days) of the same kind of weather, either inclement or fair, without any significant changes in water temperature or wind.

Additional Saltwater Tips

Intertidal zones are very diverse and cause fish to behave in ways that are most advantageous for their survival. The bite of one species may occur during a different part of the tide cycle and in a different place than it occurs for another species. Local knowledge is paramount for best success. If you intend to fish an unfamiliar location, a few questions asked at the local fishing tackle shop should avail you with useful advice. Hiring a guide could be best.

In select locations, good bites occur just as high tide is going slack. The reason may be that fish must then swim around more actively to move water over their gills to absorb more oxygen, and their movement incidentally causes them to encounter more food to eat.

According to some fishermen on the east coast of the United States, one of the most productive bites occurs when high tide slithers in at the break of daylight in morning. Fish swim into eelgrass patches which contain abundant grass shrimp and various crab species.

Good bites are more commonly experienced when the tide is moving, either in or out. *Out* seems to gather more support than *in*, although that may change by location and species. Reports from fishermen I've consulted indicate the bite is often better at the beginning of an ebbing (incoming) tide, perhaps because fish are hungrier earlier during the tide than later after they've been feeding for a while. The lowest topography such as troughs, cuts, canals, and ditches are where the best currents are located, which makes them premium feeding locations for predators. They are among the best fishing locations and easily located by watching where the tidewater is first to enter or last to drain out. Larger fish may not feed any longer than smaller fish because they may aggressively take the best feeding lanes where food is more plentiful and easier to catch.

Freshwater

The Moon's effects on freshwater fishing are far less understood than it's effects on intertidal saltwater fishing. Tide in freshwater is generally extremely small and inconsequential unless it's coming in from the ocean. There is no model of moon behavior in freshwater fishing as well proven as the tide model for fishing in saltwater. Contemporary Sun and Moon charts are no exception. There seems to be few certain instances when the Moon is undoubtedly influential in the behavior of a freshwater bite.

Three Influences on the Bite

I know of only three circumstances in which the Moon influences the bite, and all involve a bright moon. There are probably others.

The first circumstance is one that charter captains and recreational fishermen are subject to on the Great Lakes, particularly during salmon migrations in August and September. When the Moon is bright, especially during the full moon and a couple days before and after it, fishing success in the morning becomes marginal, and often totally frustrating. Generally, there is no significant bite during those mornings. The reason given by fishermen is that the moonlight is so bright that fish can see the forage and feed on it through the night. By the time morning arrives, the fish are sated and have temporarily lost their appetite. This frustrating behavior occurs repeatedly during the bright period of every full moon.

The second circumstance involves my own personal experiences while trout fishing at night (legal in Michigan). I spent a couple decades fishing 30 to 35 consecutive nights each year trying to catch trophy brown trout during the hexagenia limbata mayfly hatches occurring in late June and early July. The hatches normally commenced during late dusk and continued for about an hour or so, which usually meant well into darkness. When the hatches quit, however, a new challenge was afoot. Trophy brown trout were still receptive to artificial fly offerings in the hour after the fly hatches were done, but only in certain places.

I usually caught nice fish in spots that the fish normally occupied, but almost never caught anything when the Moon was bright. When it was bright, no matter its phase, the bite seemed to go dead in most of the water. Eventually the reason became apparent: The trout were avoiding direct moonlight. If they weren't avoiding it, they surely weren't biting in it. The only bites I could get were in shaded locations where fish could not see the Moon. As the Moon continued to rise, fewer locations remained in shade and fish seemed to move to them and were still prone to bite if they were in them. As far as I could tell, they kept to the shaded side of the river, or moved to a shaded bend. In summary, when the Moon was up, they stayed out of its shine. After realizing this behavior, I concentrated my efforts on shaded areas not exposed to moonbeams and again began catching better fish.

A third set of circumstances in which the Moon may influence the bite also occur at night.

Night-feeding predators such as burbot and walleyes may tend to feed more actively at night when the moon is a little brighter because it illuminates their prey. They can see it to catch it. The heavier night-feeding would likely result in fewer fish caught during daylight hours.

Conversely, night-feeding activity would be reduced during the darkest nights near the new moon (no moon) period, resulting in better daylight catches. Fishing success may be particularly good near dawn because many hours will have passed since the fish were last able to see food well enough to catch it.

An active feeding period may also occur just as the Moon rises several hours after sunset, which means after a very dark period of several hours, especially if the sky is overcast. It's likely that fish will not have fed during the darkest period, but may become active when prompted by the earliest moonlight. It seems that the longer the period of darkness, the more active the fish would become when moonlight finally illuminates the water. Planning to fish at the crack of moonrise after long periods of darkness may be a profitable strategy.

Check the United States Naval Observatory website at www.usno. navy.mil for complete sun and moon data.

Sun and Moon Charts

Do fish bite at certain times in freshwater because of the Moon; does the Moon trigger them to bite? I will argue that the Moon almost never triggers them to bite. The Moon's light may extend or facilitate nocturnal activity, but, does the heavenly body itself, without the light, cause a bite? Not that I can find evidence to support. When the nightly moon is bright, fish may feed a little more because they can still see their prey, but shining a bright light over the water would accomplish the same thing. Light from either source could be dimmed and nullified by heavy overcast, which would end feeding attributed to the elevated light level. What other effect may the Moon then have? I know of none supported with good empirical data.

Do fish bite vigorously during the times posted as peak fishing times on Sun and Moon charts? Yes they do, and they do it a lot, but again I argue it's not primarily because of the Moon.

Do good bites coincide with times when the Moon is directly overhead or directly underfoot on the opposite side of the Earth? Yes, they surely do, but again I posit that the bites almost never occur because of the Moon.

Belief that freshwater bites are caused by the Moon requires something akin to blind faith. I have never encountered a testable method that could even remotely prove that bites in freshwater are caused by the Moon — other than moonlight enabling a bite at night, or possibly being a factor in spawning timing. I'm flabbergasted that so many fishermen place so much faith in the moon-bite principle, which is supported mostly by conjecture and riddled with shortcomings. To me, it's a principle that only a politician could love.

Sun and Moon charts assert that the best chances for good fishing correspond with the major and minor time periods on the charts. The times are calculated based on the positions of the Sun and Moon in relation to the Earth, and closely correspond to tide times. Supposedly, the best fishing probability is during the two major times, and the next best probability is during the two minor times. Approximately two major times and two minor times occur every day (approx. every 25 hours). The major times are separated by the minor times, and one or the other occur approximately every 6¼ hours. Major periods are said to last about two hours, and minor periods about one hour. The times advance about 50 minutes every day; for example if a major time is at 6 p.m. today, it will be at about 6:50 p.m. tomorrow.

I've read countless anecdotal stories by fishermen who claimed they had sensational fishing success during the exact time periods that the charts predicted. I'm confident that many of those stories are true. It's also true that catching fish during many major and minor periods almost cannot be avoided!

If a major/minor period lasts one-to-two hours, and it occurs during the preferred molting/hatching time of an aquatic insect, the bite could be terrific and the angler might be very successful. If the insects are hatching every day during a certain period, and if the major/minor time period keeps advancing by 50 minutes every day, the two will undoubtedly intersect; and, in the case of a two-hour major period, they could intersect up to three days in a row; and a few days later the intersection could happen with a one-hour minor period that might occur for two days in a row, and so it goes, repeatedly. Numerous molts and hatches occur on most days during the comfortable weather portion of the fishing season, so the intersection of chart times and molts/hatches is inevitable almost every day. When they intersect and a fisherman is successful, it's a short leap for him to assume that the chart's predictions were dead-on correct. Unfortunately, the chart times have only created an illusion that could lead to frequent disappointment for the angler.

Some of the published testimonials, drawn upon to support the validity of the charts, create the impression that fish are slavish to the influence of the Sun and Moon. They imply that a fisherman can reasonably expect the entire fish population to be aroused, active, and will eat something if the opportunity arises. This notion fails miserably in the face of reality.

If fish behave as slaves to the times on the charts, and in the manner implied in the testimonials, then they should be aroused, active, and seriously predatory during every major and minor period that occurs every day; which means this activity should occur about four times every day with no exceptions. The charts and testimonials have been used to persuade anglers that this is true.

To the contrary, however, many clear-thinking fishermen are convinced it's not true. Their skepticism is best represented by tournament fishermen, especially those seeking largemouth bass and walleyes, who have spent many agonizingly difficult days on the water trying to catch a couple fish. These are expert fishermen who sometimes catch little or nothing during an entire day of strenuous, high-intensity fishing. It's not unusual for them to go two or three days in a row with marginal success. If the fish were aroused, active, and seriously predatory four times per day, these fishermen should have had far better success. Average fishermen have even more days when fishing is a struggle than days when they catch lots of fish. Most fishermen will tell you that great fishing days only happen occasionally, and those are the days that keep them coming back, hoping to someday have another day like it. I doubt you could find a sane fisherman on the planet who would tell you that great fishing happens every 6¼ hours in freshwater.

Most fishermen are clever and quick enough to adopt a fishing system that pays big dividends if it works. If, as implied by the charts, fish suddenly become active and feed at four specific times every day, fishermen would soon crowd the waters at those times and abandon fishing at other times. If the expectations inferred from the charts became reality, fish populations would be decimated in short order. It hasn't happened.

The first charts were introduced around the year 1935, over 70 years ago. That seems like plenty of time for a fishing system to prove itself and convert most skeptics into believers, but that hasn't happened either.

I suspect that most fishermen are not aware that the charts have always been saddled with *caveat emptor* (buyer beware) warnings. Knowledge of the warnings seems to have evaporated over the decades.

When the charts were first introduced, the public was told that the timing of bite activity could change due to adverse temperature, low water, high water, unsettled barometric conditions, and other factors (unnamed) that were not revealed. We were also told that weather and feeding conditions must be favorable, but the specifics of "favorable" were never cited; and individual fish may not be affected, only schools. How can a thinking fisherman place his trust in a system like that? Drawing on an old saw, "It's like trusting a lucky rabbit's foot while ignoring the unfortunate luck of the rabbit!"

Avid fishermen are familiar with the frustrating fishing that follows a strong cold front. It's not uncommon for fishing success to come to a near halt for two or three days in a row. During this slow fishing period, eight to twelve consecutive major/minor periods can cycle through without any evidence that they improved the fishing. Yet a large number of fishermen seem to prefer believing the anecdotal evidence in great fishing stories, rather than challenging the foundations and veracity of Sun and Moon charts.

In the spirit of fairness, the best thing about fishing is that it's fun. I can only guess that, for some fishermen, it's more fun to fantasize about catching more fish with a fairy-godmother-like system than dwelling on the poor fishing days that we'd all rather forget.

Full Moon as a Spawning Timer

The Moon's influence on day-to-day fish activity may not be a reliable factor, but there is an abundance of anecdotal evidence that suggests spawning activity of many fish species occurs near the time of a full moon. This is a completely different situation than the Moon's gravitational influence on daily activity as implied by Sun and Moon charts.

I have never found any scientific or anecdotal evidence demonstrating that fish go through any significant physiological changes during the changing tides each day. I also don't know of any biological mechanism that might support claims that the Moon causes fish to bite four times per day. They might exist, but I'm not aware of any. Conversely, there is a mechanism that supports the concept that the Moon influences the timing of spawning.

In the simplest of terms, it involves the fish's eye and brain. The retina of the eye receives light which then activates light sensitive cells in the pineal gland which is located near the center of the brain. The pineal gland controls production of the hormone melatonin, which is linked to sleep/wakefulness cycles and sexual development. Light entering the eye signals the pineal gland to make more melatonin, or make less, depending on how much light is present. Melatonin increases during times of darkness and encourages sleep, but decreases as light gets brighter, which causes more wakefulness and activity. In a nutshell, this mechanism makes non-mammalian vertebrates (which include fish) less active in darkness, but more active in light. In addition, melatonin is thought to suppress sexual development. If it does, then sexual development is suppressed less in the

244

brighter light of a full moon. This would favor sexual maturity and spawning during the brighter periods of full moons.

The fact that fish consistently spawn during the same time periods every year, for example in late spring, is evidence that some mechanism in the fish is controlling when spawning will occur. The mechanism may be completely internal, or one that responds to something in the external environment. It appears that it's partly both.

It must be both because fish don't spawn on every full moon. They reputedly only spawn during a specific full moon at a certain time of the year. So, how does a fish know what time of year is the right time, and which full moon is the right one?

A possible answer is that its biological clock recognizes the length of the daily photoperiod. Recognizing the length of the photoperiod, however, is not the complete answer because the length of photoperiods occurring in spring will also occur in fall. Every photoperiod, except the shortest one and longest one, occurs twice per year. For example, a photoperiod of a particular duration will occur between December and June when days are getting progressively longer; and its counterpart of the same duration will occur between June and December when days are getting progressively shorter.

The same problem occurs with water temperature: For example, fish may spawn when water temperature rises to 60 degrees F in spring, but the temperature also falls to 60 degrees F in fall. Based on temperature, how does the fish decide whether it should spawn in spring or fall?

A biological clock must be the answer because fish must spawn when their eggs have the best chance to survive, and they do. Somehow, something is keeping track of the timing for favorable survival. One solution would be that the biological clock is counting the full moons and causing spawning 12 full moons apart.

This idea isn't so far fetched: Every year a majority of cliff swallows return to the Mission San Juan Capistrano in San Juan, California, on March 19, exactly 365 days from their return the previous year. How do they arrive at exactly 365, repeatedly? Could the 12 annual full moons be the natural sequence that the clock uses for timely spawning? Possibly, but the problem with counting every 12 full moons is that in some years there are 13 full moons (every 2.72 yrs). The extra moon, in some circles, is known as a blue moon. Obviously, the clock must somehow deal with the extra moon. Along with photoperiod and temperature, full moons must be considered as factors used by the biological clock to determine the correct time to spawn.

Our understanding of the Moon's influence on spawning is complicated further by common anecdotal accounts, which are confusing. Regarding largemouth bass, some fishermen claim that bass stop feeding three days before the full moon, which, supposedly, foretells the correct moon. Others say conditions must be right or bass will delay spawning until the next full moon. Others say peak spawning "nearly always" occurs during a full moon, which means "not always." When does it not? Still others insist if spawning doesn't occur during the full moon it will occur during the new moon. The new moon, however, is a dark period known to produce high melatonin levels, effectively blunting spawning activity. I also know fishermen who fish only during full moon periods, so their anecdotes are all based on results of fishing during full moons. Most are unremarkable. The inconsistencies are difficult to reconcile.

Still, much of the anecdotal evidence supporting the notion that spawning occurs during full moon periods seems too consistent to be coincidental. The possibilities require an open mind. I suspect there are places where local fishermen can reliably predict, in most years, when spawning events will occur under a full moon. I'm skeptical that anyone always gets it right, but I have little doubt that some have honed their intuition for predicting the spawn and the good bites that come with it. I don't say this without added basis, as shared below.

One of the strongest correlations between reproductive behavior and full moons that I'm aware of is described in a book by Dr. James Kroll and Ben H. Koerth, 1996, Solving the Mysteries of Deer Movement, Nacogdoches, Texas, USA, Stephen F. Austin State University. Kroll and Koerth are leading researchers in whitetail deer behavior. I've severely abridged their findings, perhaps to a fault, but you'll get the gist.

Their extensive studies revealed that most female whitetails, at my latitude, are prompted into estrus by the second full moon (beaver moon) after the harvest moon. Their internal chemical compounds responsible for estrus typically manifest their effects within a few days after the beaver moon. If the beaver moon was too many days removed from the traditional estrus date (November 15), estrus was generally less pronounced and dribbled over a longer period. Females that didn't come into estrus near the beaver moon typically went into estrus during the comparable period of the full moons that occurred just before or just after the beaver moon.

Blue moons are not a problem in this system. It's a remarkable correlation that I monitored for years and found valid on wild deer populations near my home.

If it's possible in deer, the odds may favor its possibility in fresh-water fish.

Chapter 12

Finding the Bite

This chapter explains how to use much of the information from previous chapters for successful fishing in freshwater, worldwide. The goal is to impart you with a well-honed ability to predict and find good bites, or, at the very least, provide you with a good reference for accurately predicting and locating good bites.

This is not a substitute for the comprehensive treatment of each topic in earlier chapters. It's a focused review of the primary factors already covered, and an *expansion* of some of the earlier concepts. It also includes ways to use the information that were not mentioned earlier. The full armament is then applied to rivers, small lakes, and reservoirs. Knowing how to use this information can put you on the most productive water at the most productive time. It's based on the premise that fish must eat, and they will move to the forage when it's available. Find the food and you'll find the fish. Other than spawning, the location of food is the major factor controlling most fish behavior.

If you're a recreational fisherman, it can help you catch far more fish than ever before. It's especially helpful if you're taking an extended fishing trip to new water. If you're a fishing guide or lodge owner you can use it to give your clients significantly better days on the water and your reputation will grow accordingly. If you're a tournament fisherman, expect to catch more fish because you'll understand far more about finding the bite, and your odds of winning prize money will increase. It's all made possible by a simple understanding of only four environmental factors needed for predicting most bites:

Water Temperature

Natural Sequences

Total-Pressure

Wind

Light level can also be important, but is usually mentioned or implied where needed, and requires little explanation.

Water Temperature

Water temperature gradually changes throughout the year in all water systems, whether rivers, lakes, or reservoirs, from coldest in winter to warmest in summer. Each system exerts its own unique influence on the temperature of the water it contains, thus no two systems behave exactly alike. For example, a river may have a fast flow that keeps its water cool, but a neighboring river may have reservoirs behind a series of dams that impede flow and allow more solar heating, resulting in much warmer water in various sections of the system. Rain and runoff may make either river cooler, although they can sometimes make them warmer. Cold rain in early spring or late fall may not affect water temperature much because water in lakes and streams is already cold. There are endless variations in all systems.

Altitude and Latitude

Altitude and latitude also influence water temperature. Lakes situated in low altitudes will warm faster and sooner in spring and remain warmer longer in fall than comparable lakes at higher altitude.

A similar progression of temperature change occurs from north to south and vice versa. Lakes in lower latitudes warm sooner in spring and stay warmer longer in fall. If the same lakes are located at higher latitudes, they will warm slower in spring and cool down faster in fall. This is addressed further in section Natural Sequences.

Stratification

Water temperature also varies from one depth to another in lakes because water has different densities at different temperatures. The warmest, less dense water is normally at the top of the water column, except when water is at 39 degrees F. Water is densest at 39 degrees F, so it's normally found at the bottom of the water column, and all warmer and colder water is found above it, with the warmest at the top unless it's ice, which floats. This arrangement of temperature layers (stratification) is normally present in lakes from sometime in spring to sometime in fall, but eventually yields to lake "turnover" by late fall in most places. Turnover results when temperature layers become fully mixed by wind action and colder autumn air. After turnover, but before freeze-up, water temperature is nearly uniform from top to bottom throughout the entire lake.

Dissolved Oxygen

As water becomes colder it also becomes capable of holding more dissolved oxygen. During the stressfully hot months of summer, colder water with higher oxygen will frequently harbor more fish, which means fish, and therefore the bite, will often be deeper. Conversely, oxygen often depletes at deepest depths under the ice as winter wears on, so fish may rise in the water column to access better oxygen availability in late winter.

Preferred Temperatures

Water temperature is also a major indicator for spawning events. Each fish species has a unique temperature range within which it spawns, and often has a singular, optimal temperature that occurs during the peak of its spawning activity. If you know the temperature range preferred by various species, you will know when to pursue them when they spawn.

In like manner, aquatic insect species also have preferred water temperatures and will hatch during periods when temperatures are optimal. Predicting the bite period, based on preferred hatch temperatures is a simple, straightforward technique commonly used by flyfishermen. Temperature also works in concert with total-pressure to influence the duration that aquatic insects and crustaceans remain in the state of ableness before molting or hatching (recall that a hatch is also a molt). Increased temperature reduces the time in ableness because the organisms get their required degree-days faster. Having a sense of the three to four day history of water temperature can be as important as knowing the history of total-pressure.

Although water temperature can create favorable conditions for a bite, it can also serve as a barrier to fish movement in rivers and lakes due to fish having preferences for certain temperatures. Despite their reluctance to leave the comfort of water at their preferred temperature, they may leave it often if their food is located in a different temperature zone. This is commonly the case during hatches and molts, which cause small predators to congregate, which then attract the larger predators from their haunts.

Sampling Water Temperature

The common-sense place to take water temperature is at the level in the water column that you expect your target fish to occupy, and in locations where you expect fish to be when the temperature reaches a certain value. For example, if fish normally spawn in a certain location every year, sample the water temperature in that location, but do so at the same depth that the fish normally occupy. If fish are suspending, measure the temperature at that level. This advice also applies to locations where aquatic insects hatch in lakes and streams. Measure the temperature where you expect the insects to appear, and at the depth fish normally occupy. In unimpeded rivers, for a given location, temperature measured anywhere in the main current is usually adequate for most purposes, although locations where current is significantly slower than the main current need to be temperature sampled separately. Samples should also be obtained at the same time of day, each day, for reliable predictions.

Air Temperature

And finally, I would be remiss not to mention that air temperature changes have very little immediate effect on fishing, with one notable exception — mating flights and egg laying by adult aquatic insects, especially mayfly spinner falls. If air temperature falls too low, it can make the adults too lethargic for normal activity, which kills the expected bite. It may lead to flight delays of hours or longer, or mortality. Atmospheric temperature also affects barometric pressure, which certainly has effects on fishing, but it's addressed in the form of total-pressure.

Natural Sequences

Natural sequences are events in nature that follow one after another, and periodically repeat in the same order. A good example is seasons of the year: Winter, spring, summer, and fall. They repeat every year, always in the same order. It's a reliable sequence that fishermen exploit to their fullest advantage. For example, when spring arrives they know it's time to pursue various fish species in the shallows because many will be congregating and spawning. For many species it's the only season in which they spawn. They repeat it every year in sequence with the season. Fishermen easily recognize the correlation and synchrony of the two events. They know they can catch spawning fish sometime in spring, every year. They can predict it years in advance. It's the very essence of how natural sequences can be used for fishing success.

Correlations and Indicators

Predicting that you can catch spawning fish sometime during spring is a nice idea, but spring is three months long. Predicting the exact timing of spring spawning is still difficult for most, but far easier by correlating the spawning event with other sequences.

Plants and their various stages of development can be directly correlated to the exact time period that spawning occurs for most species. In like manner, spawning of one fish species can often be used to foretell the advent of spawning of another species. Plants and their stages can also be correlated to aquatic insect hatches, molts, and mating flights (spinner falls) that produce goods bites. The annual chronological order of insect hatches is an extremely valuable prediction tool. The sequence of rising or falling water temperature can also be used to foretell spawning and insect molts that produce good bites.

Consider: You may know that spawning of a certain species slowly begins when water reaches a certain temperature and certain insects are hatching. You may learn, however, that *peak* spawning coincides with the bloom of a certain wildflower that occurs a few days later. In subsequent years, the bloom of the wildflower may be the only indicator needed for signaling peak spawning activity. It may eliminate marginal fishing success that can occur during the slow onset of spawning or the waning end of it.

The most valid indicators and precursors are those that you observe in the same location every year. For example, if it's a wildflower, insect, or other indicator observed in your yard or local stream, then you should only use the ones from the same location in your yard and local stream in subsequent years. If it's alongside a street on your way to the grocery store, that's the one you should use every year. If it's too difficult to use the same indicator, use one (same species) that's as near as possible to the one you've been using. The point is, don't use one too many miles away, say, more than 15 miles north or south at the same altitude; more than 15 miles east and west at the same altitude is okay. For indicators at significantly higher or lower altitudes you may need to make an adjustment for its use based on the different altitude. Such adjustments are addressed later under **Altitude Allowance.**

Also, when making correlations with sequential events, be aware that a first occurrence like the first wildflower blossom, or a first hatching mayfly or spawning fish, may be a fluke caused by a genetic mutant. It's best to wait until the trend of the sequential appearances or occurrences appear to have begun in earnest.

If you are using plants as indicators or precursors, you should only use naturally occurring wild plants, not domesticated plants bought in garden centers. Domestics are commonly so hybridized that the species may look similar, but they develop at different rates and are easily misidentified, which can skew your predictions.

As a point of interest, many wild plants that seem to be naturally occurring, especially wildflowers, are actually early European domestic imports that eventually "escaped" into the wild. Most grow along roadsides where the virgin soil was disturbed and facilitated their escape. Nonetheless, their feral nature makes them excellent indicators and precursors.

Variations in humidity and precipitation will play a constant role in the health of many organisms, but will normally not affect the order in which sequential events occur.

Precursors

Precursors are the early warning indicators that exist in all sequences. They are events that occur just prior to the main event that you're trying to predict. They flag you to get ready for the main event because it's coming next. For example, if your favorite fish spawns when water temperature hits 65 degrees F, the precursor is water at 64 degrees F, or perhaps it's a fish that spawns slightly sooner when water temperature is 61 degrees F

Aquatic insect hatch sequences and wildflower sequences are stuffed with precursor possibilities — hundreds. A wildflower blossoming 100 miles south of your location can signal that the same wildflower will blossom in your neighborhood in about two weeks. That particular flower may be the one that coincides with a certain caddisfly hatch period that produces a phenomenal annual bite. The precursor puts you on notice of roughly when the hatch period and good bite will occur. When the same flower blossoms locally, it reminds you that the hatch period has arrived.

If you're unable to identify a primary indicator that occurs at the same time as your hot bite, try to identify one that occurs a few days or a week prior. It'll serve just as well. I have several in this category.

Using sequence events as indicators and precursors becomes quite fun. More often than not, you'll know something that the rest of the world hasn't figured out yet. You'll have a better idea of when to go fishing or when to stay home, and where to go or not to go.

Dormancy and Emergence
In most instances, precursors help you plan ahead by a few days, but the dormancy rate and emergence rate can help you plan ahead by weeks. Recall from Chapter 2 that these rates occur at roughly 70 miles every 10 days on the 45th parallel (45 degrees north latitude), halfway between the Equator and North Pole. In the Northern Hemisphere, dormancy occurs from north to south, but emergence occurs from south to north. Both occur in exactly the opposite directions in the Southern Hemisphere.

I've made comparisons with botanical indicators (a stage of a plant's development) as far as 360 miles south of my location and the average rate of 70 miles every ten days has held basically true after making an allowance for altitude (See Altitude Allowance and Sidebar #26: Estimated Rates).

Altitude Allowance
Higher altitude causes additional delay of natural sequences in similar habitats. For predictions, I compensate for differences in altitude by including an extra 2-4 days for each 100 feet of *difference in altitude*. It seems to be a workable approximation for most latitudes. If weather is hot use 2 days, if weather is average use 3 days, if it's cold use 4 days. At worst, your prediction will likely be in the right ballpark. If your prediction is still unsatisfactory, use a number that fits and keep good logs. It doesn't take long to refine predictions with good logs.

26

Estimated Rates

- Distance between degrees of latitude is approximately 69 miles
- Applicable only for the same species of plant or animal
- Applicable up to approx. 1000 feet above sea level — use slower rate at higher altitudes. See **Altitude Allowance** on next page.

Near this Degree of Latitude	Estimated Average Rate of Dormancy and Emergence
50	65 miles / 10 days = 6.5 miles / day
49	66 miles / 10 days = 6.6 miles / day
48	67 miles / 10 days = 6.7 miles / day
47	68 miles / 10 days = 6.8 miles / day
46	69 miles / 10 days = 6.9 miles / day
45	70 miles / 10 days = 7.0 miles / day
44	71 miles / 10 days = 7.1 miles / day
43	72 miles / 10 days = 7.2 miles / day
42	73 miles / 10 days = 7.3.miles / day
41	74 miles / 10 days = 7.4 miles / day
40	75 miles / 10 days = 7.5 miles / day
39	76 miles / 10 days = 7.6 miles / day
38	77 miles / 10 days = 7.7 miles / day
37	78 miles / 10 days = 7.8 miles / day
36	79 miles / 10 days = 7.9 miles / day
35	80 miles / 10 days = 8.0 miles / day
34	81 miles / 10 days = 8.1 miles / day
33	82 miles / 10 days = 8.2 miles / day
32	83 miles / 10 days = 8.3 miles / day
31	84 miles / 10 days = 8.4 miles / day
30	85 miles / 10 days = 8.5 miles / day
29	86 miles / 10 days = 8.6 miles / day
28	87 miles / 10 days = 8.7 miles / day
27	88 miles / 10 days = 8.8 miles / day
26	89 miles / 10 days = 8.9 miles / day
25	90 miles / 10 days = 9.0 miles / day

Table contains estimated average rates of dormancy and emergence at different latitudes. The rates are only suggestive (except latitude 45 degrees) and are the result of anecdortal conversations I've had with anglers across the country, from the Gulf of Mexico to the Great Lakes. The table reflects rates as best as I could determine from the anglers' short-term observations without the benefit of accurate logs. Long-term logs are needed to validate or make adjustments to the rates as shown. The rates take into account that progressively more degree-day heat is available at progressively lower latitudes, resulting in a progressively, but only slightly faster rate at each latitude, from the poles toward the equator.

Altitude allowance is depicted in Figure 12-1. The similar habitats chosen are two identical lakes, Lake **A** and Lake **B**, located immediately next to each other. Lake **A** is situated 400 ft above sea level, whereas Lake

ALTITUDE ALLOWANCE

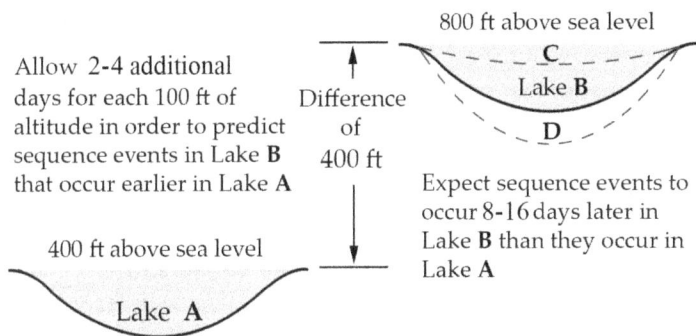

Figure 12-1

The *identical* lakes are located close enough together that each will ordinarily host most of the same fish, insects, crustaceans, and plants as the other. That both lakes host the same organisms makes it possible to use the organisms in one lake as bite precursors for the other. When emergence unfolds during spring and summer, all sequences will first occur in Lake **A** because they normally commence at the lowest altitudes first. Emergence occurs there first because more heat is available at lower altitudes. More heat causes faster degree-day accumulation, resulting in earlier emergence. Eventually Lake **B** will experience the same sequences, but only after a short delay of about 8-16 days (2-4 days/100 ft x 400 ft = 8-16 days) because temperatures are cooler at the higher altitude.

If Lake **B** only filled the basin to dashed line **C**, forming a shallow Lake **C**, the shallow lake would heat up much faster. Sequence delays may then be less than 2 days per 100 feet of difference in altitude. If Lake **C** is shallow enough, it could heat up faster than Lake **A**, resulting in sequences occurring in Lake **C** sooner than in Lake **A**. Fortunately the lakes' behaviors would be about the same every year, which would facilitate reliable predictions.

If Lake **B** filled the basin to dashed line **D**, forming a deep Lake **D**, the greater volume of water would remain cooler much longer. If the water remains cooler, sequences may be delayed longer than 4 days per 100 feet of difference in altitude.

With respect to altitude, the dormancy rate works the same as emergence, but in reverse. Dormancy occurs at the highest altitude first and lowest altitude last.

Seasonal Lag

The rates I've cited are widely applicable, but unusual environmental conditions exist that require other considerations. A good example is the sequence of seasonal lag that the Great Lakes exert a few miles inland along their eastern shorelines. It's the phenomenon whereby the deeply chilled waters of winter warm so slowly that prevailing westerly winds blow chilly air off the lakes well into spring and summer. Much of spring can still feel like winter, and much of summer can still feel like spring. Temperatures of the seasonal climate lag behind the warmer seasonal temperatures experienced farther inland. After the water warms throughout summer, prevailing winds then blow warmer air a few miles inland, mitigating the chilly onset of autumn; and so it goes. Mountain ranges, deserts, and other large features also have their own unique effects on natural sequences in their local region. Good logs will eventually reveal an average annual date (expected date) upon which a natural sequence event will occur in areas with lag. Once again, such events can be expected to occur not more than 14 days from the expected date (exceptions are uncommon), and occur within five days or less from the average date in most years.

Earth Orbit and Clocks

I suspect that deviation from the average date is kept in check by two primary factors: Earth's constant orbit and biological clocks.

The steady orbit keeps the average monthly temperatures within a very narrow range from year to year — normally less than a couple degrees Fahrenheit. This keeps degree-day availability relatively constant and reliable.

Biological clocks stubbornly regulate the annual and daily timing of sequence events and seem to resist severe deviations from the normal average timing of their occurrence. This seems more pronounced in some organisms than others, but it's why organisms are so dependable and valuable for making fishing predictions. I'd betray a friend's confidence if I provide more details, but I know of one fish species that has always spawned in a Great Lakes' tributary within three days of a certain date over the six years that I've been keeping track of it. Spawning occurred before, on, or after the date, but always within three days of it. Another friend records the return of specific bird species every year, and, so far, they all return within about three days of an average date.

Hidden Sequences

Sequences that probably cause the most bites are the hidden under-water molts that fishermen never see — when immature insects and crustaceans molt out of their early instars. You now have the means to predict the timing of those molts.

As you begin using this sequence information, your instincts for judging habitats will quickly become more acute. You'll develop keener senses for nuances that influence innumerable sequences that can be tapped for your benefit. The most important sequence you will ever use, however, is the calendar. Always record a date.

Total-Pressure

Temperature and some sequence knowledge are utterly efficient tools for identifying periods during which spawning and insect molting produce good bites. Unfortunately, spawning periods and bites are brief, and molts of specific species of aquatic insects are notoriously undependable from day to day. Predicting their annual hatch period is one thing; predicting the day they hatch or molt during that period is quite another.

Understanding the concepts of total-pressure and the state of ableness makes it possible to predict the exact days, and commonly the hour that they will hatch, and the days when they won't.

Total-pressure is the sum of two pressures — barometric pressure plus water pressure. It varies in direct proportion to changes in barometric pressure and/or water level. When water temperature remains steady, total-pressure appears to act as the major factor controlling the day that insect hatching and molting occurs, which occurs after they enter the state of ableness.

State of Ableness

Ableness is the condition wherein an aquatic insect or crustacean has developed to the point of being able to molt or hatch (Chapter 5). The condition, depending on the species of insect or crustacean and its latitude/altitude, may last for hours or days or more. My experience indicates that ableness, in ordinary conditions, is about four days near the 45th parallel at about 500-1000 ft above sea level. Warmer water temperatures will accelerate development in ableness; colder temperatures will impede it. When water temperature has hovered near the species' preferred temperature for a few days and remains in that range, total-pressure alone can be used to determine the day in which molts and hatches will occur.

When aquatic insects and crustaceans enter ableness, they acquire barometer-like properties and become slavishly responsive to total-pressure. They remain in ableness until they have enough strength to overcome the conditions presented by total-pressure, and then molt or hatch.

Pressure Rules

Molting and hatching (during a normal water temperature range, which is usually the case) occur according to the high pressure rule and low pressure rule, which are:

High Pressure Rule:

When total-pressure increases or is high, it hinders the molting processes and slows them down, which results in molts and hatches occurring later during the state of ableness.

Low Pressure Rule:

When total-pressure decreases or is low, molting processes are aided by it and speed up, which results in molts and hatches occurring earlier during the state of ableness.

Effects of these rules — **Effects of Total-Pressure on the Bite** — are explained in a brief, condensed manner in larger font on the next page A few related details for predicting bites are also included. A copy of the page may be handy in your wallet, fishing vest, or tackle box:

Effects of Total-Pressure on the Bite

The following explanations are based on stable water temperature, i.e., daily water temperature is reaching an insect's preferred temperature range at the right time of day during its normal seasonal hatching period; and when insects or crustaceans are in the state of ableness during all other instars after hatching from an egg.

Molting and hatching will be suppressed at the onset of a high total-pressure trend, but will normally resume within two to four days in temperate latitudes, depending on how high the total-pressure becomes, and if it does not spike severely higher as can happen during flooding. Molting and hatching, after resuming, will then continue to occur daily through the high total-pressure period and through the lower total-pressure period that will normally follow. When total-pressure trends upward again, molting and hatching will again become suppressed, and the entire cycle will repeat.

Pie molts and pie hatches can be caused by as little as 15-20 points of pressure drop. Multiple pie molts and pie hatches can be caused by as little as 40-60 points of pressure drop. The necessary pressure drops may be less at higher altitudes. Good bites will occur on the days and times that molts and hatches occur.

Total-pressure is affected equally by either a change in water depth of 1.36 inches or a change in barometric pressure of 10 points (.10 inches of mercury).

§

Water Level History

To make good predictions, it's imperative to know the recent history of total-pressure, at least for the prior three to four days. You must know if and when the water level has risen or fallen by an appreciable amount, and also if and when barometric pressure has risen or fallen by an appreciable amount. Any *combination* of the two equaling or exceeding 15 barometric pressure points is an appreciable amount. Fifteen barometric pressure points is equivalent to an increase or decrease of the pressure of basically

261

two inches of water (2.04 inches). (Sidebar #15: Pressure Points and Water Level Equivalents, Appendix B).

Water level changes can sometimes be determined by observing the high water line, or by simple common sense about recent precipitation and how it probably affects your water system. High water lines can be tricky because a wide wet line always exists above the water level due to capillary action on all protruding objects and where the water meets the bank or shore. Water lines are more useful if water has fallen instead of risen because the wide wet line will be temporarily wider. Protruding objects can be useful if you have a reasonable idea about how much should be protruding above the water's surface or not. If you have a means for direct measurement so much the better. If there hasn't been any rain or runoff for a few days you can normally assume that the water level has been constant for the purposes of making predictions, or that the level has dropped which may cause a good bite if it has contributed to an appreciable amount of reduced total-pressure. If water level has dropped a small amount and barometric pressure has also dropped a small amount, the small drop of each may create enough drop in total-pressure to cause molts or hatches, and therefore a good bite.

Barometric Pressure History

Knowing the history of barometric pressure can only be done with a barometer or by checking weather websites. National weather service sites that record airport weather conditions have limited but good information. Hourly barometric pressure readings serve best. Water levels don't vary by much most of the time, so barometric pressure is the indicator that will help you determine when much of the fish's food will show up or not.

If water temperature is within the normal range during the seasonal hatch period of a given species, and the water level hasn't changed for a few days, the day that hatches of the species occur can be determined solely by barometric pressure. Hatch charts available in local tackle shops or flyfishing shops, or good logs will reveal the time of day of the insect's appearance. Some hatches last for hours, others may last only a fraction of an hour. Hatches of some species may occur so sparsely over the course of many hours that they seldom cause good bites, but their spinner falls may occur collectively and condensed into such short periods that good bites are normally assured.

When barometric pressure trends downward after an extended period of high pressure, normally three to four days on the 45th parallel, pie hatches and pie molts (Chapters 6 and 7) are likely to occur. If barometric pressure goes extremely low, perhaps 75 points lower or more (my guess), pie molts and hatches may occur after only two days of high pressure.

In summary, the timing of molting and hatching of aquatic insects and crustaceans occurs as the result of the interplay between three basic factors: Temperature, water level, and barometric pressure. When temperature and water level are unchanged, barometric pressure is the key determinant for predicting good bites. In most instances, if total-pressure indicates that hatches and molts should occur, yet they do not occur, water temperature has probably been reduced, causing a delay of the expected hatches and molts. Also, when hatches and molts cease because total-pressure begins trending higher, spinner falls and their resultant bites will still occur on a predictable basis, commonly a day or two later, depending on the species and air temperature. Spinner falls, however, do not always cause a bite on lakes, and reservoirs. They can occur unbeknownst to fish because of wind, as explained under **Heat Accelerated Bites**.

Barometric pressure history is so important to reliable predictions, that I make this one last exhortation for equipment manufacturers to bring a user-friendly, recording barometer to market. During the course of writing this material, I spoke with a couple manufacturers and one assured me that the technology exists to make it happen. Let's hope it happens sooner than later.

Wind

Wind exerts very little influence on free-flowing rivers of average size. It may whip the surface and spook fish into cover, or blow terrestrial insects into the water and create a minor bite, but it's relatively inconsequential most of the time. Sections of larger rivers may be affected more if they have open expanses as large as some lakes, in which case they may partially behave as lakes.

When wind blows across lakes, it creates a variety of circumstances for good bites. Wave action and movement of the warm water near the surface play the key roles.

Plankton, Turbulence, and Turbidity

Wind regularly blows warmer surface water from one location to another. The shift in location can be substantial, depending on wind direction, velocity, and duration. When the warm water is blown to a shoreline several things occur: A certain amount of plankton, often substantial, will be carried into the leeward shore area. Also, wave action will churn the shallowest water, which acts to dislodge and suspend various food items from the bottom sediment. The suspended plankton and dislodged food may then attract baitfish which may attract larger predators and produce a good bite. Wave action near shorelines may also cause a degree of turbidity, and fish will often move into shallow areas while the water is dirty and visibility is limited. Perhaps they sense that they are less vulnerable in it. If the water is overly turbid with suspended particles, it may interfere with gill function and cause fish to retreat to more hospitable locations. If wave action is too turbulent near shore it may cause fish to patrol in deeper water flanking the worst turbulence.

Heat Accelerated Bites

Another effect of warm water blown to the leeward shore is that it carries heat that, if sustained long enough, may be substantial enough to trigger spawning, or staging for spawning of certain fish species which congregates them in the area and creates an earlier good bite. Staging or spawning will still only occur during the normal annual spawning period, but will occur earlier within that period rather than later.

The heat may also accelerate the occurrence of insect molts and hatches on the leeward side if the wind becomes calm. Calm wind will allow wind-driven, piled-up water to recede back toward the lake so as to reduce total-pressure along the leeward shoreline to a more normal level, which further facilitates earlier molts, and more good bites.

Locations where insects hatched in lakes and reservoirs will also experience spinner falls, and good bites where they occur, usually a day or two after the hatch. Occasionally, however, spinner falls may go substantially undetected by fish because wind direction may have changed by the time the spinners return. The new wind direction may have blown the warm water to another location, dragging forage and predators with it. The spinner falls may produce only a minimum bite or no bite because fish have moved off.

The area overspread by windblown warm water will include additional area that results from Ekman drift, which is caused by the earth's spin (Coriolis affect). Recall that meaningful Ekman drift only occurs when wind blows over water that is temperature stratified.

Highest Percentage Locations
Some leeward shores are better for good bites than others because they're comprised of better habitat for small organisms that attract baitfish. Some are also closer to deeper water than others, which positions them closer to the travel routes of larger predators. Knowing the direction from which winds must blow in order to attract fish to these shoreline areas can improve your success significantly. Accordingly, every separate wind direction will produce its own highest percentage locations that can produce a good bite. This will be elaborated upon in section **Small Lakes.**

Plotting the highest percentage locations for good bites on a lake map isn't particularly difficult. Locations with sand are least hospitable for small organisms, gravel is better, reeds growing in sand is also better, rocky, weedy bottoms are better still, as are dark muddy bottoms, and muddy bottoms with weeds or forms of timber are among the best, but there are others. Bottoms best for spawning seem to be gravel, stony, or shallow mud overlying sand or gravel or other hard bottom underneath. Nearby deeper water makes them better still.

When warm water is blown to the leeward shore, it will cause the thermocline to downwell a certain amount near that shore. Temperature zones preferred by certain fish species will then shift upward or downward accordingly. During colder months the temperature shift may be shallower and toward shore; in warmer months the shift may be somewhat deeper and away from shore; and the fish will likely shift with it.

While wind is blowing warm water toward the leeward shore, it's also blowing it away from the windward shore. As it blows away, the water level may recede (a matter of inches) from the wndward shore, which would reduce total-pressure and possibly facilitate molting or hatching near the windward shore. This is especially possible if the water temperature doesn't get any cooler near the bottom that overlies the insect habitat. The thermocline will upwell somewhat near the windward shore, causing cooler water to creep closer to shore, but the slope of the shore will determine how close it will approach. It will approach over a greater distance on low, gradual slopes, but very little on steep slopes. So, if substrate inhabited by insects and crustaceans along the windward shore isn't overspread by colder water, molts and hatches are more likely to occur there because of reduced total-pressure.

Conditions Change Slowly

When a windward shoreline becomes a leeward shoreline, or vice versa, because wind direction changed, fishing conditions along that shoreline do not change immediately. They change gradually over a period of hours, depending on wind velocity and how long it persists. Wind direction normally changes over a period of hours, so the thickness of the warm water layer slowly builds up or is peeled away over a period of hours as well. In effect, the water conditions and fishing conditions in place will change very little at the onset of the wind direction change, but will gradually and slowly change during the coming hours. When wind direction changes, there is always a time lag between existing fishing conditions and the new conditions that replace them.

Currents Caused by Wind

Other than the up and down motion of the thermocline, currents created by wind are probably negligible in the vast majority of small lakes and reservoirs. Fall winds that cause turnover and bring nutrients toward the surface via vertical currents may be an exception, although I know of no fishing techniques that exploit vertical currents directly.

Wind at River Mouths

Wind blowing over a large lake toward a river mouth can blow warm water in that direction and replace cooler water that previously surrounded the area, and vice versa. If it's blowing away from a river mouth, it can move warm water away and allow colder water to replace it (thermocline upwelling), and vice versa. Either effect is possible, but one or the other is usually prevalent during certain seasons and depends on whether the lake water is warmer than the river water, or vice versa. Depending on time of year and the preferred temperature range of fish species, the water temperature surrounding the mouth, whether warm or cold, may either block fish migration upstream or facilitate it. The wind, however, can reverse either effect within hours. Wind direction and the temperature of the water it displaces at the mouth have a major impact on the timing of upstream migration of many species, especially anadromous species like salmon.

Variable Winds

If you're trying to determine effects of wind on your fishing water, but winds are currently variable, recall that variable winds are commonly (but not always) located near the core of barometric pressure systems, so they will be short lived. Nonetheless, they affect fishing by redistributing warm surface water and horizontally redistributing the plankton in it, i.e., the winds spread them out over a much wider area. The result is fishing conditions that become confusing and difficult to interpret. When this situation develops, a good option is to review the wind direction that prevailed immediately prior to the advent of variable winds. The best leeward habitats affected by the previous prevailing winds are probably still the best choice for good bites during the unsettled period of variable winds because food is likely still available for fish in the same locations.

As these examples reveal, recent wind history is exceedingly important for locating good bites in small lakes and reservoirs. It's also important to remember that the illustrations in this chapter show the effects of several hours, or more, of sustained wind from a single direction.

§

Water temperature, natural sequences, total-pressure, and wind are the most useful factors for making bite predictions in all water systems, so some of the same material is repeated in each of the following discussions about **Rivers**, **Small Lakes**, and **Reservoirs – Impoundments**.

Sidebar #27: Structure, Cover, and Water Features, which is a useful reference for all water systems, is only contained near the end of section **Small Lakes**.

Most of what you have ever learned about structure and cover fishing still applies, but you will now be able to apply it to structures and cover within higher percentage areas, and confidently disregard similar characteristics in lower percentage areas. Wherever the terms *structure* or *structures* appear alone in the remainder of this chapter, they shall also mean to include *cover* and *water features*.

Rivers

Predicting or finding the bite in streams is relatively easy compared to some lakes and large reservoirs. Streams can be dealt with somewhat briefly because only a few factors need be considered in most instances.

Various Habitats

Streams, like small lakes and large reservoirs, contain various habitats. Each habitat harbors its own unique species of food items for fish to eat. For example, one section of a stream may be fast flowing over a gravel bottom and produce good stonefly hatches. Another section may be slow moving and have silt beds that produce good mayfly hatches. The section near the mouth will usually be warmer than the section near the headwaters, which is usually colder, thus each will commonly contain different insect and crustacean species adapted to one section or the other. It's also common for individual habitats, for example silt beds or stretches of gravel, to be located at occasional intervals over the full length of the stream. Gravel may be present where the stream gradient is steep, silt beds may be present where the gradient is more gradual. Other sections, especially where stream flow is relatively slow, may be weed choked or covered with sand.

Predictability of Food and its Location

Whatever the habitat and its location, specific food will become available in each in a predictable manner every year; and always near the same calendar date that it was available in previous years, usually within 14 days (usually a lot less) of its average date of appearance. Predicting the exact calendar period when specific food should be available in each section of stream can be accomplished by noting which botanical indicators occur during the same calendar period, or close to it. Normally, when the indicator appears every year, the food also makes its appearance and produces a good bite.

Insect hatches and molts are the most common form of food that can be correlated to botanical indicators, but they are also good precursors for the appearance of the next species. Insect hatches and molts occur in wonderfully chronological order, so the occurrence of one species always foretells the coming appearance of the next one. Fly hatch charts available in local fly fishing shops show the order in which they emerge, and each emerging species can easily be correlated to its own unique botanical indicator.

Some botanical indicators may occur during the same period as the food, but others may regularly occur a little sooner than the food. They could occur a day or two, a week, or 10 days etc., before the period when the food is expected to appear. Whatever the case, the indicator you use will generally allow you to make the same reliable predictions every year. For example, if you base your predictions on an indicator that occurs six days before the food appears one year, that same indicator will be good for predicting the same food six days before it appears every year thereafter or very close to it. The earth's location in its orbit, degree day absorption, and biological clocks make it so.

Nearby rivers are also excellent indicators. It's common for many of the same species of insects and crustaceans to live in other rivers in the region, even if the rivers are dozens of miles away in some cases. Due to altitude, latitude, and drainage differences between rivers, the organisms almost always make their appearance in some local rivers before others.

Fortunately, you can use the appearance of the organisms in nearby rivers as reliably as botanical indicators. For example, if organisms make their appearance a few days or a week earlier in a nearby river than they appear in your river, they will appear in your river after about the same predictable interval every year. You can use the appearances in the nearby river to foretell appearances in yours. Be aware that appearances of the same organisms will occur in the same type of habitat in the two streams — same organism, same habitat. You will not see the same organisms emerging in dissimilar habitats. Not all nearby streams will harbor all the same species, but most will have many in common.

Also, water level will usually fluctuate far more significantly and rapidly in most unimpeded river systems (no dams) than in lakes, so you must always be cognizant of its role in total-pressure in order to make good predictions. This is especially important if rain runoff or snowmelt affects one river more than the other if you're comparing the timing of events between them.

Once you know the calendar period when appearances will occur, you will know the period during which the bite will occur. Your three to four day knowledge of the history of total-pressure and water temperature can then be used to determine the *day* the bite will occur. Knowing the preferred *time* of day when the organism (insect or crustacean) normally makes its appearance will then tell you the time to be there for the bite. If the stream remains unchanged over the years, the appearances will occur in the same section of river year after year. This is a case of being able to predict the bite to within the hour that it occurs, but it's not an exceptional case. Similar precise predictions can easily be repeated throughout the fishing season.

Spawning Predictions

Spawning of a particular species in a nearby river can also be used to predict spawning of the same species in your river. Elapsed time between the spawning events in the separate rivers will occur at about the same predictable interval every year. For example, if spawning occurs eight days earlier at a certain location in a nearby river than in a certain location in your river, you can expect it to continue to occur about eight days earlier in future years. The same principle applies for pre-spawn staging when fish gather in larger groups, and post-spawn recovery behavior. The *interval* between similar occurrences from one river to the other will always be roughly the same, provided you always make your comparison between the same two locations of the two rivers. Spawning of one species also signals the upcoming spawning of the next species in the chronological spawning order of the stream. Finding the bite associated with spawning is often as simple as knowing where the best stretches of gravel or rocky bottoms are located over the length of the stream, or impassable obstacles like dams and waterfalls. If upstream migration is halted by obstacles, spawning will occur in the closest suitable habitats downstream.

Another phenomenon associated with spawning is the staging of large numbers of fish that occurs just prior to their mass movements upstream. Even though most staging occurs in lakes, it's briefly addressed here. In a nutshell, fish that are about to run upstream for spawning will frequently approach the mouth of a stream and congregate near it if water temperature is not conducive to their advancement upstream. The congregations are often large and occur in the same proximity to the river mouth every year. Experienced charter captains and avid recreational fishermen usually know the location of the nearby staging areas and fish them accordingly. You can shadow these experts to discover staging locations, but please be respectful and courteous when attempting to fish near where they are already fishing. Treat your fellow fishermen in a manner that you would want to be treated, had you been there first.

Temperature Progressions

Insect hatches and molts in unimpeded rivers normally occur first near the river's mouth because the water is usually warmest in the lower river system. As the water warms farther upstream over the coming days and weeks, hatches and molts then occur in the upstream sections as well. The sequence is always the same from year to year, commencing from downstream to upstream and is directly associated with water temperature, although not every river or section of river behaves in this manner.

Exceptions may occur in upstream areas that are shallow and slow-moving, and especially where backwaters like sloughs, bogs, feeder ponds and adjacent shallow-water swamps dump warm water into the mainstream. The mainstream may then reach a higher temperature sooner than downstream waters, in which case hatches and molts will occur upstream sooner than in stretches farther downstream. A similar situation can occur in shallow, slow-moving water near where mainstreams flow into reservoirs. Cold tributaries that feed into the lower reaches of a river may also keep the lower part of the river at a lower temperature than the upstream reaches, facilitating upstream molts and hatches first.

The progression of the warmer water temperature upstream eventually reaches an upstream limit where it can't advance any farther. The cool temperature of water flowing from groundwater springs or the bottoms of dam reservoirs keeps the advancing warmer temperature at bay downstream. This generally occurs in headwater regions and dam tailwaters where water remains colder throughout the warmest part of the year. During winter, however, they may have some of the warmest water because the ground keeps spring water and lower level reservoir water within a relatively narrow temperature range throughout the year.

Tailwaters, Headwaters, and Dams

Tailwaters may harbor a greater quantity of aquatic organisms than headwaters due to the sheer size of riverbeds near the base of dams. Upper headwaters are normally inhabited by fewer and smaller fish species, and fewer insect and crustacean species because of limited habitat. It then follows that the sparseness of species creates sparseness in bites, both in fish size and quantity in upper headwater stretches. There are few exceptions, but a particularly notable one is the incredible Kitchitikipee big spring near the city of Manistique in Michigan's Upper Peninsula.

My memory is surely corroded by the 40 years since I visited Kitchitikipee, but the experience left me in awe for a lifetime. Would I ever see anything that exceeded such a wonder? Not likely. I can only retell it as I recall it, accurate or otherwise. It was in late fall.

A raft, attached to a large diameter cable, traversed back and forth across the huge pool created by the spring. As the raft was maneuvered to mid-pool, an enormous volume of gin-clear water could be seen erupting upwards through violently roiling sand 50 feet (?) below the surface. The sheer volume and impression was volcanic. It was claimed that enough water was gushing from the earth's belly at this spot to supply New York City's need for freshwater every day. It was a staggering sight. I recall seeing a handful of suspended trout (not sure which species) in it that appeared to be as long as my arms, but fishing was prohibited. They must have been there taking advantage of the comfortable temperature, because there could not have been much of a food base in the spring pool.

The behemoth spring immediately feeds its cold water into Indian Lake (13 square miles) which also receives water from expansive swamp and marshlands (warmer water), which then drains into the very short (approx. 6 miles long) Indian River, which drains into Lake Michigan. It's a very unusual water system that probably produces an unusual sequence of hatches and molts, but they would still be predictable by the usual means of correlations with common indicators and the total-pressure rules.

A difficult river location in which to predict a good bite is often just below a dam. Reservoir draw-down schedules can create conditions too unsettled for the average fisherman to easily decipher. Irregular drawdown can play havoc with total-pressure and the predictability of insect molting and hatching.

Dams create radically dissimilar environmental conditions in the stream, both downstream and upstream. Water conditions immediately upstream of a dam are often similar to the warm water and slow flow conditions near river mouths, but conditions immediately downstream are often similar to cold water and fast flow conditions near headwaters of streams. You may multiply your fishing opportunities if you treat each section of river below and above dams as individual rivers unto themselves.

For example, as depicted in Figure 12-2, the section of river between the river mouth and Dam 1, section **A**, can be treated as an individual river for bite prediction purposes. Section **B** between Dam 1 and Dam 2 can also be treated as an individual river for bite predictions, as can section **C** between Dam 2 and the headwaters.

Despite circumstances that may create confusion, you can predict the best days and times for natural bites in rivers if you know the trends of (1) barometric pressure, (2) water level, (3) water temperature, and (4) the chronological sequences and timing of hatches and molts.

A, B, and C can each be treated as individual rivers for the purpose of predicting good bites

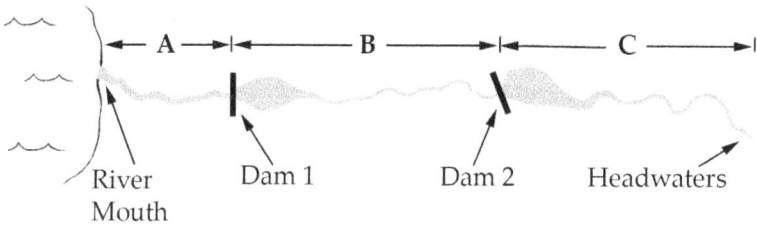

Figure 12-2

Regardless of all other conditions, hatches and molts and the resulting bites are always subject to the high and low pressure rules. The rules are always in play.

Wind Effects

Wind blowing on streams is almost never a factor unless it's ripping the water surface and scaring fish that want to feed, or interfering with casting. Wind-blown plankton is also not a factor in most medium to small rivers because the plankton count is usually so low that it doesn't trigger fish to feed to any significant extent. Current flow keeps the count from accumulating and growing to high levels, especially in the middle and upper stretches of free flowing streams. Plankton may become a factor where stream flow is slowed by dams or stream beds with low slope gradients.

Small Lakes

Predicting the availability of food in small lakes is a little more challenging than predicting its availability in rivers. The difference is wind, more specifically wind *direction*.

Water temperature, natural sequences, and total-pressure are equally important in small lakes as in rivers, but wind direction — the one-to-four day history of wind *direction* — must always be considered as an *equal* or *greater* factor. Learning about the effects of wind direction is simple, and they're addressed in detail later in this section.

Many Habitats

Like rivers, small lakes contain various habitats that harbor unique species of food items for fish to eat. For example, one section of a lake may have a gravel bottom that produces good stonefly hatches. Another section may have silt beds that produce good mayfly hatches. Each section will commonly contain different insect and/or crustacean species that is especially adapted to that section. There may also be other sections that are sandy and barren of most life forms and seldom experience good bites. Some sections may be colder than others because of nearby springs, inlets, or long periods of shade.

The variety of habitats is broad, and many are unique and may only occur at a single place along the entire circumference of the lake. Others may occur in numerous locations throughout the lake system.

Predictability of Food

Whatever the habitat and its location, specific food will become available in each in a predictable manner every year; and always near the same calendar date that it was available in previous years, usually within 14 days (within five days or less in most years) of its average date of appearance. Predicting the exact calendar period when specific food should be available can be accomplished by noting which natural sequence indicators occur during the same calendar period, or close to it. Normally, when the indicator appears every year, the food item also makes its timely appearance and produces a good bite.

Insect hatches and molts are the most common form of food that can be correlated to botanical indicators, but they are also good precursors for the appearance of the next species of insect to appear. Hatches and molts occur in wonderfully chronological order, so the occurrence of one species always foretells the coming occurrence of the next one, and the next good bite. Fly hatch charts available in local fly fishing shops show the order in which they emerge on local water, and each emerging species can easily be correlated to its own unique botanical indicator.

Some botanical indicators may occur during the same period as the food, but others may regularly occur a little sooner than the food. They may occur a day or two, a week, or 10 days etc., before the period when the food is expected to appear. Whatever the case, the indicator you use will generally allow you to make the same reliable predictions every year.

For example, if you base your predictions on an indicator that occurs six days before the food appears one year, that same indicator will be good for predicting the same food six days before it appears every year thereafter or very close to it. The earth's location in its orbit, degree day absorption, and biological clocks make it so.

Nearby lakes are also excellent indicators. It's common for many of the same species of insects and crustaceans to live in other lakes in the region, even if the lakes are dozens of miles away in some cases. Due to altitude and latitude differences between lakes, the organisms almost always make their appearance in some local lakes before others. Fortunately, you can use the appearance of the organisms in nearby lakes as reliably as botanical indicators. For example, if organisms make their appearance a few days or a week earlier in a nearby lake than they appear in your lake, they will appear in your lake after about the same predictable interval every year. You can use the appearances in the nearby lake to foretell appearances in yours. Be aware that appearances of the same organisms will occur in the same type of habitat in the two lakes — same organism, same habitat. You will not see the same organisms emerging in dissimilar habitats. Not all nearby lakes will harbor all the same species, but some will have many in common.

Also, water level may fluctuate more significantly and rapidly in some lakes than others, so you must always be cognizant of its role in total-pressure. This is especially important during times of rain runoff or snowmelt if you're comparing the timing of events between lakes. Water level changes in critical areas of one lake may also differ from the water level changes in critical parts of the other because of wind, which can cause a broader (or narrower) time period for some sequence events to occur from one lake to the other. Good logs can reveal the details over time.

Once you know the calendar period during which appearances will occur, it follows that you will also know that the bite will occur during that period. Your knowledge of the three to four day history of total-pressure and water temperature can then be used to determine the *day* the bite will occur. Knowing the preferred time of day when the organism (insect or crustacean) normally makes its appearance will then tell you the *time* to be there for the bite. It's not uncommon for some molts to last for hours, which means the bite may also last for hours, especially if the molters are small and fish must eat a large quantity to satisfy their hunger. If the lake has remained unchanged over the years, the appearances will occur in the same section of lake year after year. It's a case of being able to predict the bite to within the hour that it occurs, but it's not an exceptional case. Similar precise predictions can easily be repeated throughout the fishing season.

Spawning Predictions

Spawning of a particular species in a nearby lake can also be used to predict spawning of the same species in your lake. The *interval* of time between the spawning events in the separate lakes will occur at about the same predictable interval every year. For example, if spawning occurs eight days earlier at a certain location and habitat in a nearby lake than in a similar location and habitat in your lake, you can expect it to continue to occur about eight days earlier in future years.

The same principle applies for pre-spawn staging when fish gather in larger groups, and also post-spawn recovery behavior. The interval between similar occurrences from one lake to the other will always be roughly the same, provided you always make your comparison between the same two locations of the two lakes. Spawning of one species also signals the upcoming spawning of the next species in the chronological spawning order of the lakes. Finding the bite associated with spawning is often as simple as knowing where the best stretches of gravel, rocks, or sandy bottom etc., are located in the lakes. These types of bottoms are frequently covered with mud that spawning fish remove to create beds for egg laying.

Wind Direction and High Percentage Locations

The location and timing of sequence events in small lakes is highly dependent on the water temperature and total-pressure, which are heavily influenced by wind direction. Wind direction, therefore, is a primary factor in the location and timing of good bites. Wind speed is also an influencing factor, but not nearly as important as wind direction. Increased wind speed only hastens the effects of wind direction.

The following material about wind direction is particularly interesting because it reveals why fishing can be so good or so lousy near points of land that protrude into a lake. Tournament fishermen may find it particularly valuable. It reveals a better understanding of when and where to fish certain points and island locations, and avoid wasting precious time on others.

Figures 12-3 through 12-6 depict the wind's influence on warm water and plankton locations in a small lake in the Northern Hemisphere. A detailed explanation is given for Figure 12-3, which makes only cursory explanations necessary for Figures 12-4 through 12-6. The same information for the Southern Hemisphere is represented in Figure 12-7.

The explanations advise you to fish in the warmest water, but you should only do so as long as the heated water is not stressing your target fish, which can happen if water temperature climbs too high. Water temperature that's too high will cause fish to avoid it and migrate to cooler water, which could happen during the dog days of mid-to-late summer. If that occurs, the windward side of the illustrations would offer the most productive fishing areas because water temperatures in those areas would be cooler. If the surface water isn't cooler, you can at least expect cooler water to be closer to the surface than it is near the leeward shore. This is a small-lake example of the see-saw movement of the thermocline as explained for Figure 10-5.

Two important factors are reflected in the illustrations: (1) wind is sustained from a single direction for several hours or more, and (2) the water is temperature stratified, the usual condition that exists throughout most of a fishing season. Despite factoring in temperature stratification, the depictions are still useful after lakes turnover in fall when stratification is temporarily eliminated. The only thing that's different after turnover is that Ekman drift is no longer a factor. For all practical purposes, in the absence of temperature layers, there is basically no Ekman drift. Water and plankton will generally move in the same direction as the wind without veering to the left or right. Ekman drift returns again in early spring as temperature layers begin to recur for the season. Planktoon still occupies the upper portion of the water column.

The lake depicted in the illustrations may have little resemblance to the lake(s) you fish, but the principles of locating bites based on wind direction apply to all forms of lakes. Also, no underwater structures are depicted, but a lengthy list of structure, cover, and water features is included in **Sidebar #27: Structure, Cover, and Water Features** near the end of this section. Once you've determined high percentage areas of the lake where good bites may occur, the list will help you identify important structures and cover that may hold fish within those high percentage areas. Identifying and fishing the structures and cover will improve your chances even more.

Figure 12-3 depicts a *north* wind blowing over a small lake containing an island and three points of land that jut into the lake. The north wind sets the warm upper layer of water in motion toward the opposite end of the lake. Recall that the Coriolis force also influences the surface water movement by causing it to veer to the right of the wind direction (Ekman drift). The movement of the water is slightly or completely obstructed by the island, the points, and the opposite shorelines.

While the water has been moving along the east side of Point **2**, dispersed plankton has also been moving with it. The moving plankton, however, has become more numerous along the eastern side of Point **2** because Ekman drift (Coriolis affect) has carried more warm water and plankton toward that shoreline. The steady north wind keeps the water and heavier concentration of plankton moving near the shoreline and eventually blows it beyond the end of Point **2**. Once beyond the end of Point **2**, the concentration of moving plankton is no longer corralled by the shoreline, so it begins dispersing throughout the surface water once again. The dispersal pattern is a cone-shaped plume of plankton, **A**, which is a concentrated food source that will attract small organisms and baitfish. As plume **A** becomes populated with small organisms and baitfish, it then becomes a concentrated food source and *feeding lane* for predators. Plume **A** may exist only for a short duration because the concentration of plankton may soon be depleted at the north end of the lake because the wind has blown it out of there.

The wind has also blown warm water and plankton to the north shore along Point **3** where it is trapped by the shape of the shoreline in area **F**. The trap area, however, is not large enough to hold all the moving warm water and plankton from that part of the lake, so some of it slips past the tip of Point **3** and forms another concentration of plankton in the form of another potential feeding lane — plume **B**. The duration that plume **B** can persist as a feeding lane is much longer than the duration of plume **A** because the fetch from the north side of the lake is about twice as far to Point **3**, which means a concentration of plankton can be blown past the tip of Point **3** for a much longer period.

Note that the north wind will set all the water in motion and force some of it between Point **2** and Point **3** (dotted line), setting up a weak current in the narrow passage (narrows) between the points. Winds from the other directions of the compass will also force water through the narrows.

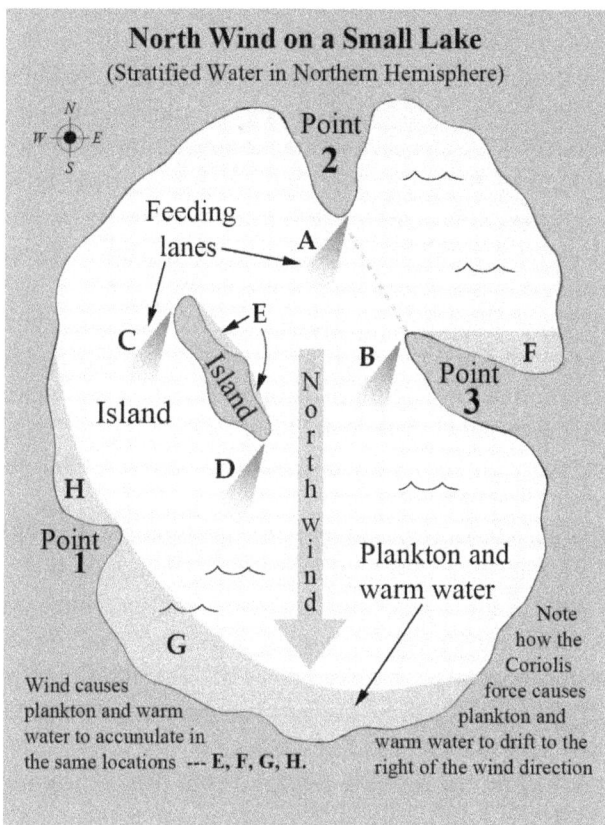

Figure 12-3

creating their own characteristic current, and current creates feeding lanes. The narrows is an area of the lake that will probably hold fish somewhere in close proximity despite the wind direction, but the wind direction will influence where they hold. The deepest point in the narrows, i.e., between Point **2** and Point **3**, is not indicated in the illustrations, but may also be a potential feeding lane because of the current. Remember that fish face upstream in currents, so position yourself accordingly.

The north wind has also created two more feeding lanes, **C** and **D**, near the tips of the island. The shape of the island and its orientation to a north wind and its associated Ekman drift is such that its northeast-facing shoreline can trap a small area of warm water and plankton against it as depicted by area **E**. All other warm water and plankton is able to slip past the tips of the island and form the plumes of feeding lanes **C** and **D**. The duration that **C** and **D** persist as feeding lanes is probably somewhat comparable to the duration of plume **B**. Feeding lane **C** is probably least attractive because there is so little island shoreline to deflect plankton into it.

The wind and Ekman drift move the largest portion of warmest water with plankton to the south and southwestern shores of the lake as depicted by shaded areas **G** and **H**. The warm water and plankton in areas **E**, **F**, **G** and **H** make those areas attractive to small organisms and baitfish, which in turn makes them attractive to predators.

In addition, wherever the warm water eventually arrives, it will cause faster degree-day absorption in the aquatic insects and crustaceans which can cause hatches and molts sooner than in areas where the water is cooler. This is possible if the wind hasn't substantially raised the water level and therefore the total-pressure. Remain cognizant that the high and low pressure rules are always in play.

The increased likelihood of earlier hatches and molts, plus increased plankton that attracts food for predators makes plumes **A**, **B**, **C**, **D**, and areas **E**, **F**, **G** and **H** higher percentage locations for good bites when a north wind blows. The plumes and areas closest to deep water or structure are likely the better locations for good bites. The concentration of plankton in plumes **A**, **B**, **C**, and **D**, will be higher near the narrow head of the plume and much less near the wider tail of the plume.

Point **1** may be one of the hottest places to fish in the entire lake. It's fully surrounded by warm water and plankton, and hatches and molts may be occurring near it soon. If the bottom substrate harbors abundant insect and crustacean life near Point **1**, and if it is near deeper water or structure, it may always be one of the best places to fish when the north wind blows. Good logs will reveal the tale over the coming years.

Figure 12-4 depicts a south wind blowing over the lake.

Feeding lane **A** near Point **1** will persist only for a short time because the wind fetch from the south is a short distance. The shape of Point **1** will not trap any warm water or plankton because Ekman drift will drive them away from shore. It's the least attractive location to fish with a south wind.

Feeding lane **B** will persist much longer because of the long fetch across the water from the south, but it's also one of the least attractive feeding lanes. The island shoreline that deflects plankton to **B** is so short that not much more plankton will be deflected and concentrated there than is drifting in the open water.

Feeding lane **C** will be one of the longest persisting feeding lanes and one of the best with a south wind. It will experience a high plankton count because the island is favorably oriented for a south wind to corral and drive a significant amount of plankton past its north end. The angle of the island to the wind is what allows so much plankton to slip past it. A high concentration of plankton will be trapped along the west side of the island within the very small area **E**.

Feeding lane **D** will persist a long time due to the long fetch from the south shoreline. It will also experience a high concentration of plankton due to the shape of Point **3** that will continue deflecting it toward the tip of

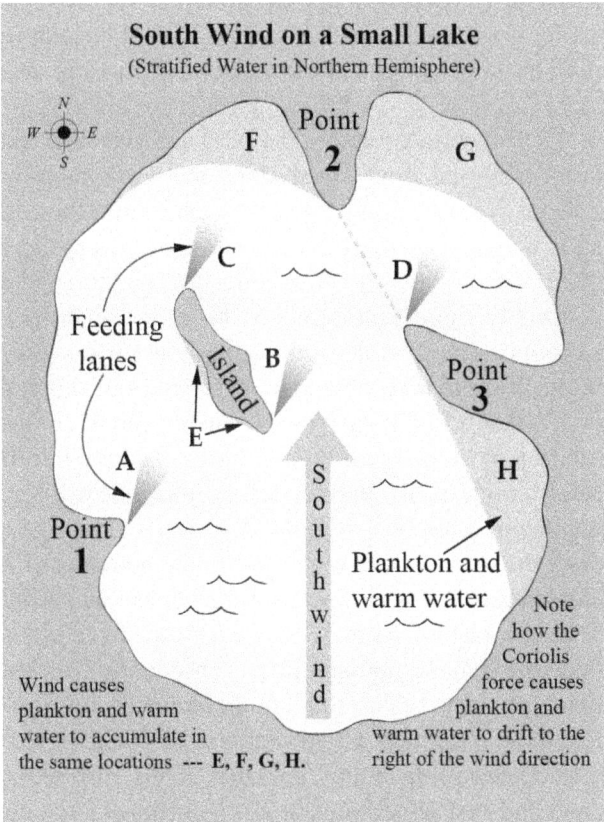

Figure 12-4

Point **3** where the wind steers it into **D**. The value of **D** as a feeding lane, however, may be questionable. Notice how Point **2** and Point **3** appear oriented toward each other, as if they may have once been connected. They may have once enclosed the small northeastern area of the lake, which may be much shallower. If so, it may not contain suitably deeper water for predators and **D** may simply go unnoticed, but it should be checked. If it's not shallow, **D** could be a dependable and productive feeding lane during a south wind. The south wind will also create a stronger current through the narrows between Point **2** and Point **3** that could improve **D** as a feeding lane.

The wind has also moved warm water, plankton, and the probability of earlier molts and hatches into areas **E**, **F**, **G**, and **H**. These areas and the feeding lanes closest to deeper water and structure are the higher percentage locations for good bites. Hatches and molts will be suppressed if the wind has raised the water level and increased total-pressure in any of these areas.

Figure 12-5 depicts an east wind blowing over the lake. Feeding lane **A** is formed by plankton forced along the north shoreline of Point **3**. It will be short lived because of the short fetch from the eastern shore. Feeding lane **B** will also be short lived because of the shorter fetch. Both **A** and **B** will also have relatively low amounts of plankton and perhaps not enough to cause any significant attraction for most organisms that could lead to a good bite. The Coriolis force along the north shore of Point **3** causes plankton closer to that shore to move away from shore, diluting the plankton count when it finally arrives anywhere near **A**. In the case of **B**, only a very short part of the tip of Point **2** steers plankton into **B**, and is almost completely comprised of that carried in by Ekman drift, so the plankton count may be elevated only slightly. A westerly flowing wind-caused current through the narrows will contribute to the potential of **A** and **B**.

Feeding lanes **C** and **D** will persist for an extended period due to the long fetch from the eastern shore. **C**, however, may have a relatively low plankton concentration and not enough to cause a bite. It's comprised of what little plankton drifts to that small point on the island from the southeast direction. **D** will contain a high amount of plankton that the wind drives along the eastern side of the island that finally slips around its north end. The island and east wind funnel a disproportionate amount of plankton to **D**. It's easily the feeding lane with the most food and highest fishing prospects during an east wind, especially if deeper water or other good

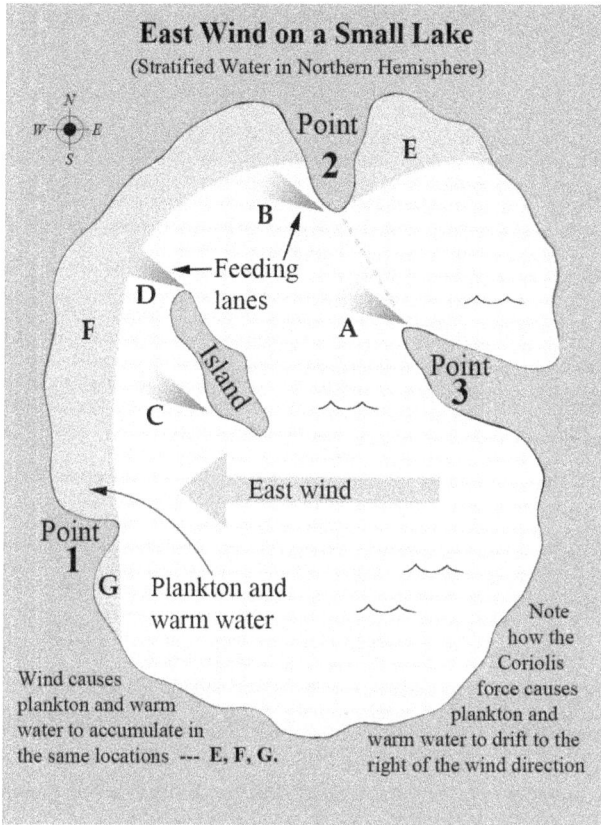

Figure 12-5

structure is nearby.

Point **1** may also be a prime location for good bites during an east wind. It eventually becomes surrounded with warm water and increased plankton, and could be quite productive if it's close to deeper water or good structure.

Areas **E**, **F**, **G**, feeding lane **D**, and Point **1** are the higher percentage locations for good bites during an east wind, especially if any of them are close to deeper water or good structure. Hatches and molts will be suppressed if the wind has raised the water level and increased total-pressure in any of these areas.

Figure 12-6 depicts a west wind blowing over the lake.

Feeding lane **A** will be extremely short lived because it's minimally

283

populated with additional plankton because of the short fetch from the west shoreline, and all warm water is driven away from it by a west wind. Thus, the fishing prospects of **A** and Point **1** are significantly diminished by a west wind.

Due to the shape and orientation of the island, the west wind will cause a large amount of plankton to funnel into feeding lane **B**. The shape of the island obstructs the plankton's eastern movement, but the island's angle to the wind also lets the plankton move along the west shoreline of the island until it slips past the island's southern tip into **B**. **B** will persist for an extended period because of the plankton's slow movement along the island before it finally slips past the tip.

Feeding lane **C** is similar to **A**. It will be short lived and minimally populated with additional plankton because of the short fetch from the west shoreline and the very short distance of the island shoreline that helps funnel any plankton in Ekman drift to **C**. **C** probably experiences little or no bite.

Feeding lane **D** is similar to **B**. The shape of Point **2** obstructs the easy movement of plankton to the east. The angle of the west side of Point **2** and its orientation to the wind allows plankton to slowly move along Point **2** until it slips past its southern tip and into **D**. **D** and **B** may persist for about the same length of time because of the slow movement of plankton along the west side of Point **2** and the west side of the island.

Both have about the same distance of fetch from the west. Current through the narrows should be strongest with a west wind.

The tip of Point **3** may not be a high percentage fishing location, but its flanks are surrounded in warm water and an elevated amount of plankton, which may make them prime locations for good bites during a west wind.

Areas **E**, **F**, feeding lanes **B** and **D**, and the flanks of Point **3** are the higher percentage locations for good bites during a west wind, especially if any are close to deeper water or good structure. Hatches and molts will be less likely to occur if the wind has raised the water level and therefore increased total-pressure in any of these areas. If the wind has been low velocity, however, total-pressure may be insignificantly affected and have little influence on molts and hatches. The warm water blown into these areas may then facilitate molts, hatches, and good bites to occur.

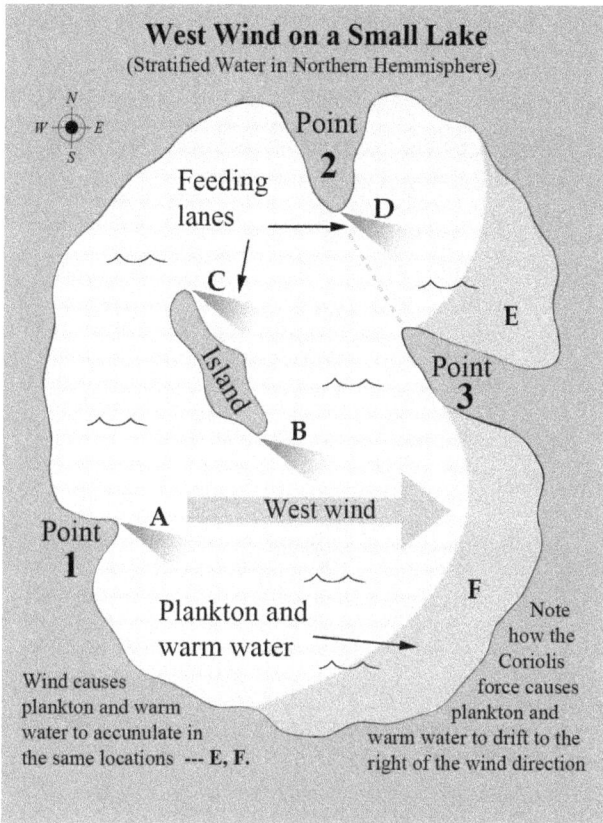

West Wind on a Small Lake
(Stratified Water in Northern Hemmisphere)

Point 2

Feeding lanes

D

C

E

Point 3

Island

B

A   West wind

Point 1

Plankton and warm water

F

Note how the Coriolis force causes plankton and warm water to drift to the right of the wind direction

Wind causes plankton and warm water to accunulate in the same locations --- E, F.

Figure 12-6

Southern Hemisphere

Figure 12-7 illustrates similar feeding lanes and high percentage fishing areas for winds blowing over the same lake, but it's located in the Southern Hemisphere. They occur for all the same reasons as in the Northern Hemisphere, with one small difference: Ekman drift veers to the *left of the wind direction* in the Southern Hemisphere instead of to the right as in the Northern Hemisphere. Further explanation for Figure 12-7 would be unnecessarily redundant.

Determining where feeding lanes and higher percentage fishing areas will occur requires little imagination. Just envision which way the wind is pushing the water and which way the water will veer (Ekman drift)

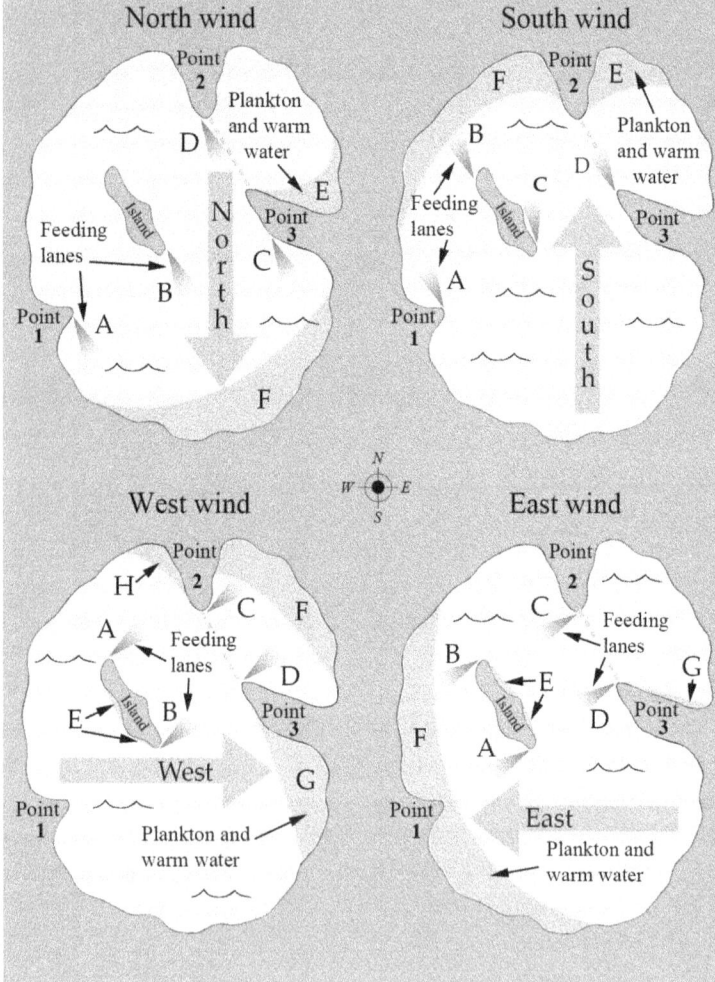

Southern Hemisphere

(Stratified water)

Drift patterns of plankton and warm water caused by wind and Coriolis force on a small lake. Conical feeding lanes and shaded areas are high-percentage areas for good bites.

Figure 12-7

away from the wind direction. There is no left or right drift if the lake has turned over and eliminated temperature stratification, as is the case some-time in fall. Consider the size and shape of the obstacles (like islands and points) in the path of the moving water and adjust your estimations accordingly. You'll generally be close.

Dead Calm Days

It's a little trickier to determine where the feeding lanes and higher percentage areas occur on dead-calm days or days with just a breath of air movement. Knowing the wind history for the previous couple days may be your answer. If wind has blown steadily from one direction before becoming calm, the best fishing is likely to be where the high percentage locations were created by higher wind during the previous days. Conditions in those prior locations will not have changed much, so they may still be productive. Fish may not be as active, but are likely still nearby, especially in nearby deeper water or cover because the small organisms and baitfish they feed upon will have had little reason to move. Much of the plankton will still be in the vicinity because of the dead-calm conditions.

If you're unable to acquire the wind history, another method is to make a quick tour around the lake and sample the water temperature in enough places so you can determine which way the warm water has migrated. Be mindful that your conclusions can be skewed by too few samples and because shallow areas with dark bottoms generally warm up faster than most others. Take enough care with your sampling so the true pattern can be identified.

Calm days allow the entire surface to heat up again, causing plankton to quickly multiply throughout the entire lake system due to the heat. If calm conditions persist for two or more days, previously windblown plankton patterns will become less meaningful because small organisms will be able to feed in many more places. The bite may be good, but it could be scattered hither and yon and difficult to find; a reminder that wind is your friend. Areas unaffected by the current wind may experience a steady rise in plankton populations that hold baitfish in place and cause predators to remain nearby, thus keeping the bite nearby. Areas that are never affected by wind or current movement tend to become stagnant from algae growth (oxygen depletion) or too warm too quickly.

Variable Winds

Perhaps more puzzling than windless days, are days when wind direction is variable. Recall from Chapter 9, Figure 9-2, variable winds are a normal occurrence near the center of comma-shaped, well organized high pressure systems and low pressure systems. In either case, whether high or low pressure, the system in place has been in place for an extended period, normally more than a day before variable winds occur.

In the case of high pressure, three to four days of stable weather probably preceded the variable winds, therefore hatching and molting is probably occurring at a normal rate. Fishing is probably quite good; and the best fishing is probably located in the highest percentage locations caused by steady winds during the previous couple days.

In the case of low pressure, the variable winds would probably be preceded by at least a day or two of overcast skies and possibly higher winds caused by dropping pressure. The variable winds will occur when pressure is lowest, meaning blustery conditions will often occur on wide expanses of open water. Pie hatches and pie molts will have been occurring since low pressure began creeping in. They should continue occurring through the deepest low pressure, but fishing may have to be limited to protected areas out of the wind, primarily for safety. If the system is a weak low pressure system, fishing conditions should be good over most of the lake because winds will be low velocity. Once again, the best fishing may be located in the highest percentage locations caused by steady winds during the previous couple days.

Always Rely on a Barometer

Always beware that weather can be markedly deceptive, and you should always rely upon a barometer when determining if atmospheric pressure is high or low. I've been quite surprised a few times when cold temperatures engulfed my region, yet barometric pressure dropped at the same time. Without a barometer I may have easily assumed that the temperature drop indicated high barometric pressure had blanketed the region, but, in fact, the opposite occurred.

Multitude of Conditions

The warmest water is generally the most productive during spring, but it may be too warm during late summer months, in which case cooler water on the windward side of lakes may be more productive. Knowing more about fish's preferred temperatures and the probability of where those temperatures may occur can be very helpful. Each lake will undergo its own unique heating and cooling cycle each season, so keeping track of it with good logs can save you a lot of effort in future years on the same lake.

In the colder waters of late fall, after turnover, fishing near leaf drop areas and collapsed weed beds can be productive early and late in the day. Also, there can often be patches of dead brown weeds and live green weeds in the same vicinity. The live green weeds will often produce a better bite, perhaps because they are still photosynthesizing, and/or are more nutritious and supporting a broader spectrum of food organisms that attract more fish. Alternatively, fish may occupy the green weed zones as a survival mechanism because their coloration gives them a concealment advantage in it from predators, or they may occupy it simply because they are more accustomed to it after the long growing season.

Be aware that hatches and molts may occur on the windward side of lakes if the temperature of the substrate harboring immatures is unchanged by wind conditions. The wind can reduce the water level, and therefore total-pressure, which can result in an early hatch or molt when the water temperature has been unaffected by the wind. This can happen even if there is a slight drop in water temperature because the immatures may have matured enough in ableness to molt if pressure is reduced. This is probably not a common occurrence in most water systems, but my guess is that it's probably not rare either. Such an occurrence could result in good bites occurring on both the windward and leeward sides of a lake at the same time. All anglers should be so lucky from time to time.

Ideal Conditions

The above circumstances are just another example of the bedfellow relationship of temperature and total-pressure, and why the high pressure and low pressure rules must always be taken into account. There are two weather situations, however, that are no-brainers for good bites: (1) The days after high barometric pressure has remained steady for 3-4 days and continues to remain steady, and, (2) When prolonged (3-4 days) high barometric pressure drops to a lower level and stays at that level or drops lower, and total-pressure is not changed by precipitation runoff.

These are ideal conditions that facilitate the best natural bites. Some of the bites will be better than others, but good bites will normally occur in these conditions. Some will be so significant that anglers will have trouble competing with the abundance of natural food and suffer minimal catches. These conditions will cause similar bites in most water systems most of the time unless something unusual occurs that discourages the bite. If you have the flexibility in your life to pick the best days to go fishing, pick days when either of these two conditions occur. Let natural sequences be your guide to specific time periods within which certain bites will occur; then go fishing when either of these conditions occur during those time periods. The resulting angling experience may fulfill your wildest flights of imagination.

Patterns

The best anglers know that the vast majority of water holds no fish, so they strive to avoid fishing the empty water as best they can. Many compete in tournaments and have developed techniques for identifying patterns of fish behavior that they use before and during tournaments. Patterns can be almost anything. For example, perhaps fish are only being caught at the same depth over a dark bottom — that's a pattern; or they're only being caught near brush lines — that's also a pattern. Maybe the majority is being caught in deep shade, or on humps, or only near the downwind side of points, and so forth; they're all patterns. When daily insect hatches occur in the same locations, they signal that a pattern of good bites are probably occurring in those locations every day during the same time period. Logging the time and location of such hatches can frequently put you in the right spot at the right time the next day, and days thereafter. When an acceptable fish is caught in these locations, anglers usually continue fishing them and similar spots to determine if a pattern exists that they can capitalize on for the day, and perhaps for the next day. Many will wisely invest a little time to uncover such a pattern. If it doesn't prove successful, they quickly look for the next pattern opportunity.

Patterns develop in a variety of haunts, better known as structures, cover, and water features. An extensive list of them is included in **Sidebar #27: Structure, Cover, and Water Features**. It's likely that one or more of them are in, or near every *high* percentage area where you've predicted good bites to occur. Those within the high percentage areas are likely the *highest* percentage locations in which you will encounter a bite. Your predictions will be even more fruitful when you've identified fish behavior patterns in those highest percentage locations. Your new ability to predict bites, combined with any knowledge of structure fishing, should enhance the rewards of both.

#27
Structure, Cover and Water Features

Backwaters	Dam corners	Marinas	Shade
Banks and under-	Deep basins	Marl	Slab lumber piles
cuts	Deep channel bends	Marsh edges, open-	Slack water
Bayous	Deep holes	ings	Silt beds
Bays (protected)	Deep river bends	Mud lines	Silt lines
Bends, inside or	Deep water	Mud over hard	Sloughs
outside	Depressions	bottom	Slopes
Boat houses	Ditches,	Narrows	Stoney areas
Boulders	Ditches, submerged	Narrows with cur-	Stream beds, sub-
Break lines	Docks and rafts	rent	merged
Breaks on Breaks	Drain channels	Outlets	Stumps, submerged
Breakwater	Dropoffs	Overhangs	Timber, fallen
Bridges	Eddies	Piers	Timber, submerged
Brush, edges and	Edges of mud and	Pilings	or flooded
sunken	sand	Pits	Sunkeen objects
Buildings, sub-	Edges of vegetation	Pockets	Surface
merged	Edges of weeds	Points	Swepers
Buoys, large	Feeder ponds	Pools	Temperature layer
Canals	Flats	`Pools below falls	Trestles
Causeways	Grass beds	and rapids	Turbid water
Channels	Grass lines	Railroad grades,	Turbidity lines
Cliff bases	Gravel areas, shoals	submerged	Weed beds
Coffers	Harbors	Rapids	Weed lines
Confluences	Holes in weed mats	Reeds	Weed mats
Coves	Humps	ridges	Weed patches
Creek Channels	Jetties	Riffles	Weed tops
Creek channel	Launch sites	Rip rap	Wing dams
points	Leeward or wind-	River mouths	All things that
Creek inlets	ward shores	River courses	provide fish with
Creeks	Ledges	Rock piles	relief from strong
Culverts	Lily pads	Rock wall	currents
Currents, edges	Logjams	Rocky shoals	
Cuts	Log piles	Runs	
Dams	Logs, submerged	Sandbars	

Forage and Fish movement

During recent years, structure fishing has included the concept of predator fish traveling to and from a single location that provides safe sanctuary from various threats. Supposedly they migrate from these sanctuaries to feed and spawn and return to them on a regular basis, sometimes as regularly as twice per day. I suspect this is substantially true in ponds and very small lakes, where migration can be a short trip in all directions, but it's not very realistic in bigger water.

In bigger water, it seems more likely that predator fish will find temporary comfort or safety, or good ambush sites in the vicinity of good forage, and remain near the vicinity until the forage is depleted. In bigger lakes, when local forage is depleted, long jaunts may be required before encountering adequate forage once again.

Important forage species such as minnows and other baitfish are generally on the move a great percentage of the time. They, too, must find food, which is usually zooplankton drifting in wind-driven, warm surface water, and aquatic insects and crustaceans. Predators commonly follow and feed on the forage that's following the wind-driven plankton. An incidental benefit for the forage occurs when the warm water is blown to a new shoreline location. The increased water temperature accelerates insect molting and hatching in that location, and probably crustacean molting as well if the location is suitable habitat for supporting such organisms . It can cause a new abundance of available insects and other food organisms. It's an incidental event that probably occurs quite frequently. It would be one of nature's great ways to sustain the forage, and hence the predators. It's a natural order that puts all things in the right place at the right time on a regular basis, and which is almost always moving to a new downwind location.

I know of nothing else in the dynamics of the food web that can continually lead forage and predators to a steadily recurring abundance of food like wind can. It's these dynamics that undermine the concept of single, safe sanctuaries. I suspect that "sanctuaries" are simply haunts in various locations that serve as convenient and comfortable places from which predators can temporarily access forage while it's abundant in those vicinities. Some haunts are probably occupied more than others, but it's reasonably probable that their occupancy can be frequently correlated to wind direction.

Water in wind-protected areas of larger lakes, like bayous, bays, coves, sloughs, feeder ponds, and marshes will often behave more like water in small lakes instead of larger lakes. Their water generally warms sooner because its movement is more restricted, which causes sequential events to occur much earlier, like they would in a smaller lake. Therefore certain bites will occur sooner in most of them.

The following section on reservoirs and impoundments contains additional valuable discussion for finding bites in streams and small lakes.

Reservoirs - Impoundments

Reservoirs and impoundments are individually unique, with widely varying characteristics, but most exist to store large amounts of water and regulate its use. They are so synonymous in meaning and purpose that they are deemed to be the same thing for this discussion. Therefore, for the sake of simplicity, only the term *reservoirs* will be used here.

A majority of the information in section Small Lakes above also applies to reservoirs, but most of it will not be repeated in this section.

Fishing in reservoirs is normally more challenging than fishing in the average farm pond. Reservoirs behind dams can be a mile wide or more, and many miles longer. Most have a history of surrendering their secrets reluctantly. In essence, however, a reservoir is simply a lake with a controlled outlet at its downstream end (a dam) and a mainstream inlet at its upstream end, and may include smaller tributaries that feed into it. The largest reservoirs typically feature a multitude of coves, bays, points, shallows, channels, flats, humps, tributaries, islands and so forth, many of which are also found in small lakes. Finding fish among all these features can be a daunting challenge.

Questionable Behavior
Most fishermen go fishing to locate and catch fish. This is especially true for tournament fishermen when money and prizes are on the line. Their livelihood often depends on it, and most of them spend most of their tournament time fishing in reservoirs of one kind or another. They think hard about the reasons why fish will be in one location or another, and what they should use to catch them. To improve their chances, they commonly pre-fish the reservoirs, sometimes for days before tournaments begin, to identify fish behavior patterns and productive locations.

Unfortunately, the patterns and locations will often change mysteriously as a tournament progresses. When this happens, finding the right fish often becomes an exercise in chaos. It usually involves scattershot attempts with different techniques at different locations, hoping that something will work to catch a good fish, and a few more after that. Results are generally disappointing because success has been reduced to a random game of chance. Many tournaments are lost by tournament leaders who fail to discover the pattern that works on the final day of competition. It's common for other fishermen to figure it out and go home with the money. Savvy tournament anglers know that the longer a tournament lasts, the less likely it will be won based on a behavior pattern that is several days old.

Similar behavior occurs almost invariably among recreational fisherman. They usually go to the same spot in the reservoir where they caught fish during a previous trip, hoping success will be good once again. They fish the old pattern. If the location is unproductive, which is often the case, they begin trying different baits, flies, or lures presented in different ways at different depths in an assortment of different habitats. When they finally catch a fish, they continue the same technique and hope to catch more. Sometimes they do catch more, occasionally many more, but they frequently don't catch nearly as many as they think they probably should. They conclude their trip by consoling themselves with thoughts that the few fish they caught still provided a pleasing experience. Yet they harbor quiet disappointment because they haven't caught more fish, or bigger fish. Recreational and tournament fishermen could both do better in reservoirs by concentrating their efforts in areas containing a higher likelihood for success, i.e., where bites are most likely to occur. Identifying many of those areas can often be done before leaving the launch site. Temperature and wind direction are generally the key, as well as some rudimentary knowledge about the species being sought.

Wind Direction and Good Bites

Wind direction plays a major role in fish movement in reservoirs for a majority of the open-water fishing season. Wind pushes plankton-laden water around on reservoirs in the same manner as it does on small lakes because reservoir water is also temperature stratified from early spring through summer and most of fall. The warmest surface water is blown downwind to a leeward shore, but drifts to the right (Northern Hemisphere) due to Ekman drift, exactly the same as occurs in small lakes. When the wind-driven warm water is forced against a shoreline, the shape of the shoreline either traps the plankton-laden warm water and holds it in place, or lets it slip past the shoreline to form a feeding lane and/or move on to accumulate at a destination farther downwind as illustrated in Figures 12-3 through 12-6 in Small Lakes.

Figure 12-8 depicts which locations have higher potential for good bites based on wind direction in a hypothetical reservoir in the Northern Hemisphere.

Water temperature in Figure 12-8 is assumed to be below stressful levels for fish. In temperate latitudes, the least stressful temperatures normally occur during winter, spring, early summer, and mid to late fall. Temperatures may be too hot and stressful during mid to late summer and early fall, which could require fishing in deeper, cooler water near leeward shorelines, bearing in mind that the locations of leeward shorelines are frequently changing.

Letters N, S, E, and W denote which locations offer a higher probability for good bites when winds are from the north (N), south (S), east (E) or west (W). For example, wherever the letter "N" is located, it represents a higher probability location for a good bite when wind is blowing from the north, especially if it has been sustained for at least a day or two. Similarly, wherever the letter "W" is located, it represents a better location for a good bite when wind is, and has been, blowing from the west, and so forth for letters "S" (south) and "E" (east). Notice that each letter is in a location where the shape of the shoreline traps the warm water and holds it in place, or lets it slip past the shoreline where it would then form a feeding lane and move on to accumulate at a destination farther downwind and generally to the right. Note especially how the jutting points of land are affected by wind from one direction more than wind from other directions. Ekman drift is a factor in determining the location for every letter.

Seven creek arms feed into the reservoir, all having wide and/or narrow sections, and each section can be expected to behave differently with different winds. Generally, narrow sections will have faster flow, more depth, and concentrate food in a narrower slot through that part of the arm. Narrows always have high potential as a feeding lane, but particularly high potential at the downstream end if wind is pushing plankton-laden warm water through the narrow section. Not many letters (N, S, E, W) are positioned in the creek arms because downstream current flow can also negate many influences of wind from certain directions. In other words, some winds will have little effect in parts of creek arms because normal current

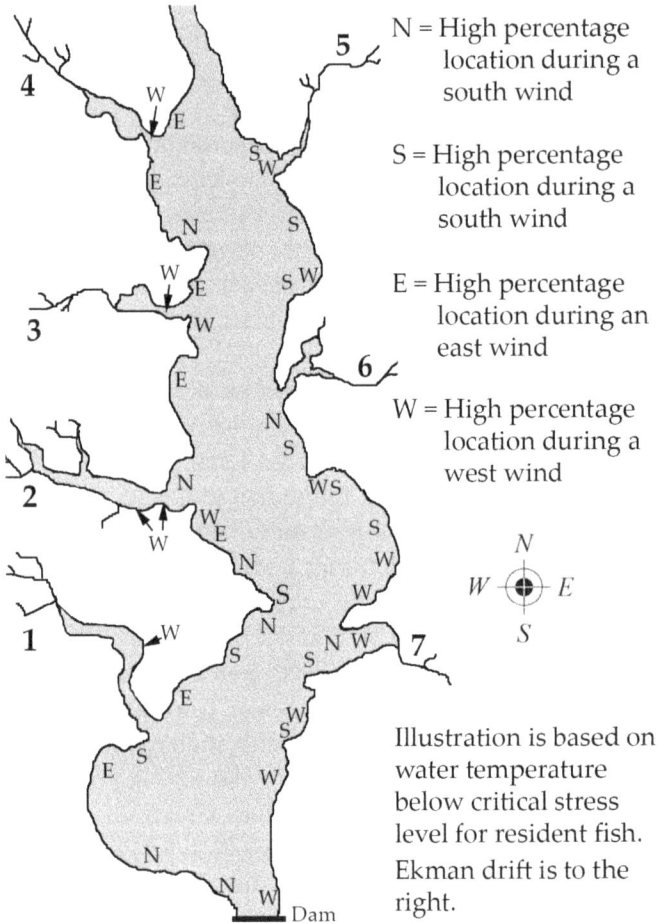

HYPOTHETICAL RESERVOIR
Northern Hemisphere

N = High percentage location during a south wind

S = High percentage location during a south wind

E = High percentage location during an east wind

W = High percentage location during a west wind

Illustration is based on water temperature below critical stress level for resident fish. Ekman drift is to the right.

Figure 12-8

or stream flow effectively counteracts the wind effects. Wind will have more effect in sections of creek arms where current flow is slow.

Annual natural sequences unfold in predictable fashion in reservoirs just as they do in rivers and small lakes, and they usually occur in shallow water first. Shallow water areas warm up first, causing new plan growth and re-oxygenation from photosynthesis, earliest spawning, and earliest significant insect hatches and so forth, and the most predictable bites. Shallow areas are commonly found in upper creek arms and along the flanks of the upper reservoir where the mainstream first dumps into it. More shallow areas can be located on topographic lake maps. Older U.S. Geological Survey maps and aerial photographs can also be referenced to find shallows, and to locate structures that were flooded when the reservoir was filled.

Your Reservoir

When deciphering your own reservoir, you only need to reason for yourself where wind will cause the warm water to accumulate, or flow as a feeding lane, with influence from Ekman drift (in stratified water). Each wind direction must be considered separately because each will yield different results. Every reservoir is different from all others, but warm water movement is generally predictable in every one.

Water Isolated from Wind

Some areas in small lakes and reservoirs may be significantly protected from wind and minimally affected by it. Wind may not move the water around very much in those areas, so the bite may almost always occur in them where the most food organisms are available. There is likely a higher percentage area in each one, although it may shift around through the seasons according to the natural sequence of food availability in its various small habitats. Good logs can eventually reveal the seasonal locations.

If the water in some locations becomes stagnant, it may foster algae growth that negatively affects the bite. Large algae die-offs in stagnant water can cause exploding bacterial counts that severely reduce dissolved oxygen, forcing fish to relocate to water with higher oxygen content.

Fish are near Food

Unstressed fish in reservoirs, as elsewhere, are ordinarily located in a limited variety of places. They're usually in haunts with access to food, or along routes to and from food, or somewhere in a pattern of movements associated with spawning. By necessity, they're opportunistic feeders so they move to feed when food becomes available or when they expect it to be available, or they sometimes remain near it if it's available and abundant, or they prowl for it when it's not readily available. Even during pre-spawning and spawning, many fish species are never far from adequate food. During post-spawning, however, they must sometimes move long distances — miles — to find it, which occurs when they have depleted the food supply near the spawning grounds. It's probably safe to assume that fish feed in many different areas of a reservoir at some point in their lifetime, but they feed in some areas more than others. Their feeding patterns will fluctuate throughout the year because the location and availability of their food also fluctuates. Therefore, if you can predict when and where their food will be available, you can be relatively confident that at least some fish are nearby to pounce on it.

Insect hatches are one of the most obvious and valuable indicators of where the food is. They are often the food that predators eat, or the food that attracts the baitfish that the predators eat. They occur in places where they probably occurred on a previous day, and where they will probably occur again on a subsequent day. They are a beacon that belies the location of good bites.

During spring, fall, and winter, hatches are usually more prevalent during mid-day. During summer, they are more prevalent in morning and evening. The difference in activity is likely due to the sun's heat which has its most activating effect during midday in spring, fall, and winter, but it's most searing and detrimental effect during midday of summer. Recall that moisture preservation is supremely important for hatching insects to survive, and daily hatch times reflect that requirement throughout the seasons. Overcast skies, which interfere with the sun's effects, may cause normal hatching times to shift to later in the morning or earlier in the afternoon or evening.

In addition, photosynthesis by underwater plants essentially shuts down during the hours of darkness, which reduces dissolved oxygen in the water and likely compromises insect activity in the wee hours before dawn. This help explain why fish begin to bite as dawn penetrates the darkness. As light levels rise, oxygen levels also begin to climb, making it possible for many organisms to elevate their activity level, which would stimulate feeding because the elevated activity makes some of the organisms more vulnerable as prey. The new light of dawn also makes them more visible and easier to catch. It's likely that many fish are also hungry after fasting during the hours of darkness which would certainly contribute to good bites near dawn. The long daylight fast would also help explain a spike in feeding activity near dusk, when insect activity increases during the warmer part of the fishing season.

Pre-Fishing and After-Hours Scouting

Hatches can make your pre-fishing excursions far more productive. Every insect emerges from a unique habitat, therefore when they're seen rising from the water at a certain time and location, the time and location should be logged. It would be helpful if you could identify the species, which is almost impossible at times, but a simple description is much better than nothing if you're able to collect a sample. Just make up a description if need be. The description will help determine if the same insect is being sighted on subsequent days and in future years. You may also notice that small fish are feeding on them or trying to escape from predators below. It's best to cover a lot of water to find as many hatch locations as possible. They signify prime food areas and reveal one end of fish's routes to them. These locations and routes could be productive when you come back during active tournament competition.

If tournament rules allow, you can continue making these excursions during the evenings on days of competition. Rather than retire for the day after weigh-in, it may prove profitable to venture back onto the water in the evening to observe if hatches or fish activities have changed from the day before, which they often do. Most changes occur because of a significant change in wind direction or speed, or a significant change in barometric pressure. These are critically important changes because they change the direction of plankton drift, and the locations of favorable total-pressure and water temperature. Productivity of locations unaffected by the wind may not change by much. If any of these changes do occur, however, your next day of fishing will probably not be a repeat of the day before. You will need to make adjustments in your tactics that allow for the changed conditions. Local weather reports and forecasts will be very helpful in this regard.

You will frequently not encounter hatches on the days and evenings you prefer, but you may still spot fish that don't appear to be in any particular hurry to move on. Their lazy demeanor may be an indication that they are exactly where they want to be because they may be expecting food to appear soon in that location. The sightings should be logged, and the locations entered into a GPS (Global Positioning System) unit if you have one.

You can make two assumptions about the fish you've sighted: (1)

They have been there awhile, or, (2) They have just arrived, which means they have migrated from somewhere, and it probably didn't take them long to make the trip. If they've been there awhile, your scouting work may be done. You know where the bite will likely happen and where to fish if wind direction doesn't change. If they just arrived, you need to know the route they followed to get there. That's your challenge, and it's probably a structure identification challenge, but at least you know where to begin. Refer to the list of structures in section Small Lakes.

Advantage of Wind History

Unlike insect molts and hatches that commonly advance from downstream to upstream in unimpeded river systems, many significant molts and hatches in reservoirs generally occur in the shallowest, slowest, warmest water first, particularly locations with dark bottoms. Many then advance to the deeper areas that have become warmer through the respective hatch or molt period. Conversely, deeper locations may warm before shallower ones if wind blows warm water into the deeper locations first, which will cause molts and hatches to occur there sooner, or perhaps at the same time as they occur in the shallows. When you see good hatches, be sure to obtain the water temperature where they occur. This brings into question which flies have hatched in recent days; did they cause a good bite, and where in the progression of water temperature throughout the reservoir can they be expected to hatch next? Knowing the temperature will significantly improve your odds of correctly predicting the timing and locations of their next appearances, and where they will cause the next good bites.

Spawning, too, can occur in any one of the above scenarios first, so long as the locations have a suitable bottom for it, except some fish species prefer to spawn in a current, whereas others prefer to spawn in still waters. Seasonal timing and preferred water temperature are the keys to locating the spawners and their good bites.

Whether you're looking for spawners or insect activity, knowing the history of wind direction and velocity for the few days preceding a fishing trip to a reservoir or small lake can guide you to good bites. You can better determine where warm and cold water have been located and where it is more likely to be when you arrive. This is particularly valuable for locating spawners because they prefer specific temperature ranges and specific locations that they use every year. Wind history also gives you a strong indication of where total-pressure has been high or low, which, when combined with the locations where warm water has been, can tell you where hatches and molts have likely been occurring. Local weather forecasts that include wind direction forecasts can then be used to foretell where hatches, molts, and feeding lanes have a higher percentage of oc-curring next. Locations where they occur next are where the next good bites will occur, as well as locations where spawning is taking place.

Local Resources

Pre-spawning, spawning, and post spawning behavior only occurs for a short time for most species each year, and local fishermen commonly know when and where each occurs. You can learn a lot from them by hanging around boat launches and marinas at the end of the day and asking questions when they come off the water. Many are wily and won't tell you much and may mislead you, but there are also those who are not jealous of their knowledge and will gladly give you honest, detailed answers. Local tackle shops can also be helpful. You will likely learn what has spawned or not, and where success has been best in the last few days, among other nuggets of information. You may get even better information if you ask for their complaints about fishing being poor. Each bit of information is a piece of a pattern that is now easier for you to figure out. If the fishermen are not helpful enough, you can ask local government fishing agency per-sonnel, especially fisheries biologists and fish and game law enforcement officers, who are usually happy to provide that type of information.

Never discount how helpful your natural resource law enforcement officers can be. Several years ago I was conversing with our local conser-vation officer about natural sequences and how I was able to use them to predict when smelt would run up local creeks to spawn every spring. My knowledge of sequences enabled me to predict the exact day the smelt runs begin every year. The officer is a friend of mine, and a bit of a naturalist, so I went into a lengthy explanation about photoperiods, pressure systems, flowering plants and a few other factors that I'd investigated for my pre-dictions. I probably sounded proud of my accomplishment. He politely listened to my story, and then said, with a knowing grin, "I have a better way. I have 25 years of arrest records of poachers illegally netting steel-head while they were netting smelt. I know the dates because concerned sportsmen tell us the day the smelt arrive, but we wait a day for the word to spread. Poachers usually arrive the next day, and that's when we show up." Arrest records, who'da thunk. You could pursue this angle with local authorities.

Also, don't neglect information available on the internet, particularly chat rooms, bulletin boards, and forums. They are especially good sources for spawning, baitfish, and hatch information.

If you know how to be respectful and polite, don't be afraid to seek advice from local experienced fishermen who are in the sunset of their lives — the old timers. They can be some of the best and most trustworthy sources for critical local information. Many get a bigger thrill from helping someone like you catch more fish than catching another fish themselves. I've been given many great insights by retired guides and retired charter captains who have graciously shared their knowledge. Hiring an experienced local guide for a day can also be a shortcut to a trove of useful knowledge.

Another useful strategy in reservoirs is to obtain draw-down schedules from dam authorities. When water is being drawn down it creates more current in the reservoir and more food for baitfish will be temporarily drawn into the increased current. The current will be more pronounced near the edges of cover and large structure like weed beds and humps, and over open flats. Fish will migrate to feeding lanes set up by the newly formed strong current. Predators may then take up stations where they can ambush baitfish that have been activated by the stronger current and may be swimming in it. Some Current lanes then become feeding lanes that may produce good bites.

Southern Hemisphere

Figure 12-9 illustrates similar high percentage fishing areas for winds blowing over the same reservoir as depicted in Figure 12-8, except it's located in the Southern Hemisphere. The high percentage areas occur for all the same reasons as in the Northern Hemisphere, with one small difference: Ekman drift veers to the left of the wind direction in the Southern Hemisphere instead of to the right as occurs in the Northern Hemisphere.

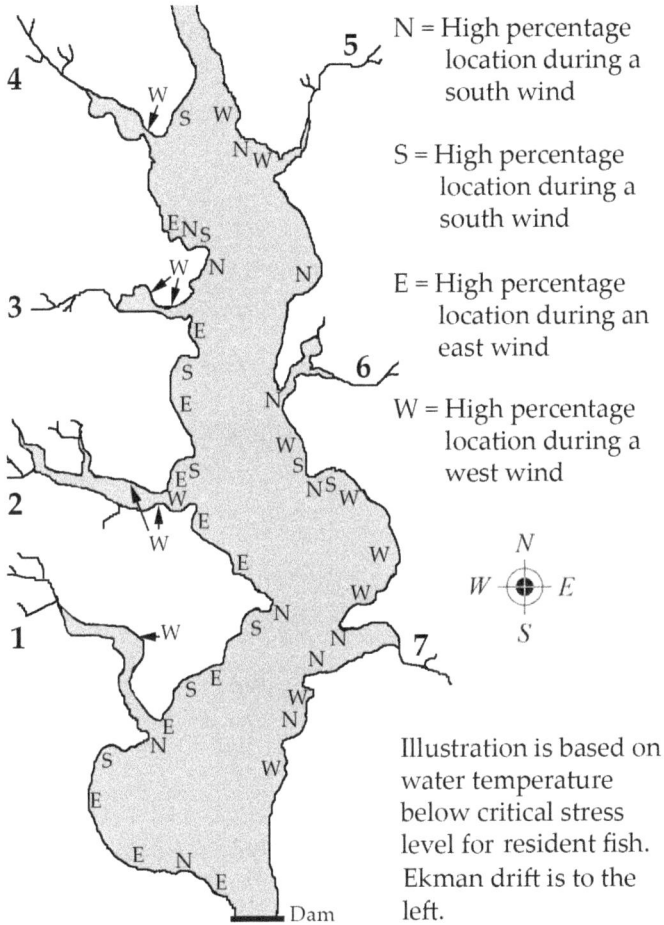

HYPOTHETICAL RESERVOIR
Southern Hemisphere

N = High percentage location during a south wind

S = High percentage location during a south wind

E = High percentage location during an east wind

W = High percentage location during a west wind

Illustration is based on water temperature below critical stress level for resident fish. Ekman drift is to the left.

Figure 12-9

Chapter 13

Log Page and
Prediction Steps

I've had the rich pleasure of knowing several fishermen who have made a thoughtful and diligent effort to keep good logs in order to improve their fishing. Some information has been helpful and led to improved catches, but more has resulted in no benefit. The problem is that the wrong information or not enough of the right information has been logged. Figure 13-1 depicts a sample log page containing provisions for most of the information you will ever need for predicting and finding good bites. Its dimensions should be about twice the size shown here in order to accommodate ample information in the respective boxes. If more space is needed, the back of the page is available. Not all of the boxes are relevant for all outings, but for best long-term prediction results, enter pertinent information in as many boxes as possible. The form is suitable for fishing and scouting excursions alike.

My Steps for Predictions
Friends frequently call and ask me to predict whether fishing will be good, or not, if they go fishing today, tomorrow, or during the coming weekend. I relish the challenge. Some predictions are easier to make than others, but most only take a few minutes after becoming accustomed to

Sample Log Page

DATE	FISH SPECIES	QTY	SIZE RANGE	NAME OF RIVER, LAKE OR RESERVOIR	LOCATION OF CATCH

TIME OF CATCH	GPS COORDINATES		DEPTH OF CATCH	TEMPERATURE AT DEPTH OF CATCH	STOMACH - INTESTINE CONTENTS

RELEVANT STRUCTURE	LOCATION OF FISH SIGHTINGS	WATER CONDITIONS CHOPPY ____ FLAT ____ CLEAR ____ TURBID ____ OTHER ____

HATCH / MOLT SPECIES TIME LOCATION HEAVY ____ MEDIUM ____ LIGHT ____	SPINNER FALL SPECIES TIME LOCATION HEAVY ____ MEDIUM ____ LIGHT ____

BAITFISH SPECIES TIME LOCATION CRUSTACEANS OTHER BEHAVIOR	INDICATOR	PRECURSOR

BAROMETRIC PRESSURE HISTORY: UP TO 96 HOURS	NOTES
LITTLE CHANGE ____ TRENDING HIGHER ____ TRENDING LOWER ____	

WATER LEVEL HISTORY: UP TO 96 HOURS	NOTES
NO CHANGE HIGHER LOWER	

WATER TEMPERATURE HISTORY: UP TO 96 HOURS	NOTES
NORMAL HIGHER LOWER	

WIND DIRECTION HISTORY: UP TO 96 HOURS	NOTES

AIR TEMPERATURE HISTORY: UP TO 96 HOURS	NOTES

RECENT PRECIPITATION	SKY CONDITIONS CLEAR ____ CLOUDY ____ PARTLY CLOUDY ____	SUNRISE ____ SUNSET ____ MOONRISE ____ MOONSET ____ % ILLUMMINATION OF DISK ____

TACKLE & PRESENTATION

REMARKS

Figure 13-1

accessing the information. Nearly all the information I need is available on a small handful of websites, which I keep bookmarked. The steps I take to make predictions are listed below. I include them only as a final example that might be helpful.

The first facts I learn are whether the prediction is needed for a river, small lake, reservoir, or one of the largest lakes (Lake Michigan in my case), and which species of fish is being sought. My routine is similar for each, but there are differences, as explained below.

River Predictions

For routine river predictions I do the following: I first check the local airport weather data website for precipitation history and barometric pressure history. If precipitation has been zero for the past few days, I then assume water levels have been stable and are not a factor. If substantial rain has fallen in the past several days, I know that water levels have gone up and increased total-pressure, so molts and bites have probably been suppressed and may remain suppressed until the water level begins falling. High water argues against a good bite. If water level is falling, molts and bites are probably close to recurring normally if they haven't recurred already, therefore bites are also close to resuming or have already resumed. A falling water level is always reason for optimism.

I then check the trend of barometric pressure and determine if it's relatively unchanged and for how long, or if the trend is up or down, and by how much. If it's relatively unchanged for four days, I'm relatively confident that some kind of molting, and therefore a good bite, is probably occurring sometime during the day or will occur the following day. If the trend is downward by 15 points or more for more than eight hours, I'm also confident that molting and a good bite are occurring sometime during the day. If the trend is upward and has exceeded 15 points upward for the past six to eight hours or more, I am usually doubtful that significant molting and a good bite will occur during the remainder of that day. The odds are poor. The increased total-pressure may keep immatures in ableness for another day. Odds of a good bite are certainly better for the following day, especially if the water level is falling, which may partially or fully offset the increase in total-pressure caused by higher barometric pressure.

I also check air temperature because persistent cold air may cool the water enough to suppress molting and any related bite. If the air has warmed substantially, water temperature will rise and accelerate immatures through ableness and cause an earlier bite. If I'm aware of a sequence indicator or precursor that can bear on the prediction, especially for time of day, I'll certainly use it.

Lastly, I check country-wide and regional radar, the local forecast, and an infrared satellite loop to observe movement of cloud formations.

The Infrared reveals approaching bad weather that doesn't completely appear on radar. Both reveal whether it's safe to venture out, or if bad weather is approaching that warrants canceling the outing. It usually takes only about four to five minutes to access the information on the web and in my logs and make an informed prediction.

I frequently don't know the water temperature, which would be a strong indicator foretelling which insect or crustacean may hatch or molt but all the other conditions can still be used to predict situations that are conducive for molts, hatches, and good bites to occur. You can discover which insect, crustacean, or baitfish is relevant when you arrive at the river bank, then log it.

Small Lake and Reservoir Predictions

For routine small lake and reservoir predictions I check and consider all the same factors and websites that I use for river predictions, and repeat most of that information here, but wind direction is also now a critical factor.

I first check the local airport weather data for precipitation history and barometric pressure history. If precipitation has been zero for the past few days, then I assume water levels have been stable and are not a factor. If substantial rain has fallen in the past several days, water levels may have gone up and increased total-pressure, so molts and bites have probably been suppressed and may remain suppressed until the water level begins falling or several days of ableness have passed. The runoff may also have lowered the water temperature, which would delay molts and bites. High water argues against a good bite. If water level is falling, molts and bites are probably close to recurring normally if they haven't recurred already so bites are also close to recurring.

I then check the trend of barometric pressure and determine if it's relatively unchanged and for how long, or if the trend is up or down, and by how much. If it's relatively unchanged for four days, I'm confident that some kind of molting, and therefore a good bite, is probably occurring sometime during the day or will occur the following day. If the trend has

308

been flat for a couple days, but is now downward by 15 points or more for more than eight hours, I'm also confident that molting and a good bite are occurring sometime during the day. If the trend is upward and has exceeded 15 points upward for the past six to eight hours or more, I am usually pessimistic about molting and a good bite occurring during the remainder of that day. The odds are questionable. The increased total-pressure may keep immatures in ableness for another day. Odds of a good bite are certainly better for the following day, especially if the water level is falling, which will offset the increase in total-pressure caused by higher barometric pressure. If I'm aware of a sequence indicator or precursor that can bear on the prediction, especially for time of day, I'll certainly use it.

I also check air temperature because persistent cold air may cool the water enough to suppress molting and any related bite. If the air has warmed substantially, water temperature will rise and accelerate immatures through ableness and cause an earlier bite. The air temperature gives me a good idea about whether the wind is blowing warm across the lake surface, or if surface water is being cooled and compromising favorable bite conditions.

Next, I check wind history for determining where warm or cool water is located around the lake or reservoir and decide which locations are favorable for good bites — often based on structure and cover. I'll then evaluate where feeding lanes may have developed as a result of the wind direction in recent hours. If possible, it's all depicted on a topographic map of the lake. Favorable locations can be plotted for all wind directions long before needed and simply referenced "at a glance" when needed, e.g., Figure 12-8.

Lastly, I check country-wide and regional radar, the local forecast, and an infrared satellite loop to observe movement of cloud formations. They reveal whether it's safe to venture out, or if bad weather is approaching that warrants canceling the outing. It usually takes only about four to five minutes to access the information on the web and in my logs and make an informed prediction.

Largest Lakes Predictions (e.g., Lake Michigan)
My predictions in the largest lakes have been primarily directed to fishing near shore. They have also been for specific species of fish, for example, smallmouth bass, salmon, lake trout, and several others. Each species has a preferred temperature range, spawning behavior, and forage

preferences, and they all come into shallow water (20 feet or less) when chasing forage, and during their spawning periods, but only if the water temperature is suitable. They usually inhabit their preferred temperature zone if they can find it, which makes their appearances predictable if you can find where the water is the correct temperature. Near shore in these huge lakes, the water temperature is most frequently in the preferred range for a particular species when sustained wind blows from a certain direction. The wind either brings warm water near shore and the warmer water species with it, or moves it farther offshore which leaves colder water near shore and the colder water species with it (Chapter 10).

Accordingly, my predictions are generally based on only four factors: Wind history that includes direction and velocity, water temperature, and sequences such as spawning periods that also include spawning periods of bait fish like alewives and smelt.

I check wind data on the local commercial airport weather website; and also check the local forecast and infrared satellite cloud looping to see if wind direction will remain the same or change soon, and if bad weather is approaching. A quick check of national and regional radar helps to visualize any weather threats that need to be considered.

I check surface water temperature at **www.coastwatch.msu.edu,** which is a cooperative project of government agencies and State of Michigan universities. The site contains processed satellite temperature surveillance data of the Great Lakes and provides surface water temperature maps. The maps contain temperature data in isobar form, and are fantastic aids. They are not always available or reliable, however, because clouds often obscure the lakes' surfaces and the satellites may then read temperatures of the cloud tops, which are useless.

When clouds obscure the surface, wind is the only useful indicator, but it's still a good one. Sustained winds of a certain velocity from a single direction will move warm water out or bring it in to every location on the lake. Each location will have its own unique combination of wind velocity, direction, and duration that cools or warms the location. In the locations for which I have made predictions, approximately one to three days of sustained winds exceeding 10 miles per hour will usually be enough to bring a significant water temperature change to those locations. The time required to effect the change is dependent on how thick the warm surface water region is, and how far the wind must move it. Changes occur soonest in large bays like Green Bay and the Grand Traverse bays, which behave more like smaller, independent lakes. The significant temperature change then brings a significant change in the fish species near shore. When these temperature changes occur simultaneously with baitfish spawning, or significant insect or crustacean molting, the bite is on.

If I or my friends plan to fish at night, I always check the United States Naval Observatory website at **www.usno.navy.mil** for complete sun and moon data. I'm interested in the times of sunrise, sunset, moonrise and moonset and what percent of the moon's visible disk is illuminated. The percent of illumination indicates how bright the moon is going to be. If it's going to create a bright sky for a major portion of the night, particularly if the brightness runs into dawn, fishing success for some species can be marginal (my experience), especially during the several hours before and after dawn.

For another detailed example of a big water prediction, revisit the explanation for Figure 10-10.

Your New Ability

You are now a rare fisherman who has the tools you need for predicting the *day* when natural bites will occur. Possessing the ability to predict the day is akin to possessing a major fragment of the fishing grail. With a little practice, you should have little trouble making good bite predictions and catching far more fish for the remainder of your days on the water.

An Ongoing Quest

In the spirit of your continued success, I am deeply interested in expanding this work in order to provide you with any information that I have omitted, as well as new developments that bear upon it. The multitude of scholars who checked this work have conditioned me to expect a flow of new academic studies that this work may inspire. My intent is to provide you with the results of those studies, plus an expected torrent of new bite information from fishermen all over the world, and news about proper recording barometers. As it accumulates, I hope to make it available at **www.PredictingTheBite.com.**

What I have presented is only valid if it correctly represents events occurring in nature, and I've done my utmost to achieve that end. I have struggled mightily to make this a valuable fishing book for my children and grandchildren, and fortified my discussion from every angle that seems relevant. Nonetheless, I am ready to make any changes if they are warranted by new discoveries. My children, grandchildren, and you, deserve nothing less.

Sidebar #11

A Human Hatch?

S everal years ago a national television network reported a dramatic rise or spike in birth rates in hospitals located in the direct paths of ongoing hurricanes. No explanation was offered for the spike in births, although stress was easily inferred as a cause.

I suggest that barometric pressure may be a significant contributing factor. Barometric pressure is exceedingly low near the eye of a hurricane or typhoon, but becomes progressively higher as the distance from the eye increases. The extreme low pressure near the eye should affect the mother's tissues in a pronounced way.

Pregnant women carrying full-term babies, and near-full-term babies, are themselves in a state that resembles the state of ableness. They are ready and able to give birth to babies that can survive and thrive without extraordinary care after birth. Some can be born as early as six weeks premature without extraordinary care. For each woman, all of the tissues, membranes, and fluids associated with her fetus are at or near their fullest necessary development that can produce a normal birth. Such pregnancies can be considered to be within a normal range that's ripe for birth. Naturally, each additional day of pregnancy improves the maturity, strength, and suitability of all factors required for a timely, healthy birth.

Perhaps the best known and most dramatic event that occurs prior to birth is that known as the "water break." When a woman's "water" breaks, birth of the baby usually follows within minutes or hours. What has actually happened is that the membrane that is the amniotic sac, which is filled with "waters" and surrounds the fetus and placenta, has burst. The waters then immediately drain out through the birth canal, usually wetting the expectant mother's clothing. She then knows that birth is imminent.

Obviously there is a direct, unobstructed path between the amniotic sac and the outside world through the birth canal. It's this unobstructed path that should allow barometric pressure to influence the timing of birth.

The pressure from the weight of the waters in the sac, and perhaps osmotic pressures, create a combined internal sac pressure that, from the inside, pushes outwardly on its own membrane that is the amniotic sac. Under normal barometric pressure conditions, the external barometric pressure pushes back against the woman's body and, via the birth canal, pushes back against the membrane of the amniotic sac in the opposite direction that it's being pushed by the internal sac pressure. The thickness of the membrane, and the tension within it, are maintained in a stable state by the internal sac pressure pushing against it from the inside, and the external barometric pressure pushing against it from the outside. As barometric pressure is reduced and pushes less against the membrane from the outside, and creates less resistance to the force of the internal pressure that's pushing from the inside, the membrane will distort in the direction that it's being pushed by the greater force of the internal pressure. The lower the barometric pressure becomes, the greater will be the distortion of the membrane because of the internal pressure. As distortion of the membrane becomes greater and greater, it can eventually become so locally thin that it bursts. It bursts because of the extreme low pressure of the hurricane. Not enough pressure is pushing back on it, through the birth canal, to keep it from distorting and bursting. Higher barometric pressures would not allow the amniotic membrane to distort as radically, and would be a factor that would delay birth. As distances to hospitals increase from the eye of a hurricane, barometric pressure becomes higher and more normal, and birth rates approach more normal levels.

In addition, the terrifying danger and fury of a hurricane could cause a highly elevated level of fear and stress in a pregnant mother. Her biggest concern is to protect her unborn child. The acute stress of protecting the child could cause greater-than-normal muscle tension. The increased tension and tightening in her muscle tissues may effect an almost imperceptible change in the geometry and volume of the womb space --- not a big change, but enough to facilitate a local distortion in the shape of the amniotic sac. This distortion would be exacerbated by the extreme low barometric pressure as described above. The distortion would probably include a slight bulge that would likely occur near and toward the area of least resistance --- at the threshold of the birth canal. The distortion at that location would probably become the bursting point. As stress, tension, and the distortion grow, and low barometric pressure deepens, they would cause the fragile sac to burst.

These scenarios illustrate that higher internal pressure and lower barometric pressure may cause earlier birth.

Additionally, pregnant women are generally able to give birth successfully during a final range of time of their mature pregnancy, which can span a period as long as six weeks, and is akin to a state of ableness; and, much like aquatic insects reaching their next stage of development, birth can occur earlier or later depending on the pressure differences that bear on the female anatomy.

Lower birth rates would occur during the days following an upward spike in birth rates caused by the low pressure of a hurricane. The lower rates would occur because the babies that would normally be born during the following days were already born during the extreme low-pressure, hurricane spike.

Appendix B

Sidebar #15

Pressure Points:
Barometric Pressure and Water Level Equivalents

Throughout this book, barometric pressure is expressed as a number, for example, 29.92. The units are "inches of mercury (in. Hg)." The number is always limited to two decimal places, which means the decimal places are an expression of one-hundredths of an inch. As the decimal amount changes, each one-hundredth of an inch of change is referred to as a "point." For example, if the number changes from 29.92 to 29.96, it has changed by an amount of four one-hundredths, or four points; if the number changes from 29.92 to 30.21, it has changed by 29 points, and so forth. It doesn't matter if the change is an increase or decrease; it's still a matter of points. It provides a handy way to describe changes in the weight of the atmosphere, and a way to know how much it changes total-pressure. If barometric pressure changes by 20 points, then we know that total-pressure has also changed by 20 points.

It would be equally handy to use points for describing changes in water depth that affect total-pressure. In other words, use points to express any changes to total-pressure when water gets deeper from rain or runoff, or shallower from drainage.

This is easily done with mathematical conversions of the weight of the atmosphere and the weight of water to find which amounts of each are equivalent in the way that they affect total-pressure.

The short answer is that the weight of 1.36 inches of water is equivalent to 10 points of change on the barometer. For example, if the barometric pressure is 29.80 and increases to 29.90, the increase in pressure is 10 points; therefore total-pressure would be increased 10 points. Likewise, 10 points of pressure change would also occur if water depth increases 1.36 inches (approx. 1-1/3 inches). 1.36 inches of water exerts the same pressure as 10 points of barometric pressure. (Continued on next page...)

319

Fifteen barometric pressure points is equivalent to an increase or decrease of the pressure caused by 2.04 inches of water.

Calculations for determining the equivalents are shown below:

Solving for water depth equivalent to
10 points of barometric pressure:

Weight of atmosphere @ sea level = 14.7 lbs/in.^{2}
Barometric pressure @sea level = 29.92 in.Hg
Deflection on barometer scale = 0.1 in.Hg
Water (H_2O) = 62.42796 lbs/ft.^{3} = .036127 lbs/in.^{3}
14.7 lbs/in.^{2}H_2O ÷ .036127 lbs/in.^{3}H_2O = 406.898 in.H_2O
406.898 in.H_2O ÷ 12 in./ft. = 33.908 ft.H_2O
(0.1 in.Hg)(33.908 ft.H_2O/29.92 in.Hg)(12 in.H_2O/1ft.H_2O) =
1.36 in. H_2O
Therefore:
10 pts = 1.36in.Hg

Solving for water depth equivalent to
15 points of barometric pressure:

Known: 10 points of barometric pressure is
equivalent to 1.36 inches of water depth:

[10 pts/1.36 in.H_2O = 15pts/X in.H_2O] =
[10pts (Xin.H_2O) = 15pts (1.36in.H_2O)] =
[Xin.H_2O = 1.5(1.36in.H_2O)] =
Xin.H_2O = 2.04in.H_2O
15 pts = 2.04in.H_2O

Appendix C

Sidebar #16

Standard Barometric Pressure

Scientists have established standard barometric pressure* at sea level at 29.92 in.-Hg (inches of mercury) when air temperature at sea level is 59 degrees Fahrenheit. Barometric pressure is constantly changing at all locations on the planet, so this is a long-term average number. Because it's at sea level, however, it's naturally the highest average pressure on the planet, with rare unimportant exceptions like Death Valley (no fish). All other average annual pressures are lower than 29.92 in.-Hg if they are measured above sea level.

Pressures greater than 29.92 occur more frequently in winter because air is much colder, denser, and heavier then, so it exerts greater average pressure than during warmer seasons. Pressures are lower during the warmer seasons because the air is then less dense, which makes it lighter.

If 29.92 is the highest average pressure, it seems reasonable to surmise that it figured prominently in the evolution of the state of ableness. It would be the highest average annual pressure that aquatic arthropods have needed to overcome for molting at altitudes near sea level. Arthropods would have naturally selected to handle conditions associated with this highest average pressure, or perished.

Arthropods inhabiting higher altitudes may have naturally selected to cope only with the highest average barometric pressure at their resident altitude, which would be less demanding than the higher pressure at sea level. The result may be that populations at higher altitudes have naturally selected with less strength than their counterparts at lower altitudes. Their reduced strength may affect their ability to cope with high water.

See Sidebar #17: High Water at Different Altitudes regarding the strength of high-altitude arthropods verses periods of high water.

* Standard barometric pressure is progressively less at higher altitudes. It decreases at a rule-of-thumb rate of roughly one inch of mercury (in.Hg) per each 1000 feet of additional altitude. For example, barometric pressure at sea level may be 29.92 in.Hg, but at 1,000 feet above sea level, the standard barometric pressure is less, about 28.86 in.Hg (slightly more than one inch of difference); at 5,000 feet the pressure would approach 24.90 in.Hg (slightly more than five inches of difference); and at 9,000 feet it's about 21.4 inHg (about nine and a half inches of difference). This rule of thumb is also reflected in Sidebar #10: Boiling Water.

Note: Standard temperature also decreases as altitude increases.

Figures from: National Oceanic and Atmospheric Administration and National Institute of Standards and Technology, U.S. Dept of Commerce

$\mathscr{Appendix}$ **D**

Sidebar #17

High Water at Different Altitudes
A little case study

High water at high altitudes may suppress hatches and molts to a greater degree than an equal amount of high water suppresses them at lower altitudes. The reason is because aquatic insects that have selectively adapted to conditions at higher altitudes may simply be weaker, or less strong, than insects that have similarly adapted to conditions at lower altitudes.

Insects dwelling at low altitudes need extra strength to overcome two critical conditions that are much more severe than they are at high altitude: (1) Far greater normal barometric pressure, which must be overcome during molting at all instar stages; and (2) Far greater surface tension that must be overcome when hatching.

Conversely, insects dwelling at high altitude face drastically lower normal barometric pressure, and far weaker surface films although cold water at high altitude would strengthen surface films somewhat. The normal conditions they face require far less strength to overcome than the strength needed by their counterparts at low altitude.

Consider that average barometric pressure at 7,000 feet is about 23.10 in.Hg, but average barometric pressure at sea level is 29.92 in.Hg, an immense difference of 6.82 in.Hg. It's a greater difference than occurs during the most severe hurricanes. For example, the lowest barometric pressure ever recorded at sea level was 25.69 in.Hg in Typhoon Tip (AKA Hurricane Tip) in the Pacific Ocean in 1979. The average pressure at 7,000 ft, however, is still lower by about 2.6 in.Hg. Obviously, pressure at 7,000 ft is enormously low by comparison to that at sea level.

Insects at high altitude of 7,000 ft may need to molt during high levels of snow melt each spring or summer, but the snowmelt eventually reaches the lower altitudes and its insects as well. Upper stream levels may

323

be high, but by comparison perhaps not nearly as high as the stream levels at lower altitude, which often flirt with flood levels. Insects in the lower altitudes would need far more strength to molt under such conditions.

Demands for such molting strength are probably seldom, if ever, required from insects in the higher altitudes. Generally, insects in the higher altitudes are always facing conditions that demand far less strength for survival than their lower altitude counterparts; high water levels aren't usually as high, barometric pressure is enormously lower, and surface films are far weaker.

If insects at higher altitudes are generally always subject to conditions that require less strength, then it's probably reasonable to assume that they have adapted to the reduced selective pressures with less strength. They haven't needed more strength over the ages so they may not have naturally selected for it. If they haven't selected for it, they are probably more susceptible to adverse consequences when environmental conditions pose challenges that exceed the abilities of their strength. It follows that one of the biggest challenges may then be posed by high water.

When high water occurs at high altitude, inadequate strength of insects at that altitude should have the result of keeping them in ableness for a longer duration than normal, perhaps multiple days longer during very high water (cold water temperatures and degree-days would be factors). Mortality may also become a bigger factor because of the consequences of altitude on strength. Nonetheless, there is a probability that some natural selection of stronger specimens may have occurred over the millennia which can emerge under such conditions. Their emergence may constitute either a population adequate enough to cause a bite of reasonable significance, or simply a token population of scattered emergers that fail to provoke a bite of any meaningful consequence. Perhaps a different scenario would develop. Good logs would eventually reveal the proper answer. A parallel case could also be argued for molting of aquatic crustaceans, minus consideration for surface film.

Appendix **E**

Sidebar #19

Hot Water Floats

Think of a hot air balloon; it rises upward through the atmosphere. The hot air in the balloon is less dense than the colder air surrounding the balloon so the balloon rises, and continues rising toward the top of the colder air surrounding it. Hot smoke from a fire rises in the same manner for the same reasons.

Warm water generally behaves the same way; it rises toward the top of cold water. You can see a prime example of this in hot water heaters commonly used in most homes. The cold water pipe feeds water into the tank, then a flame or electric element heats the cold water until it's hot; the hot water then rises to the top of the tank and is available to use in your kitchen and bathroom. No matter how much hot water you use, cold water to replace it will regularly flow into the bottom of the tank and is heated, which causes it to rise naturally to the top of the tank. The warm water rises because it is less dense and lighter than the heavier, denser cold water at the bottom. The warm water floats on top of the denser cold water below.

Warm and cold water behave exactly the same way in lakes and the sea. Warm water is always positioned as the top layer, with few exceptions, or working its way upward to be the top layer. Swimmers are well aware of this phenomenon; while swimming in warm water, their feet often feel a cold layer of water several feet below the surface.

Water is a strange substance, however, and exhibits two strange exceptions to the behavior described above:

1. When water freezes, at 32 degrees F, it expands and becomes solid ice. The expansion makes the ice less dense than liquid water, so the ice floats despite its colder temperature.

2. Freshwater is densest and heaviest when it reaches 39 degrees Fahrenheit (39 deg F). This means that water at 39 deg F will sink below

water that's only 33, 34, 35, 36, 37, and 38 deg F. The colder water at these temperatures will actually float on top of the warmer 39 deg F water — exactly the opposite of what you might expect.

A beneficial characteristic of freshwater is that it can contain increasing amounts of oxygen as it becomes colder and denser. Therefore water at 39 deg F can contain the most oxygen because it is most dense. Less dense, warmer water cannot contain as much oxygen as denser colder water. This can be handy information when fishing in cold water, especially for ice fishermen. Not every lake has enough dissolved oxygen in its 39 degree F water to support fish life, especially late in the season when it gets depleted, but some do. 39 degree F water, if it exists in a body of water, will always be located in the deepest hole(s). It creates favorable conditions for under-ice fishing — warmest water with the most oxygen located in the deepest holes. There is an elevated probability of fish occupying such locations during part of the winter season, particularly after oxygen is depleted in shallower water.

Bibliography

Clifford H. Mortimer, 2004, Lake Michigan in Motion, University of Wisconsin Press, Madison, Wisconsin

J. Reese Voshell, Jr., Ph.D., 2002, illustrated by Amy Bartlett Wright, 2000, A Guide to Common Freshwater Invertebrates of North America, McDonald & Woodward Publishing Company, Blacksburg, Virginia

Thomas J. Glover, 1996, Pocket Reference, 2nd Edition, Sequoia Publishing, Inc., Littleton, Colorado

Alpheus W. Smith, John N. Cooper, 1964, Elements of Physics, McGraw-Hill Book Company, New York, San Francisco, Toronto, London

Robert W. Fuller, Raymond B. Brownlee, D. Lee Baker, All of Stuyvesant High School New York City, 1932 & 1933, First Principles of Physics, Norwood Press, J.S. Cushing Co. — Berwick & Smith Co., Norwood, Mass., U.S.A.

W.B. Scott and E.J. Crossman, 1998, Freshwater Fishes of Canada, Galt House Publications Ltd., Oakville, Ontario, Canada

Gary LaFontaine, 1981, Caddisflies, Nick Lyons Books, Division of Benn Brothers, Inc., New York, New York

Fred L. Arbona, Jr., Mayflies, The Angler, And The Trout, Winchester Press — Imprint of New Century Publishers, Inc., Piscataway, New Jersey, USA

Carl Richards, Doug Swisher, Fred Arbona, Jr., 1980, Stoneflies, First Edition, Nick Lyons Books, Division of Benn Brothers, Inc., New York, New York

James C. Kroll, Ben H. Koerth, 1996, Solving the Mysteries of Deer Movement, Stephen H. Austin State University, Nacogdoches, Texas

John Alden Knight, Moon Up Moon Down, 1942, Charles Scribner's Sons, 1972 Revised Edition, Jacqueline E. Knight Solunar Sales Co., 2001 2nd Revised Edition, James C. and Linda J. Losch, Solunar Sales Co.

Index

Definitions of terms are located on pages depicted in boldface

331

332

333

338